W9-CDM-804

The Culture of Freedom

The Culture of Freedom

The Small World of
Fulbright Scholars

Leonard R. Sussman

Rowman & Littlefield Publishers, Inc.

ROWMAN & LITTLEFIELD PUBLISHERS, INC.

Published in the United States of America
by Rowman & Littlefield Publishers, Inc.
4720 Boston Way, Lanham, Maryland 20706

Copyright © 1992 by Leonard R. Sussman

All rights reserved. No part of this publication may
be reproduced, stored in a retrieval system, or transmitted
in any form or by any means, electronic, mechanical,
photocopying, recording, or otherwise, without the prior
permission of the publisher.

British Cataloging in Publication Information Available

Library of Congress Cataloging-in-Publication Data

Sussman, Leonard R.
The culture of freedom : the small world of Fulbright scholars /
Leonard R. Sussman.
p.   cm.
Includes bibliographical references and index (p.).
1. Scholarships—United States. 2. Educational exchanges—
United States. 3. United States—Cultural policy. I. Title
LB2338.S88 1992
378.3'4'0973—dc20   92-483   CIP

ISBN 0-8476-7764-8 (cloth : alk. paper)

Printed in the United States of America

The paper used in this publication meets the minimum requirements of
American National Standard for Information Sciences—Permanence of
Paper for Printed Library Materials, ANSI Z39.48–1984.

Dedication

May the new crop of Fulbrighters
continue to expand the Culture of Freedom and
be ever renewable;
ever enlarging their small world
and our understanding of the larger universe.

We know today that . . . ideas, not armaments, will shape our lasting prospects for peace; that the conduct of our foreign policy will advance no faster than the curriculum of our classrooms; that the knowledge of our citizens is one treasure which grows only when it is shared.

—President Johnson speaking the words of Charles Frankel,
September 1965

Contents

Preface:
Why This Assessment?

At the 1990 Helsinki Summit with President Bush, Soviet President Mikhail Gorbachev made the linkage: A "normal element" of the world's "new cooperation," he said, would be "human exchange" as well as trade and technology. Human exchange is a meeting of cultures as well as people, of ideas as well as goods.

America entering the twenty-first century urgently needs a cultural policy. Americans have known all along that they were different from other peoples, yet a part of all others; an amalgam of the world's peoples; a civilization.

A national cultural policy would enunciate America's role in the expanding world of international civic relationships and responsibilities.

America has a twofold future, little different from its past: to appreciate and respect the world it assimilates through generations of immigrants, and to understand America's relations in the world today and tomorrow. Knowledge of the history, the politics, and the widely diverse aspirations on all continents is above all essential. Knowledge alone is insufficient. Affective traits must also be cultivated: sensitivity, empathy, tolerance, compassion, and respect for diversity, while a stand is taken for democratic values and human rights. For now—and more so in the years just ahead—the flow of communication across national borders will be massive and instantaneous. Goods and services will flow increasingly through corporate channels that are truly internationalized. Global diplomacy will face security challenges coming from more parts of the world than ever, as even the smallest nations secure arms of major threat even to great powers and therefore to world peace. Information and sensitivity—two distinct parts of human understanding—will require careful nurturance. The challenge for Americans is clear: this nation will be expected to play a greater role on the world scene than when it was one of two superpowers. Not only because America has the armaments to do so, but also because it is the only nation with citizens from all other nations and because through this diversity it is expected to act wisely as a world citizen.

Diversity is one key to America's future, wisdom is another. The two should be melded in the day-to-day acting out of America's cultural policy so far unarticulated. How do we regard the traditions, languages, habits, and aspirations of other peoples? How do we reflect on and express our own? Most important, how do we interact with all others? What do we exchange?

The Fulbright scholarship program is America's foremost institution of academic exchanges. The program, in its fifth decade, has enabled 180,000 students and scholars from 130 countries to share America's cultural heritage, and of these it has enabled 64,000 Americans to share, no less, in the traditions and knowledge of 130 partners. To have formulated and conducted such a program required decisions taken at the highest level of the U.S. government. The time has come to examine the Fulbright program, correct it if necessary, and make the still larger decisions that will be required in the century ahead for a nation this diverse and this important to the world.

America needs a cultural policy far more extensive than it has ever attempted. And it needs a revitalized Fulbright program as an integral part of that policy.

The program should seek the best or the brightest or the most promising American and foreign students. There are, however, many tradeoffs to be considered. Should grants be awarded to an equal number of Americans and foreigners, or should the movement of grantees in either direction be governed by the special needs of each bilateral relationship? Should certain disciplines be stressed over others, such as the humanities, or the sciences and technologies, or journalism? Should certain countries or regions be favored? Should American studies be pressed abroad? Should funding of the program always be binationally shared? This book examines these and other issues and makes specific recommendations at the conclusion.

These recommendations result from my year-long (1990–1991) examination of the history and current functioning of the program. I have conducted interviews extensively in Washington and New York at the governmental and nongovernmental agencies responsible for the Fulbright program, deepening my long-standing admiration for the American Foreign Service. Through this study I have also come to admire dedicated executive directors of Fulbright commissions overseas such as Daniel Krauskopf, Israel; Barbara Peterson, Norway; Caroline Yang, Japan; and former director Cipriana Scelba in Italy. Their service over many years has provided continuity and institutional memory, which overcomes occasional attempts to distort the Fulbright process. That process is best told through personal experience. I have had heartening discussions with Fulbright alumni and current participants in the United States, Japan, Indonesia, India, and Italy. A list of those I talked with appears in Appendix A.

This project was commissioned by the J. William Fulbright Foreign Scholarship Board. (The acronym BFS, still in use, derives from the former name, the Board of Foreign Scholarships, but I shall use FSB throughout.) FSB believes that no study before this has "ever fully assessed the relationship between the Fulbright program's statutory charge and its performance." Yet eight presidents and twenty-two Congresses over forty-five years charged the Fulbright program to increase mutual understanding and peaceful relations between the people of the United States and other countries through educational exchange. The FSB operates as an independent body within the U.S. Information Agency (USIA). The FSB also grants final approval for those Fulbright programs conducted by the U.S. Department of Education (USED), which I have also examined.

This book emphasizes the subjective because Fulbrighters are individuals. As they are influenced by their Fulbright experience, they affect the ideas and institutions in many countries. This book is subjective, favorably biased, but not pie-in-the-sky. It attempts to illuminate national and binational opportunities and problems in the field of educational exchange. Long before undertaking this project, I admired the Fulbright program. I have known and respected men whose official responsibilities included general management of the Fulbright program: John Richardson and the late Charles Frankel.

There may seem to some to be undue emphasis throughout this book on the adversarial relationship between officers in the USIA whose titles are either "cultural" or "public affairs," and between the nongovernmental screening instruments in the American academy and the cultural agencies of the government. These are predictable adversaries. Particularly when they have an international caste, as in all exchanges with foreign nationals, the broad field of cultural operations is no less controversial than the adversarial players in the field of military weaponry. Culture is not an unimportant aspect of this or any society. The hallmark of any consensus building for culture or any policy in a democratic country is likely to be tension, another word for the interplay of differing interest groups. Cultural affairs, at the outset, are heavily laden with as many interests as there are academic disciplines, national political objectives abroad, and policymakers committed to diverse forms of interaction between the disciplines and the political objectives. One should not regard this tension as exceptional, necessarily damaging, or entirely dispensable. This tension can, of course, become counterproductive when it advances contentiousness for its own sake or for the benefit of the players to the detriment of the program or the overriding national interest. My conclusion up front then is that one must understand the nature of the point-and-counterpoint in order to assess the real values of the international exchange program. My conclusion: the tensions are instructive, not disposable, yet in need of some modifications.

Though I have not had a Fulbright grant, I welcomed the opportunity to examine the program. I knew, on the one hand, how significant the changes are that the Fulbright process has wrought and, on the other, how little recognized in the United States these ever-multiplying achievements are. Only at our peril do we continue to keep that wonderful idea, that incredible process, that unique network of Fulbrighters relatively secret. The purpose of this book is to examine that process and its network for their accomplishments, problems, and promise.

Acknowledgments

Richard A. Ware conceived this study when he was chairman of the Board of Foreign Scholarships in 1989. His successor as board chairman, Charles W. Dunn, assisted me extensively and provided professional guidance without attempting to influence my analysis. This project joins several initiated during Professor Dunn's chairmanship to open the Fulbright program to constructive reexamination. William P. Glade Jr., associate director, USIA, demonstrated his interest in this study by sharing his observations and encouraging others in the agency to do so. To all three, I express appreciation.

I am grateful to Ralph Vogel, staff director of the J. William Fulbright Foreign Scholarship Board (FSB), who provided a great volume of reports and correspondence, while placing them in proper perspective. In 1991, Ralph deservedly received the Distinguished Honor Award from the USIA for thirty years of "exceptional" service. Ralph has served as "the conscience of the program." He provides continuity for overseeing this complex, far-reaching work. The FSB depends on his expertise to warn of problems as well as opportunities, and to report responsibly to the Congress and public.

Jennifer Newton, deputy staff director of the FSB, provided extensive background briefings and informal conversation, both important to my understanding of the complex Fulbright system. Special thanks to Philip Marcus, member of the FSB, who introduced me to this project. His insights have been helpful. To understand the complicated Fulbright screening mechanisms I received extensive briefings from the USIA, Department of State, USED, Institute of International Education, and Council for

International Exchange of Scholars. I am grateful for their observations. In my travel abroad I was assisted by careful preparation of the respective Fulbright commission directors in each country: India, Sharoda Nayak, director, and O.P. Bhardwaj, executive officer; Indonesia, Ann vB. Lewis; Italy, Carlo Chiarenza; and Japan, Caroline Yang.

I thank all of the 109 busy men and women, prominent in many fields, most of whom devoted an hour or more to my questions. Most were Fulbrighters who shared not only their experiences but their exhilaration, which sometimes lasted more than four decades. Their names appear in Appendix A.

I am grateful to the U.S. Information Agency (USIA) and the U.S. Department of Education (USED) for providing a part of the funding for this study. They recognize that the final work and recommendations must be entirely my own. I acknowledge and express my appreciation for the major financial support provided by the Chiang Ching-kuo Foundation for International Scholarship Exchange, Earhart Foundation, Freedom House, and Sarah Scaife Foundation.

My thanks to Freedom House and its executive director, R. Bruce McColm, for providing the facilities and additional support for this effort. Both were essential.

Critical reviewers of an early version of this manuscript were immensely helpful. Richard Arndt, who has been associated with the Fulbright program for forty-two years, provided extensive editorial suggestions and raised crucial questions of analysis. All were welcome. Dick headed the Fulbright Alumni Association after retiring from the Foreign Service and a distinguished career as cultural affairs officer. Other helpful critical reviews were received from William P. Glade Jr., Philip Marcus, Jennifer Newton, John Richardson, and Ralph Vogel.

The editorial judgment of Lynn Gemmell at Rowman & Littlefield Publishers sharpened many paragraphs of this book. Once again, I am grateful to James E. Lyons, publisher, and Jonathan Sisk, editor-in-chief.

I appreciate the forbearance of my wife Marianne who, while I wrote, walked alone on the beautiful beaches of Prince Edward Island.

Finally, I gratefully acknowledge the contribution of Jessie Miller, my research associate, whose patient transcribing of the lengthy taped interviews provided raw material for analysis, and whose challenging questions and thoughtful comments at every stage improved this examination.

All the reporting and judgments are mine and do not necessarily reflect the views of the J. William Fulbright Foreign Scholarship Board or any other agency.

I do *not* acknowledge here my indebtedness—or that of so many others, and the nation he represented—to J. William Fulbright. My regard is amply stated in the following pages. I hope this book will encourage others to assess and record the program's extensive contributions.

—L.R.S.

Prince Edward Island
New York City

May 1992

1

Toward a National Cultural Policy

Cultural ignorance can kill. Tens of thousands died in the 1991 Persian Gulf War, not only because of a dictator's aggression and intransigence. The ironic truth—words attributed to President Bush's intermediary with Saudi King Fahd—was that going to war had been sealed by "cultural misunderstanding."[1] On that same conviction, six months later, Senator David Boren introduced a bill to take $180 million from the intelligence budget to create an international-education trust. The fund would train young Americans in the languages and cultures of distant peoples. Said Senator Sam Nunn, "We had to put 500,000 American men and women . . . in harm's way [in the Persian Gulf] because our diplomatic and policy communities [were not] expert in cultures and languages that encompass the regions of the world."

They couldn't communicate even within the existing small but growing Culture of Freedom. That culture fosters mutual understanding among and within nations. Security is bolstered by the amicable resolution of differences based on greater awareness.

Yet one American program, little noticed, has created vast if underutilized human assets. The J. William Fulbright scholarships are a worldwide educational exchange of persons and programs. It displays the small-world phenomenon: two strangers meet in an unlikely place and discover they have a common acquaintance. They recognize a bond across space and time:

"What a small world!"

Social scientists estimate tantalizingly that a chain of *seven* such intermediaries can link most pairs of people now separated anywhere in

1

the world.[2] The Broadway hit "Six Degrees of Separation" evokes the same theme. By exchanging 180,000 students and scholars from 130 countries for nearly five decades the Fulbright program has created a putative network that is a small world growing ever larger and ever more useful to humankind.

Just since the revolutions of 1989, the world has changed dramatically. The Fulbright program can contribute to the world-in-formation. The program is so diverse, so useful to so many different academic and political constituencies, domestic and foreign, that it needs careful reexamination and positive refocusing.

At the outset, cumbersome processes were established to protect the program from efforts in either the political or the academic bureaucracies to skew grant selection that would favor individuals or policies that could be construed as political choices. Yet this program, committed to serve the public interest, must inevitably address political factors in the academy and in the government.

Today, as part of American leadership toward a new world order, the Fulbright program should be placed within a clearly enunciated National Cultural Policy. The goals of international educational and cultural exchanges should reflect the post-cold war world. New centers of scholarship and technology abroad, tied to new communication linkages, challenge America to define its own cultural objectives. Both the private and public sectors should be examined, though government should not interfere with the vastly larger and complementary nongovernmental cultural establishments. Americans need to become better aware of their own heritage, private and public, before launching new exchange-of-persons programs.

Whatever the design of a National Cultural Policy, the Fulbright program must face harsh choices. Funding today is inadequate for the size and breadth of the program. Only $1.35 billion taxpayer funds have been spent for these exchanges in nearly fifty years. Private and public American universities, individuals, foreign governments, and U.S. and foreign corporations have added 71 percent to the U.S. dollar commitment. Most important—and little recognized—the actual return on these investments may have been many times as great: in skills generated, technologies created and expanded, trade and other cooperative patterns inspired, good will earned for America, and personal and professional life-changing experiences realized by 180,000 Fulbrighters.

This considerable achievement notwithstanding, the Fulbright program is at a crossroad: It must secure significantly increased funding, perhaps some from private American sources, or reduce the scope of its work. For operational and funding purposes, the program should sharpen its goals and demonstrate ever-higher standards of scholarship. The new communication technologies should facilitate continuing cooperation between Fulbright alumni and their former hosts. All such innovations would be enhanced by formulation of a National Cultural Policy. The J. William Fulbright Foreign Scholarship Board, appointed by the president to supervise academic exchanges, should recommend to him the creation of a National Cultural Commission.

As the military/strategic component of American foreign relations is reduced, cultural interactions with other peoples, especially in formerly closed societies, must increase. Ignorance of other peoples, and indeed ignorance of America's own cultural heritage and aspirations, inevitably exacerbates conflict and sabotages national purpose and policies. Failure to dispel that ignorance, failure to enlarge educational exchanges to meet expanding opportunities would be a significant national failure.

The small world of Fulbrighters can make limitless connections with the larger universe.

One man launched that idea. It has improved hundreds of thousands of lives directly, millions indirectly. That idea has helped introduce entire scholarly disciplines in countries abroad, and has led to better teaching and research methods here and abroad. It has improved the way architects build, scientists research, teachers teach. The idea has influenced the way countries act: Their behavior improves as elites learn greater sensitivity and act with greater respect for other cultures. That idea has brought people together from many nations not just for a semester, but a lifetime.

That idea created a network—potential, if not yet fully consummated—across many lands and within nearly all countries. It has brought European, Asian, African, and Latin American scholars to learn while they enrich scholarship in the United States; and Americans to broaden their scholarship even as they share it abroad. The idea created a process that influences the scholar's understanding of other peoples and, no less, his or her own people. The man is Nobel Prize caliber, yet neither he nor anyone knows fully what his idea has created and his name sustains. The man is J. William Fulbright, a controversial and influential U.S. senator from Arkansas from 1945 to 1974. The idea was the Fulbright scholarships, the exchange of students, scholars, and intellectuals between the United States and 130 other countries.

And yet, notes James H. Billington, the librarian of Congress, "It is ironic that the American people who created and supported the Fulbright program for forty-five years with public funds, the largest and probably most successful cultural exchange program in history, seem to be almost the only major people in the world who do not fully appreciate it." Wrote the distinguished British historian Arnold Toynbee, "Along with the

Marshall Plan, the Fulbright program is one of the really generous and imaginative things that have been done in the world since World War II."³

My purpose here is to show that the Fulbright program may be judged extraordinarily effective, yet burdened recently by that very success. That burden tends to limit current achievements and devalue the program's largely unheralded successes. An overly burdened and underappreciated Fulbright program would be detrimental to America's national interests and harmful to individual scholars and their disciplines everywhere.

Americans rarely ponder their place in the world. Political campaigners momentarily raise the issue, generally in terms of national security. That term is usually linked to military or geopolitical concerns. Important as they are, such factors do not stand alone. Security strategists understand that powerful armament or shrewd diplomacy is ineffective without applied national will derived from an intelligent public that is informed about world affairs and America's role and ready to take appropriate action. In the new world order, evoked by President Bush, whatever that may become, military factors seem to be far less important than during the cold war. Indeed, America's failing competitiveness—loss of trade, jobs, and income from abroad—is deepening domestic concerns arising from the nation's role in the world. "National security" henceforth is likely to be linked far more to mind power than material power. With demilitarization should come greater intellectual empowerment.

The reciprocal exchange of ideas across national borders can lead to greater security and human progress. Toward this end, the principal focus of the Fulbright program has been and should be the enhancement of the individual intellect. Fulbright exchange cannot realistically be based on the export of American systems or institutions; just as the current "U.S. democracy initiative" cannot expect to transfer American political forms to other cultures. Rather, in both cases the American experience—its diverse scholarship and its democratic institutions—provides a model that scholars or government leaders elsewhere can draw upon to develop their own cultural and governmental institutions. But the prime focus remains: the intellectual empowerment of individuals, foreign and American; empowerment of scholars by interacting, one with the other. All learn. All teach. "Exchange" is the operative word because the process is two-way. That double flow on such a scale—more than 180,000 high-quality travelers over forty-five years—is unique in history. Most valuable, this select group tests its own values and scholarship abroad. It also maintains contact with former host scholars and institutions, and so contributes—jointly—to new discovery. The exchange and its values continue for lifetimes.

Thousands of Fulbrighters went on to build extraordinary careers. Some are interviewed in this book. One Fulbrighter walked on the moon. In addition to two U.S. senators and two librarians of Congress, Fulbrighters became presidents of universities in the United States and abroad. More than a dozen future Nobel laureates were presciently selected for Fulbrights before they made their most notable contributions. Major American composers—not only academics—held Fulbrights early in their careers, as did many prominent authors and journalists.

From overseas, the Fulbright concept brought Alexander Yakovlev to Columbia University from 1958 to 1959 to study the New Deal. Yakovlev later argued in the Politburo for the release of Andrei Sakharov, the Russian physicist-human rights activist, when he was exiled in Gorky. Yakovlev became the principal adviser to the reformist President Mikhail Gorbachev, the sounder of alarm just days before the August 1991 coup challenged the Gorbachev regime, and a major actor in subsequent events in his country. Egypt's former deputy prime minister, Boutros Boutros-Ghali, the new secretary-general of the United Nations, was a Fulbright scholar at Columbia University, 1954 to 1955.

Fulbright alumni include a former prime minister of Sweden; dozens of cabinet members in Europe, Asia, and Latin America, including the finance minister of Mexico who negotiated the new U.S.-Mexico trade agreement; and in Japan alone, the chief justice and three other justices of the Supreme Court, seven Diet members, presidents of twenty-seven universities and more than 100 senior executives of major corporations. One Fulbrighter we shall meet later in the book left Italy to study in America, had a brilliant corporate career in Europe, and returned here to head the largest publishing house in the United States.

These are a few of the men and women awarded Fulbrights early in their careers. Others became prominent in their respective scholarly disciplines or in professional endeavors such as journalism, publishing, banking, and finance. They demonstrate the fundamental commitment of the Fulbright process—indeed, the American sociopolitical ethic—the traditional commitment, too often honored but neglected, to the value of the individual in society. No one act, no single event or personality alone produces a major change in the history of human relations. Furthermore, "all education is a gamble," Harvard President Derek Bok, himself a Fulbrighter, reminds us: "You can't prove the value of anything educational because it's all mixed up with everything else."[4] The Fulbright program, too, is a gamble. But intelligent minds, thinking and acting in concert, can enlarge the possibilities for individuals to improve the condition of the many. So that retrospectively one may say that such men and women help move history in an appropriate direction. The gamble seems to pay. The Fulbright program was well ahead of its time. It set the standard for other American educational exchanges, but accomplished much more. In the four decades after World War II, when the United States was the world's primary source of research and development, the Fulbrights were a ticket to the highest adventure in many disciplines. Many foreign Fulbrighters studied American science, technology, and management, as well as literature, economics, and art. Americans studied the high culture of European and Asian traditions. They researched the social and political developments of fast-changing continents. Whatever their professional interests, however, Americans were exposed to the ideas and ways of thinking and living of other societies. Similarly, foreign Fulbrighters in the United States, observing American ideas and lifestyles, were able thereafter to understand the complex American social and political system that influences so much of the world, even when it doesn't expect to.

Today, in many fields, America is no longer the only source of cutting-edge research and technology. In its fifth decade, therefore, the Fulbright program has a new and more important potential: to design for its future—and the future of America—a still more effective teaching-learning process, a true "exchange" based on the original Fulbright objective of enhancing mutual understanding of peoples. Just as elite universities in the United States no longer stand as high above many first-class institutions, so American scholarship must compete with a greater number of outstanding academics abroad. The Fulbright program therefore becomes more important to America than ever. In the beginning the program introduced other countries to American research frontiers. Now, the program helps Americans to keep in touch with the advancing research frontier abroad. American academics and their foreign colleagues will teach and learn together. The Fulbright process must accommodate this and other changes in the world.

In that process, Americans will learn more about themselves and their role as world citizens, a goal of the Fulbright program from the beginning. The program should help Americans understand the rapidly changing demographic map of the United States. The great influx of Spanish speakers, for example, is not a short-term phenomenon. By the year 2000, Hispanic citizens representing many distinct national origins may comprise 20 percent of the U.S. population. This soon-to-be America's largest ethnic minority so far retains its linguistic and distinctive cultural identity. Ignorance of these distinctions by the American majority can lead to social malaise and faulty public policy. Similarly, the Asian influx has several different ethnic and religious qualities. Fulbrighters studying in Asian countries and the Asian scholars coming to America provide

bridges of understanding that will be increasingly necessary in multiethnic America.

Such preparation is essential though traditionally alien to the American system. The time when the United States could move planlessly into
the future is rapidly passing. Military and strategic planning took center
stage since World War II. Almost everything else was left to happen-
stance. Intellectual and cultural development, except for some notable
philanthropies and the national endowments, was regarded as solely a
personal concern: an odd state for a nation created by intellectuals, fa-
thers of a highly intellectualized system of governance, still more strange
since that theory of governance assumes an educated citizenry capable
of understanding and voting on complex public issues. Yet Americans
generally seek short-term objectives, framed either by a Washington
administration's four years in office, a career bureaucrat's temporary
perch on the organizational job ladder, or a private corporation's fourth
quarter profit-and-loss statement. Academics are trained to focus on the
longer view. They should have a major contribution to make to the
understanding of their fellow citizens, provided academics are not alien-
ated by choice (reflecting dissatisfaction with government policy) or
isolated by government (a consequence of officials' opposition to academic criticism of public policy). The relationship of the intellect to
materialism in an interactive progression was eloquently stated by John
Adams in a 1780 letter to his wife:

> I must study politics and war that my sons may have liberty to study
> mathematics, philosophy, geography, commerce and agriculture, in order
> to give their children a right to study painting, poetry, music, architecture,
> statuary . . .

Adams progresses from assuring the nation's security and political
stability to developing trade and the national intellect so that a citizen
may be free to participate in the "high" culture. All three levels of development are sought in different ways in diverse countries. It is essential to know how different cultures develop and reflect the citizens and
national leaders of other countries. For, interestingly, political leaders in
many new societies of Eastern Europe and the Third World were cultural
leaders *first*. Political leaders came from the ranks of poets, dramatists,
novelists, and journalists. That is not to suggest that the United States
pursue a cultural policy in order to create new political leaders, rather
that America should no longer undervalue intellectual creativity at home
or abroad in designing national priorities and international activities. The
fact is, the United States does not routinely incorporate educational and

cultural considerations into international policy formulation. That void reduces our capability to anticipate major changes in crucial places. Though they had some sound professional advice in the Middle East and Vietnam, our policymakers could not cope with seismic changes in those regions. Official misperceptions led to human and political disasters.

Culture is differently defined by different observers. Sometimes it is taken to mean the narrow range of "high culture"—the arts, mainly the classics and a few selected moderns—or more broadly, the full range of a society's activities from its popular entertainments to its mode of health-care delivery and its transportation system to the market or command economy. In some definitions, culture addresses the degree to which government controls or influences the channels of mass communication. Culture is the mediator between the harsh imperatives of nationalism (domestic and global) and, for example, the consensus building of democracy (at home and abroad).

Culture can be on the side of democracy in ways suggested by Leon Wieseltier: "Nationalism redeems the group; democracy redeems the individual . . . Nationalism demands authenticity; democracy demands diversity. Nationalism challenges the universal with the particular; democracy connects the particular with the universal."[5] Democracy encourages its cultures to support individuals in their diversity and weave them into interacting societies. Culture becomes an instrument for international civility.

Relating America's intellectual life to its political role in the world should not shock either academic or political purists. To be sure, bitter debates have raged on university campuses over whether to accept government funds for research. And officials have withheld financial support of lab or classroom for many reasons. The Fulbright program, from the outset, was to be protected from politicization by an intricate system of screening by nongovernmmental agencies and final approval of all Fulbrighters by an independent Foreign Scholarship Board (FSB) appointed by the president. Critics said the FSB reflected the political coloration of either Democratic or Republican administrations. Politicization at its crudest meant awarding Fulbright grants to partisans favorable to the administration or constructing Fulbright programs especially to meet particular political objectives at home or abroad. There have been complaints that the removal of the Fulbright program in 1978 from a little observed bureau in the State Department to the U.S. Information Agency (USIA) politicized the program by proximity to the full-time propaganda mission of USIA. Politicizing did not imply injecting partisan politics, much less ideology, but in subordinating Fulbright allocations to USIA's general political objectives. Such objectives push money in the direction of targeted countries, and expand research or a scholarly presence either to produce greater information about a newly interesting area, or win political favor and influence academic development in a targeted country. The move to the USIA diminished the State Department's role in cultural relationships and is said to have polarized the bureaucracy: Some saw Fulbright scholarships as a short-term propaganda tool in the cold war or as a form of international patronage useful, as a pork barrel, in establishing intergovernmental relations even apart from cold war activities. Others welcomed the program as a long-range investment in better understanding between peoples and nations. Still others have seen Fulbright awards as a favor to be dispensed in pursuit of career advancement in the public bureaucracy.

The polarization of the bureaucracy was clearly demonstrated in 1981. Supporters of the Fulbright program felt victimized when congressional budget cuts were mooted to have been aimed by the USIA disproportionately at the Fulbright and other exchange programs. Fulbright supporters believed that academic exchange budgets would be reduced to favor USIA's broadcasting and international-visitor programs. Both programs are eminently desirable. This writer has frequently given public support to both. These are, however, more politically oriented than intellectual exchanges, and meet the short-term policy objectives of public affairs officers abroad. Defenders of the Fulbright program persuaded Senator Claiborne Pell, chairman of the Senate Foreign Relations Committee, to protect the level of funding for the Fulbright program in allocations to the USIA. This arrangement does not affect the actual distribution of funds, but it does protect the proportion of USIA money reserved for the Fulbright program.

Despite pledges to keep the Fulbright program nonpropagandistic and nonpartisan, critics maintain that cultural affairs officers (CAOs), serving under public affairs officers (PAOs) in embassies abroad, must necessarily use the program from time to time to achieve political, ideological, economic, or other State Department objectives. Gerald Prillaman, a career Foreign Service Officer, would endow the CAO with greater operational power. He distinguishes between cultural affairs and cultural relations. "Affairs," he says, are static while "relations" are the process of mutual dialogue between two cultures. A cultural relations officer (CRO) would have the power to make such contacts between the American and another culture. But there are no CROs. Instead, "the action at USIA," says Prillaman, "is on the press and information side." He sees little hope for CAOs becoming empowered as CROs.[6] Nevertheless, cultural relations continue. Note rapidly increasing cross-border television, for example. Most mass cultural contacts are determined haphazardly, mainly by market impulses.

A strongly adversarial relationship between a CAO and a PAO sometimes develops. It occurred in the Netherlands in 1981, during the anti-American controversies over U.S. missile deployments. Most often a cultural issue may be decided by a quasi-political choice made in the field. One CAO says he doesn't need to discuss certain policies with his PAO; "I know what's in his mind," he says. Many CAOs and PAOs (including some who were formerly CAOs) strive to shield the Fulbright program from politicization. In forty-seven countries, moreover, binational commissions engage in active diplomacy to maintain academic integrity. If the two principals are attuned to one another's professional duties, yet committed to maintaining the integrity of scholarship, the CAO-PAO relationship can satisfy the highest goals of the academy within the political setting of an embassy. Professor Robin Winks of Yale University recalls an unusual case. He had been a Fulbrighter and a prominent university professor before becoming CAO in London (1969 to 1971). That CAO-PAO relationship, he says, was "superb."[7] Bill Weld, the political officer, had taken a doctorate, says Winks, and then gone into the Foreign Service. Winks recalls:

> He was a professional Foreign Service officer, but he understood academic issues extremely well. While he made it quite clear that he was my superior officer, and from time to time appropriately gave me instructions, he was always prepared to listen to my argument if I believed something should be done somewhat differently. He never interfered with the Fulbright program though he was always closely interested and asked for frequent reports on how things were going. I learned that this was not always the case with other PAOs, that there was often hostility and that the Fulbright program seemed to be the focus of that hostility. They felt they had to report proof of effectiveness in some quantifiable way. And the CAO, if honest to the program, knows perfectly well that most educational matters can't be quantified in terms of their effectiveness.

Such a relationship is far more likely to prevail in countries such as the United Kingdom, Japan, or France under stable political and cultural conditions. Where a host country's politics are unsettled, however, the PAO tends to use every instrument, including the Fulbright program, to meet political objectives. In Germany after unification, for example, there was pressure to subordinate Fulbright allocations to political objectives; i.e., influencing East German *länder* to reshape the ideological cast of their universities.

In relatively rare cases, high-level policy decisions have targeted geographic areas for substantially increased numbers of Fulbright grants. Most recently, Central America and post-revolution Eastern Europe were selected for national-policy purposes, having little or no relation to purely academic and intellectual interests. But normally the intricate and lengthy process of selecting and matching academics with overseas teaching or research slots defies the control needed to influence a particular project or scholar. The sizable number of Fulbrighters in any one year—some 5,000—also defeats any concerted effort to "cook" the political coloration of grantees or their projects. Certainly a candidate for a Fulbright grant is not asked his or her political affiliation; more likely, the academic committees conducting the peer reviews in the selection process will have far better knowledge of the candidate's political or social philosophy. And, finally, the Fulbright program is indeed propaganda or, if you will, good public relations. When Fulbrighters perform well as academics, they bring credit to the nation and the political system that sent them on their way. Says one PAO, "To say the Fulbright program works in a political vacuum would be naive." Yet, he adds, both governments "recognize that the real utility of the Fulbright program is its prestige. Start to monkey with that and you're on a counterproductive road. I don't think we need to be taught that. It's self-evident."

Far more important, I would argue, is the Fulbright program's lack of focus or grand objective. A substantial program in the national interest, as this is and must be, should be clearly definable. Thousands of individual scholars will continue to benefit; and through them, their disciplines. But there should be a discernible goal, no matter how long-term, that is clearly marked. One goal could be the creation of an international community of scholars and other intellectuals. It would not compete with the scholarly associations of each of the disciplines; it would call on Fulbrighters in 130 nations to serve as active communicators of the Fulbright spirit. They would also employ the new communication technologies to increase contacts with colleagues in their former host countries and communicate with others in their disciplines worldwide. Such scholarly interactions would improve the quality of public diplomacy. In years past when diplomacy was left to diplomats the respective publics did not need to know as much about one another as they do today and will hereafter.

The Fulbright program as an American endeavor needs purposefulness beyond advancing the career of the individual graduate student. The American role in the post-cold war world is more complicated than using power to keep adversarial systems in a state of balance. The United States' new role in the world is as a multicultural superpower. As such, it can demonstrate a model of pluralism that does not depend on civil strife or political disintegration. Now there must be a definable educational (or "learning") component to America's international relations. This was belatedly recognized when the revolutions of 1989 opened social and political vacuums in Central and Eastern Europe. Washington struggled to find the words and tactics to support nascent democracies in Eastern Europe. The appropriate response would acknowledge, first, that "power" questions were no longer the central issues; that replacement of a command economy with one that is market-driven, important as that is, would still not be the philosophical starting point; rather, that describing the basic values and through them the long-term commitments are the bedrock concerns of a democratic society. Such an analysis for this or any modern nation demands distilling the essence of its culture.

To formulate a cultural policy will require agreement on the definition of "culture." An American "cultural policy" formulated just before World War II employed "culture" as a propaganda tool in Latin America. Such narrow uses of American "culture" are no longer appropriate. Today's definition should encompass the full range of forms and the broadest spectrum of private as well as public activities that can be considered cultural. By far, the smaller sector will be governmental activities. Should these be conducted in the foreign policy or the educational establishment or, as at present, in both? Should international programs provide only educational information or products favorable to U.S. policy? Should there be different goals for long- or short-term cultural programs? How can cultural-affairs programs be evaluated? Should elites or "people" be targeted? Should private and public cultural programs for international recipients be correlated? Is it, finally, too idealistic to create an *American* cultural policy that ultimately inspires a two-way exchange of cultures with cooperating nations on a basis of equality—and regard that function as in the *American* national interest? Can a consensus be developed for a National Cultural Policy?

Once a cultural policy for international relations has been debated and determined, short-term efforts of cultural diplomacy can be fitted to the larger pattern. The FSB is mandated by the president to establish policy guidelines for foreign exchanges, not to develop national cultural policy. This major undertaking should be launched by the White House, with the participation of a broad range of private sector cultural leaders and ranking officers of the government's educational, information, scientific, communications, and cultural establishments. The sought-after policy would have an international focus. Generating "mutual understanding" among peoples has been the Fulbright objective from the beginning. This should include the goal of applying American scholarship and intellectual power to the enhancement of an American civilization as well. That civilization would influence cultural forums far and wide—without imposing ideas by power or stealth—even as America's model of democracy has influenced massed men and women in public squares from Ladislas to Tiananmen.

Neither academic nor political interests will be properly served if the American national interest is not advanced by government-funded scholarly exchanges. To serve the national interest does not imply an immediate payoff in a particular country or international situation. Indeed, a stipulated "interest" can change with each national administration. Academics best serve the national interest by being free of temporal political concerns by whomever defined, and by concentrating instead on linkages of understanding with peers abroad. Cultural policy should have a significant international, people-to-people objective. It should enhance real exchanges of traditional as well as popular culture through several media. Though foreign area studies are increasingly necessary in multiethnic America, they are not sufficient. An appreciation of people's values and aspirations everywhere, and from time immemorial, is essential in a world steadily contracted by personal association and international communication.

Critics attack some designers of curricula in American education because they would add non-Western culture to core courses and books in the canon of higher education. There is a role for American Fulbrighters to advance cultural diversity without ideological implications. They are equipped by their experience abroad to integrate multicultural educational material with Western or American classics. They appreciate a world of diverse cultures in which non-Western societies gain access to international communication and expect some reciprocity in the exchange of ideas and traditions. The transfer of culture, acculturation, has continued from civilization to civilization. The ideologized emphasis on diversity sometimes suggested for American education tends to impose discrete aspects of America's cultural mix on the larger culture. Yet significant cultural leaders throughout history have strived to benefit the human race. Their legacies in poetry, literature, and political thought benefit all, and do not support provincial concepts of culture. America needs to examine its heritages from abroad. Such reexamination is likely to "increase the degree of rationality in U.S. [international] policy as a result of a higher level of American public understanding of the world, and correspondingly a higher level of rationality of other countries in world affairs."[8]

There are still more pragmatic needs for expanded academic exchanges. Increasingly profound interaction is needed for American scholars to keep in active contact with research innovations around the world. Though the United States still has the world's highest regarded university complex, the nation's competitiveness is being eroded in scholarship as in trade. China in 1992 will have 2,000 foreign students, most from developing countries, enrolled in eighty Chinese colleges and universities. Teaching will be mainly in English. Postgraduate courses will include electronics, computer science, physics, engineering, pediatrics, and acupuncture.[9] Everywhere, including the vast developing world, problems from ecology to peace can best be addressed by cooperative relationships across national boundaries. And these depend largely on mature understanding that results from long-term association and earnest exchange of ideas and aspirations. Living in an increasingly interdependent world requires the development of perspectives that take into account the "connectedness of things."

With eloquence, Isaiah Berlin in *The Crooked Timber of Humanity* describes the "pursuit of the ideal"—in this context the desirable peaceful uses of culture:

> If we are to hope to understand the often violent world in which we live (and unless we try to understand it, we cannot expect to be able to act rationally in it and on it), we cannot confine our attention to the great impersonal forces, natural and man-made, which act upon us. The goals and motives that guide human action must be looked at in the light of all that we know and understand; their roots and growth, their essence, and above all their validity, must be critically examined with every intellectual resource that we have . . . Only barbarians are not curious about where they come from, how they came to be where they are, where they appear to be going, whether they wish to go there, and if so, why, and if not, why not.[10]

Before the Fulbright program can undertake any new mission it must face the stern decision to secure adequate funding for its global operation or cut its program severely. This dilemma is discussed in Chapter 8. That choice will drastically alter the perception of the program everywhere. Slightly less critical are a series of tensions in the operation of the program. Where possible, they should be cured by administrative action. These tensions are examined in Chapter 7.

Chapters 2, 3, 5, and 6 discuss the history, structure, recipients and effectiveness of the program. An interview with the founding father appears as Chapter 4. Chapters 9, 10, 11, and 12 provide four country models of the program at work. A concluding Chapter 13 provides specific recommendations. Neither the problems nor the tensions should diminish the appreciation of the magnificent program known as Fulbright, or the man who gave it life and made his own name a common noun.

2

A History of the Fulbright Program

It took a *second* world war for Americans to realize they were inescapably part of a complex world. Now, what the United States did or didn't do, thought or didn't think, mattered to people far beyond American shores. And Americans, for their own good, needed to understand far more about the rest of the planet. As if to underscore that need, suddenly at the end of the 1980s, there came a dramatic democratization of international politics and diplomacy.

Alexis de Tocqueville had noted a century and a half earlier that Americans are individualists whose worldview drew upon the rationalism of Descartes and the eighteenth-century Enlightenment. That view focused on materialism rather than intangibles. Politics was regarded as a way of reconciling material interests. Life, liberty, and property were the concerns of such politics, not ideological or religious struggle. Yet World War II and the incipient cold war, fought over strong ideologies of the right and left, revealed the need for Americans to understand the world of ideas far more realistically.

After the war, colleges and universities established area and language studies and international affairs schools and programs. Private foundations created diverse projects in international education and development. Some sent Americans abroad to study or teach. Some developed American expertise in international subjects. All brought foreigners to study or occasionally teach in the United States. It would be ten years before the federal government began large expenditures for nonmilitary as well as military research and education through the National Defense Education Act (1954). It also created programs to assist public diplomacy and Americans' understanding of the world.

Informal exchanges of cultural forms and products are as old as civilization. Western culture has drawn on origins in the Fertile Crescent 3,000 years ago, the Hebraic and Islamic civilizations, Greece, with refinements by the Romans, churchmen in the Middle Ages, intellectuals of the Renaissance and Enlightenment, and latter-day creators in Asia, Africa, and Latin America, as well as Western Europe. The global cultural mix was forever altered, moreover, by two American revolutions. In the first, the Rights of Man were embedded in new institutions of democratic governance. This, too, reflected a transoceanic exchange of ideas. Locke, Rousseau, and Montesquieu contributed immensely to the ideas of Jefferson and Madison. And, in turn, the new American system was internationalized by intellectual and political leaders in Europe. That impact continues today in newly liberated countries. The second American "revolution" demonstrated how new science and technology could alter most modes of life and communication. The claim that "the media are American" may exaggerate the degree of the U.S. penetration of information services worldwide. Unquestionably, the American application of communication technology—now widely replicated elsewhere— set the pattern for acculturation in many countries. Indeed, in the always changing American culture, forms from Africa, Asia, and the Middle East are also being acculturated in the United States.

The history of the Fulbright program, not surprisingly, is a microcosm of American concerns abroad. Those concerns are not always clearly enunciated, either in terms of broad national policy or the objectives or procedures of the Fulbright program itself. For example, in serving the "national interest" must an exchange program be rapidly, visibly responsive to that objective? Other countries believe so. Official French policy almost exclusively promotes the adoption of French language and culture. The British Council and Rhodes scholarships explicitly advance Britain's national interests. The Fulbrights, however, were established on the basis of mutual interests—a two-way intellectual flow between the United States and the second country. Was this simply idealistic? Not entirely. The Fulbright program implicitly recognized that the most effective persuasion in the long run is based on sophisticated idealism; that is, advancing American national interests by attracting, not exploiting, but demonstrating mutuality in meeting the objectives and interests of individual citizens—Americans and others—as well as their governments. Although other countries promoted their national language, one segment of the Fulbright program promoted foreign language and foreign area studies in the United States and abroad for American teachers. This would enable Americans to learn, teach, or research more effectively and with greater self-confidence.

At that great moment when the American Constitution was drafted, Madison did not hesitate to consult Montesquieu's writing on checks and balances. Such informal exchange of ideas was common among European and colonial thinkers. In the far more complex twentieth century, systematic intellectual exchanges are required. The political and intellectual arrangements needed for the Fulbright exchanges sometimes generate questions, problems, and tensions. I shall spotlight in subsequent chapters those basic questions still before the Fulbright program.

Educational exchanges flowed from the humanistic tradition of American scholarship. These scholars drew heavily on European cultural sources, while contributing their own considerable insights and research techniques. One such scholar, Charles Rufus Morey, a young American professor of art and archeology from Princeton, went to Rome's prestigious American Academy in 1904. Morey became known as a great art historian of the early Christian period. Morey returned to Rome in 1945 and until 1950 he was the U.S. cultural attaché. While there, he also served uniquely for three years as director of the American Academy. Morey in 1948 founded the binational Fulbright program in Italy. He influenced many intellectual exchanges. From his Princeton University days, Morey was a close friend of Senator H. Alexander Smith, who teamed with Representative Karl Mundt to write the first peacetime U.S. law mandating activities in international information, education, and cultural exchange. The act systematized the nascent Fulbright program (1948). Morey was part of the distinguished group of American scholars engaged in personal cultural exchanges before the exchanges became officially institutionalized.[1]

Around the time Morey first went to Rome, the first privately endowed cultural exchange program started in England using the 6-million-pound estate of Cecil Rhodes. The Rhodes scholarships were created with a stated imperial, not at all binational, objective. The South African diamond merchant envisioned a world under British rule. The Rhodes scholarships enabled Americans, Germans, and British colonial subjects to attend Britain's elite universities. Thirty-two awards were earmarked each year for students from the United States.

One Rhodes scholar in 1925 was a young college graduate from Arkansas, J. William Fulbright: a B student, campus leader, and star football halfback. This man's eventual contribution to scholarly exchange may be regarded—ironically, given Cecil Rhodes's attachment to British imperialism—as Rhodes's unanticipated achievement. For the young, impressionable Fulbright, who had not seen an ocean, a major American city, let alone a foreign country, never forgot the enlightening, broadening experience of studying at Oxford and living in another civilization.

He stayed abroad for four years and returned home with two Oxford degrees. "It was almost like a dream," Fulbright recalls.[2] He ascended rapidly to the U.S. Senate. In 1944, with the war still raging, he spent a month in England at the Conference of Allied Ministers of Education. There, he was further inspired to promote the exchange of students. The purpose, he told the U.S. Senate Appropriations Committee hearing (1945), "is to try to bring about a fairer understanding of the history of each of these countries . . . instead of emphasizing the differences." Fulbright added, "It inherently has an element of promoting mutual security." He decided that year to create an American scholarly exchange. "I was looking for intellectual leaders who could be political leaders," Fulbright says. "I was in politics, and the inspiration came from World War II and how to avoid war in the future." We can profit, he believes, "from historic as well as proximate examples. That is what education is all about." There is a multiplier effect in international education, he says, the real possibility of "changing our manner of thinking about the world, and therefore of changing the world." One observer says Fulbright had "an extravagant ambition—to protect the world from self-destruction." Yet, it should be recalled, Fulbright in 1940 became an ardent military interventionist to stop the Nazi-Fascist advances in Europe. He was a strong supporter of William Allen White's Committee to Defend America by Aiding the Allies (mainly Great Britain), a committee that evolved as Freedom House.

Though little remembered, it was Fulbright, the unusual first-year representative in Congress, who secured passage of the resolution calling for the creation of, and U.S. membership in, a United Nations organization. It would have "international machinery with power to prevent further aggression." That was in 1943 while World War II raged, nearly a half century before the U.N. Security Council mobilized coalition troops for the Persian Gulf war. Fulbright would also fight for the Bretton Woods Agreement, which established the World Bank and the International Monetary Fund.

In 1945, again a freshman, this time in the U.S. Senate, Fulbright almost surreptitiously initiated an intellectual exchange program for the United States. It would become in the next forty-five years the centerpiece of American private as well as public intellectual exchange programs. Students, scholars and researchers would move across the world to or from the United States as "Fulbrighters"—the rare example of one man's name becoming the common noun for a host of persons related by intellectual pursuits rather than familial ties. By that measure, however, the Fulbright alumni are becoming an extended family.

American cultural exchange was not altogether new when Senator Fulbright globalized the process in 1946. Seven years earlier, Roosevelt's

State Department established a division of cultural cooperation to begin exchanges with other American republics under the leadership of Nelson Rockefeller. In 1938, seventeen countries signed the U.S.-drafted Convention for the Promotion of Inter-American Cultural Relations. Impetus came from the recognition that Nazis and Fascists were making political inroads in Latin America by increasing their cultural ties. World War II was just one year ahead.[3] Two fundamental principles set forth for the U.S. program under that convention have guided the Fulbright scholarships as well:

First, cultural relations activities of our country would be reciprocal, there must be no imposition of one people's culture upon another; second, the exchange of cultural interests should involve the participation of people and institutions concerned with those interests in the respective countries; that is, the program should stem from the established centers of culture.

In 1941, the State Department expanded the program to include educational and cultural exchanges with China.[4] This was the U.S. government's initial international educational exchange outside the Americas. The Latin American and Chinese projects were kept distinctly separate from the new wartime information agency that officially used the word "propaganda" for the first time. In 1946, the first official peacetime program of information and cultural affairs envisioned a long-term operation eliminating the wartime propaganda functions. The new program would focus on "peoples" rather than governments. The same year (1946), the first peacetime foreign-policy review of U.S.-Soviet relations, drafted by Clark Clifford as a top-secret report for President Truman,[5] proposed "cultural [and] intellectual interchange" along with economic measures "to demonstrate to the Soviet Union that we have no aggressive intentions, and that peaceable coexistence of capitalism and communism is possible."

That year, too, Americans initiated a massive "reeducation" program in U.S.-occupied Germany. This was first operated by the U.S. military government and later by the civilian U.S. High Commissioner for Germany. Hans Speier, an American social scientist who helped design the program, says it was "initially conceived in military and moral terms rather than as a political issue." "Reeducation" was regarded as a defense of U.S. national interests. It was "to provide long-range protection against a recurrence of aggression by building a psychological foundation on which political and economic reform could rest with hope of survival—the assumption being that neither reform would be of much avail nor long duration if each was not grounded in basic changes in values, attitudes, and institutions."[6] The objective was "to give a maximum number of young Germans on the secondary school, undergraduate and graduate level the chance to study at an institution in a democratic country and, at the same time, to receive a first-hand demonstration of democracy at work and to participate in community living."[7] Before the bilateral Fulbright program began in Germany, some 14,000 people moved between Germany and the United States on military- and civilian-run educational exchanges. An additional 2,228 persons moved between Germany and other European countries under the program.

As the U.S.-initiated reeducation succeeded, Germans played a greater role in conducting the program. On July 18, 1952, the United States and Germany signed the agreement creating the binational commission to operate the Fulbright program in that country. Shortly afterward, the U.S. High Commissioner's manual termed it a fundamental purpose to give "exchanges an opportunity to experience a democratic environment which contributes to a cooperative way of life, and to stimulate the free interchange of ideas between free nations." Although not specifically targeting the individual German's education as the American objective, the High Commission seemed to recognize, as did the Fulbright program thereafter, that national values and actions are the composite of ideas and aspirations of individual citizens.

The first binational Fulbright agreement—that between China and the United States—was signed in Nanking on November 10, 1947, one year and three months after President Truman approved what became known as the Fulbright Act. That act was not an eloquent document. It did not extol the value of intellectual exchanges, nor did it state explicitly how or where the exchanges would be conducted. Public Law 584 of the 79th Congress, approved August 1, 1946, was cleverly rushed through Congress by young Fulbright as an amendment to the Surplus Property Act of 1944. The amendment stipulated that foreign credits earned overseas by the sale of surplus U.S. wartime property could be used to finance studies, research, instruction, and other educational activities of Americans in institutions of higher learning abroad.[8] This included payment for travel, tuition, and maintenance. Foreign students and scholars would receive funds only for transportation to attend American schools and institutions. Not more than $1 million could be expended annually, or $20 million totally in any one country. A ten-person (later expanded to twelve) uncompensated Board of Foreign Scholarships appointed by the president was created to oversee the program. In 1990, the Congress honored the founder of the program by changing the name to the J. William Fulbright Foreign Scholarship Board.[9]

Fulbright understood that by funding his program from existing but frozen foreign currencies he could avoid political opposition from congressional colleagues. "Oh," Fulbright recalls, "they didn't have any idea what [the amendment] was about, and it didn't require any appropriation."[10] Funding for the Fulbright program began in 1948 with the passage of the U.S. Information and Educational Exchange Act.[11] The Smith-Mundt Act, named for cosponsors Senator H. Alexander Smith of New Jersey and Representative Karl Mundt of South Dakota, was needed to fund the maintenance in the United States of foreign grantees, and conduct exchanges in countries with minimal surplus property sales. Foreign currency could continue to pay for the travel of foreign Fulbright grantees to the United States. Debate over the Smith-Mundt Act, the first omnibus legislation for overseas information and cultural activities, focused sharply on the distinction between information and educational activities. There was considerable insistence that the two be kept separate—a theme recurring to this day. Information was regarded as propaganda designed to gain acceptance for U.S. policies, and educational exchanges were viewed as cooperative or reciprocal, and longer ranged.

The first Fulbrighter in the exchange process was Derk Bodde, a sinologist at the University of Pennsylvania. He went to China in 1948. That fall, another 46 Americans and 36 foreign nationals from Burma and the Philippines as well as China started their Fulbright year. Within a year, binational agreements were signed with New Zealand, the United Kingdom, Belgium, France, Italy, the Netherlands and Norway. In the 1949 academic year, 823 Americans and 967 from overseas traveled on Fulbright awards. Before 1952 ended, another 17 binational agreements, a total of 28, were in place. That year, some 1,253 Americans and 2,210 foreign nationals became academic travelers. Funds still came from overseas creditors of the United States. To bolster the cash flow, Congress in June 1952 accepted Senator Fulbright's amendment to the Mutual Security Act. This made accessible, for educational exchanges, counterpart funds accruing from World War II lend-lease agreements. Much Fulbright funding after 1954 also came from the sale of surplus farm products abroad.

In 1958, the past value of the Fulbright program was assessed by John T. and Jeanne E. Gullahorn. More than 100 former grantees from nine Midwest states were interviewed.[12] Some findings: between 97 percent and 93 percent said that living as a foreigner was maturing, one of their life's most valuable experiences. Their interest in international affairs increased, and by living abroad they gained considerable perspective on the United States. Their university superiors agreed the Fulbright awards had been beneficial not only for the grantee but for other faculty and students as well. The study attributed to administrators the view that "a large number of former grantees in their colleges and schools would help make their communities more intelligently aware of and more curious about the rest of the world." Only 3 percent felt that a year at a university in the United States would have been more valuable than the experience abroad. Ninety-two percent of the Fulbrighters believed that receiving the award had been beneficial to their professional careers. More than half (53 percent) said they had maintained contact with individuals abroad on a professional basis. Nearly as many (47 percent) kept in touch with their host institution abroad.[13] Of the 711 respondents, 83 percent had given a total of 13,374 talks to audiences totaling 458,260 persons concerning their Fulbright experience abroad.[14]

The German Fulbright program was evaluated from its inception in 1953 to 1959.[15] There had been 2,069 American grantees and 1,834 Germans. Of 647 German respondents, more than half were students who had just completed course work at German universities. Others were university teachers or researchers, or assistants at universities. In the study, the German Fulbrighters by an "overwhelming majority commented favorably, even enthusiastically," about American academic life.[16] Three-fourths believed they had gained professional or personal advantage through their study or teaching in America.[17] Ninety percent said that since returning home they had an opportunity to correct false ideas about the United States. Back home, nearly all discussed America in lectures and other public appearances.[18] The study concluded that German Fulbrighters had "established lasting bonds with their American friends which have made their sojourn in the U.S. a personally far more gratifying experience than would have resulted if academic work and contacts alone had been involved."[19]

The concept of binationalism and mutual benefits inherent in the Fulbright exchanges was increasingly recognized in academe and the Congress. Yet the world was different from the immediate post-war era into which the Fulbright Act was quietly born. Now (1961), President Kennedy was in the White House. Scores of new nations had thrown off colonial bonds. Technological and scientific education were top national priorities. The Soviet's Sputnik had been orbiting. Education, at home and abroad, was a concern of Congress. It consolidated educational exchanges under the basic congressional mandate—the Mutual Educational and Cultural Exchange Act of 1961. Senator Fulbright introduced the bill in the Senate and Representative Wayne Hays of Ohio, in the House. The Fulbright-Hays Act[20] sought "to provide for the improvement and strengthening of the international relations of the United States by promoting better mutual understanding among the peoples of the world through educational and cultural exchanges." Fulbright-Hays, still the operative legislation today, added significant programs to cultural exchange not envisioned in either the original Fulbright Act or the Smith-Mundt Act. Specifically,

> To enable the government of the United States to increase mutual understanding between the people of the United States and the people of other countries by means of educational and cultural exchange; to strengthen the ties which unite us with other nations by demonstrating the educational and cultural interests, developments and achievements of the people of the United States and other nations, and the contributions being made toward a peaceful and more fruitful life for people throughout the world; to promote international cooperation for educational and cultural advancement; and thus to assist in the development of friendly, sympathetic, and peaceful relations between the United States and the other countries of the world.

The act provided grants, among other programs, for Americans studying abroad or foreigners studying in the United States; for cultural and special-visitor exchanges; and for supporting modern foreign-language training and area studies in the United States by visits of American teachers to foreign countries. This last Fulbright program is conducted by the U.S. Department of Education, *not* the U.S. Information Agency which operates all other Fulbright programs.

In a statement before the Senate in June 1961, Senator Fulbright declared: "I utterly reject any suggestion that our educational and cultural exchange programs are weapons or instruments with which to do combat . . . [T]here is no room and there must not be any room for any interpretation of these programs as propaganda, even recognizing that the term covers very worthwhile and respectable activities." Fulbright was principally responding to those who regarded cultural exchanges as a form of persuasion.

The Fulbright-Hays Act is the charter that continues to set the tone, coordinate, and provide legislative support for diverse educational and cultural exchanges. The act specifically requires the president to "insure that all programs . . . shall maintain their non-political character and shall be balanced and representative of the diversity of American political, social and cultural life. The President shall insure that academic and cultural programs . . . shall maintain their scholarly integrity and shall meet the highest standards of academic excellence or artistic achievement." (From 1989 amendment. See Chapter 7.)

Then Secretary of State Dean Rusk hailed the Fulbright-Hays Act as "a milestone on the road to wider recognition that these constructive and creative activities are one of man's best hopes for world peace." By 1964,

Fulbright programs functioned in 110 countries, in 48 of which binational commissions stipulated the academic needs and nominated grantees by mutual agreement. Several commissions became dormant when the governments were destabilized or withdrew. (New commissions were created in 1990 with Canada and Mexico, followed in 1991 by binational commissions in Hungary and Czechoslovakia. Another may arise soon in Poland. By 1992 there were 47 binational commissions.)

Calls to cut back exchanges with Europeans and increase those with developing countries were examined in a 1963 analysis of educational exchanges by the U.S. Advisory Commission on International Educational and Cultural Affairs. Similar calls to apply Fulbright grants to Third World development projects came in 1990–1991. Now, as in the 1960s, the Fulbright program is regarded by some as a technical assistance program, which it is not. The 1963 assessment, mandated by the Fulbright-Hays Act, "seriously questions" downgrading the program in Western Europe.[21] This issue arose again in 1990–1991 with pressure to shift scarce Fulbright funds from Western Europe (and elsewhere) to Eastern Europe. "Europe," said the 1963 report, "is possibly undergoing more fateful changes than many of the underdeveloped nations of the world. We do not clearly know—nor perhaps do the Europeans themselves—precisely what form the new Europe will take. But we do know that we must keep in touch with it . . . [T]he need for mutual understanding, far from being past, is increasing rather than diminishing." The 1963 report of the Commission chaired by John Gardner did not diminish the value of educational exchanges with developing countries. On the contrary, the authors quote one of "our most knowledgeable respondents," stating:

> Economic and social reform in the new and needful countries of Asia, the Near East and Africa—and in Latin America and the Caribbean to which the Alliance for Progress is addressed—will be feasible only to the extent that attitudes are changed in the realm of politics and policies, that intelligence is challenged and upgraded, and that the development of human resources is accomplished. These are immense undertakings in which foreign (and especially U.S.) intervention and assistance are a difficult and delicate enterprise politically. The somewhat indirect and oblique, but vitally essential, approach through education and cultural affairs is the most welcome and accepted, the least likely to be resented or suspected, the most potent long-range.[22]

The Advisory Commission's report was the "most broadly based survey ever made of the [Fulbright] program" up to that time. The program was still in the Bureau of Educational and Cultural Affairs of the State Department. Some conclusions:

• Testimony is overwhelming from all sources that the program as a whole is effective. The evidence is also conclusive that the program has proved itself an essential and valuable part of America's total international effort.

• There is impressive evidence that the exchange program increases mutual understanding.

• Evidence is abundant that the exchange program has succeeded in helping dispel among foreign visitors many misconceptions and ugly stereotypes about the American people.

• The exchange program does not bring about a uniformly favorable point of view on all aspects of the American scene; the reaction of former grantees varies considerably with the country from which they have come, and with the particular aspect inquired about.

• The program has effectively established channels of communication between the people in other countries and the United States. Well over two-thirds of all returned grantees occupy positions in which they can readily communicate their broadened perspectives—whether as teachers, journalists or top-level administrators.

• The exchange program has effectively supported one of the nation's most basic international objectives—of helping to support strong free societies able to work together, in mutual trust and understanding.

The 1963 report, aptly titled "A Beacon of Hope," provided some suggestions for improvement: Select more "have-nots" with promise and talent so the program does not favor elite grantees or institutions. Seek candidates abroad who are "sufficiently vigorous and restless to help promote desirable social and economic change"—even some considered radical, left-wing, or politically dissident—so that they can learn there is "a democratic road to reform." Increase the low salaries paid professors and lecturers to raise the quality of academics sent overseas. Examine the quality, status, and role of the cultural affairs officer who conducts the exchange program overseas. Not enough attention is paid the CAO. The Fulbright program as a whole suffers "fiscal starvation."

The study declared: "There is no other international activity of our government that enjoys so much spontaneous public approval, elicits such extensive citizen participation, and yields such impressive evidence of success. In a time when most international activities seem almost unbearably complex, hazardous and obscure in outcome, the success of educational exchange is a beacon of hope."

The report regarded the exchange-of-persons program as unique "in the whole history of human affairs." The program responds to the spread of democratic forms of government, education, and vastly expanded global communications. Foreign relations and national development must be concerned with "the people's attitudes, their state of progress and education, their level of information, their hopes and expectations." The educational exchanges reflect what the study termed "four rather remarkable characteristics": American faith in direct exposure between peoples as a means of dispelling misconceptions, education as the principal bridge of contact, freedom of inquiry, and private participation and initiative.

Despite these high grades, the Fulbright program suffered sharp financial cutbacks in 1967 to 1968, crucial years of the Vietnam War. The International Education Act of 1966, intended to expand America's cultural programs abroad, never was funded. The State Department's cultural programs were cut almost 50 percent in two years. The Fulbright program was notably slashed from about 6,000 grantees a year both ways to about 2,000. Senator Fulbright attributes this to President Lyndon Johnson's "falling out with me" over the Vietnam War.[23] Some latter-day substantiation comes from Clark Clifford, Johnson's adviser. He quotes the president saying, "It's easier to satisfy Ho Chi Minh [the Vietnamese enemy leader] than Bill Fulbright."[24] More likely, however, the Fulbright program had more than one slasher. The Vietnam war drained funds from many federal programs, while campus war protests turned some officials against the academy. Perhaps, too, the first shock to American education by the sound of the Soviet's Sputnik whining overhead had tapered considerably by the end of the 1960s. America was putting a man on the moon and could turn to other affairs.

One politically wise and scholarly observer called such perpetual underemphasis of American educational and cultural policy abroad "The Neglected Aspect of Foreign Affairs."[25] Charles Frankel, a Columbia University philosopher, was President Johnson's assistant secretary of state for educational and cultural Affairs. His book is not a historical study or an examination of administrative organization and procedures. "It is," he wrote, "a study of principles." Its purpose was to suggest how to think about American educational and cultural diplomacy, and particularly that small but extremely significant segment of these affairs in which the federal government has a directing hand. Frankel focused on the basic principles of exchanges because he saw that the rapidly changing intellectual and cultural commerce between the United States and other nations was producing radical changes in international relations. And these changes, in turn, would influence not only nations but their citizens. "A major society in the second half of the twentieth century that fails to develop a systematic body of thought about this new dimension of international relations," said Frankel, "is like a seventeenth-century society that failed to give careful attention to the role of commerce overseas."

Charles Frankel would probably express similar concerns today, but he and his wife were murdered in their sleep in 1979. Cross-border intellectual exchanges are no longer of interest mainly to the scholarly world. Many more people everywhere are now directly exposed to the products of scholarly and intellectual activity. Frankel wrote the words President Johnson spoke at the Smithsonian Institution's Bicentennial Celebration in September 1965: "We know today that . . . ideas, not armaments, will shape our lasting prospects for peace; that the conduct of our foreign policy will advance no faster than the curriculum of our classrooms; that the knowledge of our citizens is one treasure which grows only when it is shared."

Whether or not federal intellectual exchange programs are planned with central objectives of national policy in mind, they are nevertheless presumed by observers at home and abroad to be symbolic of a national commitment—or, as Frankel reminded, "a lack of commitment," if funds and interest are miserly. "The tone of a government program is only too easily identified, by Americans as well as foreigners, as the American tone," Frankel observed. "The purposes for which the government uses educational and cultural activities are taken or mistaken for the purposes that American society as a whole assigns to such activities." Frankel termed the Fulbright program "an instructive symbol of [America's] history of educational and cultural policies." He found the Fulbright program "a sound point of departure for what should be done in the future." But those who operate the program are obliged to respond to a variety of questions from the Congress, other agencies and the public. Their answers are satisfactory, Frankel asserted, but often "the questions they are answering are the wrong questions."

Frankel sets forth "the fundamental and ineluctable fact" on which all government programs in international cultural affairs rise or fall—then and still: "The government is dealing in something which it does not produce, and which, given the habits and principles of free government, it has neither the power nor the right to regulate and control. An educational program exports what is by nature unofficial, and what has not normally been created—at any rate, if it is of high quality—to suit the special needs of a government program." That basic principle requires a framework of cooperation involving scholarly organizations, universities and individual scholars, and students. They must recognize a proprietary and professional interest in the successful outcome of the program. Frankel recognized that a nongovernmental participant must regard his or her work as an "initiator and trustee" of the cross-border exercise. A

National Cultural Policy today would not seek to alter the *content* of American intellectual exchanges. The policy would provide a welcoming intellectual climate, invite larger and better focused exchanges, and provide adequate funding.

Frankel warned that intellectuals in different countries were willing with varying degrees of readiness to participate in government exchange programs. Some American scholars regard any form of close association with government or industry as an abandonment of their intellectual independence. Academic freedom, always intensely defended, is especially evoked when a Washington administration pursues policies that run counter to the generally liberal bent of the majority of scholars. (A 1989 Wirthlin poll found that 56 percent of academics characterize themselves as liberal and 28 percent conservatives.) Many scholars in Western Europe, Asia, Africa, and Latin America, however, move back and forth between the universities and government posts. Foreign scholars are more likely to be activists in political parties, even while engaging in scholarly pursuits. This, said Frankel, reflected not only the shortage of manpower in the emerging countries but the congruence of official ideologies and the principles of the scholars. These ideologies may represent the overriding interest in "development" as a national concern which intellectuals no less than politicians are expected to address. Fewer American scholars, moreover, regard themselves as "generalized intellectuals," but rather men and women possessing special knowledge, like doctors or engineers. Foreign scholars are self-consciously intellectuals, commanding a broader view of their society and its problems. They think of their social role, in Frankel's words, as "secular priests—general guides, critics and judges of their society."

They are particularly critical of state power. Intellectual groups abroad are often "negatively disposed toward American society and American policy. To be critical of power almost automatically entails that one be critical of the country that, above all others, possesses and epitomizes worldly success, wealth and influence," Frankel held. American policy, therefore, must contend with a "basic undertow of suspicion against it on the part of intellectuals in other countries."

How, then, should one define American educational and cultural activities? Frankel suggests that government intellectual programs should be deliberately conducted for the sake of educational and cultural communication. No less important, these activities should be peculiarly concerned with long-range matters.[26] News and information—the "fast" media—generally should not be regarded as "educational" or "cultural" exchange. To be sure, the fast media can have a long-range effect on the attitudes of the respective audience overseas. Many bitter critics of

American news media in the "new information order" controversies at UNESCO in the 1980s assumed that news reportage negatively affects cultural traditions as well as social development in Third World countries. Frankel acknowledged "there is a penumbral area where 'information' on one side, and 'education and culture' on the other, fade into each other." This distinction between information and educational/cultural programs, nevertheless, should be acknowledged.

That distinction would feed a major interagency struggle that existed since the earlier reorganization of U.S. information and educational-cultural programs. In 1953, John Foster Dulles—probably to ward off further demagogic attacks on the State Department from Senator Joseph McCarthy—removed information programs from the department and placed them in the newly created United States Information Agency (USIA). Dulles was prevented from disposing of educational-cultural programs along with information by the timely intercession of Senators Fulbright and Bourke Hickenlooper. Republicans and Democrats passed a resolution stating that the objectives of educational and cultural programs were different than those of information programs and that the two should therefore be administered separately. The State Department retained educational-cultural affairs, although, says Frankel,[27] it might have made more sense from the standpoint of diplomacy to retain the information and not educational-cultural programs. When Frankel became assistant secretary of state for educational and cultural affairs (CU), he quickly faced this anomaly, as told in the revealing book he wrote as an "outsider":

[The Senate insisted on separating information from educational-cultural programs but did not say how the people should be reassigned.] The bureaucracy got to work on this knotty problem . . . All the people were neatly divided into two classes, those who were abroad and those who were in Washington. Those abroad were assigned to the new Information Agency, and those in Washington were kept in the Department of State. In consequence, the cultural section of the State Department was deprived of representatives of its own overseas. To find such representatives it had no place to turn but to the Information Agency. Cultural Affairs Officers became the administrators abroad of the American cultural program. This is the situation that still exists. The State Department, and not the Information Agency, pays the salaries of these officers, but it neither hires nor fires nor assigns them . . . The Senate had wanted cultural affairs sharply separated from propaganda activities. The bureaucracy came up with a solution that put cultural affairs overseas in the hands of people whose primary mission, as members of the information agency, was propaganda. The Senate had wanted the State Department to be responsible for cultural

policy. But the Assistant Secretary for Cultural Affairs . . . cannot communicate directly with Cultural Affairs Officers who are presumably
carrying out his policies, nor can they do so with him.[28] The man who sits
in-between is the chief of the information service in the embassy (the
Public Affairs Officer, so called). This officer, whose background is usually
in the mass media or public relations, directly supervises the Cultural
Affairs Officer . . . I suspect there are few more frustrating jobs in the
United States government than that of Cultural Affairs Officer.[29]

Elsewhere, Frankel refers sympathetically to the CAO as "the man in
the middle."[30] The CAOs still function under the authority of the PAOs.
The question of culture as propaganda arose with greater immediacy in
a further reorganization involving the State Department and the USIA in
1975. Indeed, the question would be asked, is not all cultural exchange,
even that embodying mutual exchanges between governments, a form of
"propaganda," and is it necessarily pejorative to say so?

The Fulbright program was not considered politicized when educational and cultural affairs were managed in the autonomous CU bureau
in the State Department. CU, and particularly the Fulbright program,
received few, if any, particular directives from the State Department.
The Fulbright program was seen as valuable, prestigious, and not threatening to the State Department's daily policy interests. The program was
generally assumed to be "in the national interest."[31] And by 1977 scholarly exchanges, along with USIA's cross-border radio broadcasts and
visits to the United States from foreign leaders, were regarded as "public
diplomacy."

Cultural activities had already been scrutinized. In February 1961,
President Kennedy had several recommendations to put CU into USIA.
He also had a number of expert reports recommending a contrary line of
action. He decided to follow the latter course. Indeed, he elevated the
Bureau of Educational and Cultural Affairs by designating its director,
Philip H. Coombs, an assistant secretary of state.[32] In May 1969, the U.S.
Advisory Commission on Information renewed its call for a major review of the USIA and asked, "Are information, educational and cultural
objectives compatible within one agency? . . . Do we really intend that
USIA work toward 'mutual understanding'; is it to help us understand
them as well as to help them understand us? . . . As we repeat the questions, so also do we repeat the hope that they will be answered." In May
1973, the Senate Foreign Relations Committee considered a redistribu-
tion of the functions performed by the USIA and the State Department's
CU. Two months later, the U.S. Advisory Commission on International
Education and Cultural Affairs (CU's advisory body) decided to investigate how USIA and CU might rearrange their similar and related func-

tions in ways to improve their effective performance, particularly in light of the changing directions of U.S. foreign policy.[33]

A later assistant secretary for CU, John Richardson, universally respected for his management of cultural affairs in the Nixon and Ford administrations, responded to the 1973 recommendations by organizing a basic review of the structure of international information, education, and cultural relations. The commission had a private-sector host,[34] private funding, and a distinguished 21-person panel headed by Frank Stanton, then chairman of the American Red Cross, formerly president of the Columbia Broadcasting System (CBS). Members included Peter Krogh, dean of Georgetown's school of foreign service; George Gallup, chairman, the American Institute of Public Opinion; Edmund A. Gullion, dean of the Fletcher School of Law and Diplomacy, Tufts University; Hobart Lewis, editor-in-chief, *Reader's Digest*; Leonard H. Marks, former director of the USIA; and members of the U.S. Advisory Commission on International Education and Cultural Affairs. Walter R. Roberts was the executive director.

The Stanton Commission, as it became known, made clear distinctions between the functions of the USIA and CU. Said the commission's 1975 report:

> CU, despite its location within the Department of State, has had no direct connection with foreign policy; indeed, it has been distinguished from USIA by its separation as an educational and cultural agency, from the politics of the foreign policy process and by the fact that it exchanges people, whereas USIA deals in media. CU's programs have thus been considered, not as a one-way effort to get a particular message across overseas, but as providing an opportunity for mutual contact between the United States and other nations on a personal level. As a result, CU has been expected to make an impact in the United States, to build understanding here as well as abroad, whereas the USIA was specifically enjoined by law from "propagandizing" the American people.[35]

The Stanton Commission observed that the organizational structure for public diplomacy, as historically developed, was "at variance with logic in several obvious respects."[36] Some foreign-policy activities were performed by the USIA, while educational and cultural exchanges were inside the State Department. Information about American society, including its culture, was explained by the USIA—"requiring it to be in touch with two very different kinds of information to be handled in two very different ways." The organizational separation of USIA and CU deprived USIA of control in Washington over an important tool for depicting U.S. life and thought overseas, while it seemed that USIA's dissemination of information abroad about U.S. life was not related to CU's efforts to build understanding of the United States overseas. Finally, the relationship was further complicated by CU programs abroad being executed by USIA officials. The commission found that most of the USIA's work was directed at the same longer-range objectives as CU's. Both cultural affairs officers and public affairs officers, all of whom were employees of USIA, told the commission, not surprisingly, that the overseas program must operate as a unit. The success of the program, the CAOs and PAOs said, has been "in spite of—rather than because of—the organizational structure in Washington."[37]

The Stanton Commission concluded that all information programs related to policy be placed in the State Department in a bureau established for that purpose and headed by an assistant secretary. All educational and cultural programs (including Fulbright) and those providing general information about the United States but not involving current political policy would be combined in a single operation. But the commission would place these programs neither in an autonomous USIA nor within the State Department. The commission proposed that these USIA and CU programs be placed in an entity to be known as the Information and Cultural Affairs Agency. The new agency would be "under—but not in—the Department of State." This relationship would be similar to the Agency for International Development (AID) and the Arms Control and Disarmament Agency (ACDA). (Certain USIA functions such as the Voice of America and foreign-policy guidance programs would be transferred elsewhere.) The Board of Foreign Scholarships would continue to ensure that academic grantees would be selected purely on the basis of academic excellence and without regard to political considerations.

For the first time in fifty years, a responsible body had shown how policy advocacy and cultural affairs could be separately structured in the American system. There was in 1975—and remains—some support for the Stanton proposal. Gifford Malone, a State Department officer who served as deputy associate director of USIA for two terms in the 1970s and 1980s, wrote in 1987: "The suggested [Stanton Commission] arrangement provides an essential separation of educational and cultural programs from day-to-day policy concerns and the ordinary business of diplomacy, while at the same time maintaining an equally important connection with broad policy objectives."[38]

This separation of policy-information and cultural programs was independently recommended by a high-level foreign policy commission reporting to the president on June 27, 1975, just three months after the Stanton report was released. Robert D. Murphy, former ambassador and special presidential emissary, headed the commission, which included

Vice President Nelson A. Rockefeller, William J. Casey, then head of the Export-Import Bank, Senator Mike Mansfield, and Representative Clement J. Zablocki. The Murphy Commission was established by Public Law 92-352 to suggest a more effective system for formulating and implementing American foreign policy.[39] The commission found that "neither foreign policy advocacy nor the building of long-range understanding between the United States and other nations is now being handled with full effectiveness." The commission decided that the advocacy function should be placed within the State Department alongside policy formulation. Cultural affairs should be put in a single agency separate from, but responsible to, the State Department. These recommendations, said the Murphy Commission, "coincide with the Stanton Panel findings."[40] The Murphy report then specified in considerable detail how the reorganization should proceed.

But opposition to the Stanton recommendations prevailed before the Carter administration came into office. Walter Roberts, the executive director of the Stanton Commission and a former associate director of the USIA who had been engaged in U.S. government communications since 1942, describes the "terribly funny" decision:

Cy[rus] Vance [then Secretary of State] is a neighbor of Frank Stanton's in the upper east side of New York, and I think on January 19 [1975] the two of them with their wives had dinner before he [Stanton] came down here [Washington] on January 20th. Vance told him that he would accept the Stanton panel lock, stock and barrel. He was quoted. In other words, information was to be in the State Department, cultural programs separate and the Voice of America still separate. The people who opposed it were basically my colleagues in the bureaucracy of the USIA. They did not wish to see these things divided into three parts. They wanted to have one big organization because you are more powerful if you are in one big organization rather than three smaller ones . . . They had many friends on the Hill, and they enlisted [Zbigniew] Brzezinski's [National Security Adviser to President Carter] support. So in the end the Stanton panel was only partially accepted, in my opinion, solely for organizational reasons. Nobody really thought it through, that intellectually and philosophically it made a lot of sense.[41]

Carter rejected what had been recommended. He moved the educational/cultural staff from the State Department to the information agency, even as he formally declared that the International Communication Agency (earlier and later, the USIA) should "conduct negotiations on cultural exchange with other governments, aware always that the most effective sharing of cultures, ideas and information comes between individual people rather than through formal acts of governments."[42]

Richard T. Arndt, a veteran foreign service officer and strong proponent of cultural programs protected from political influences, makes this assessment of the attitudes inside the USIA to the move of CU to USIA:

> The USIA opponents of the Stanton idea, and their friends in Congress, were of several varieties. The honest ones believed that the business of USIA was only the whitewashed American version of propaganda we have called, since the Creel Committee, "information"; everything else was fun and games, done by "little old ladies in tennis shoes" . . . The Machiavellians, on the other hand, saw that the cultural programs provided an enhancement, or even a cover under which information programs could function more effectively; but they believed that only propagandists could "manage" the cultural program if it was to be an effective tool of foreign policy. The timorous [USIA loyalists], and there were more of these than one would imagine, feared the power of the cultural affairs orientation, especially in an administration like Carter's; they saw the propaganda function seriously endangered by the seductive wiles of culture. And finally there were the inescapable opportunists and time-servers who knew which side of their bread held the butter; there were the cynics and anti-intellectuals who knew that the intellectual world overseas did not matter any more than it did in the U.S., and there were the hedgehog specialists, especially of different media techniques, who knew only their job and could not muster the curiosity to see how others' work could enhance theirs.[43]

The same decision was observed 90 miles offshore in Havana. Enrique Gonzalez-Manet, a Marxist polemicist active in international communications forums, assumed that the Stanton report had "laid the groundwork for the USIA's reorganization." At the end of the 1970s, said Gonzalez, "the government of President Carter took important steps which set the stage for the Reagan Administration's propaganda project . . . Proposed by then-National Security Adviser Z. Brzezinski . . . [the plan] unified the United States Information Agency (USIA) with the State Department's Bureau of Educational and Cultural Affairs. President Carter also obtained from Congress a substantial budgetary increase to strengthen the operations of the propaganda system abroad." Gonzalez noted that "cultural/educational exchanges" would be linked to security matters within the purview of the USIA. [44]

A concern for that linkage, for quite different political motivations, was held by some in Washington as well as Havana. The Congressional Research Service, at the request of Senator Fulbright, chairman of the Senate Foreign Relations Committee,[45] had reported in August 1975 on

U.S. information and cultural programs.[46] The CRS found that the presidentially appointed Board of Foreign Scholarships had "successfully" protected "the integrity of the [Fulbright] program against political pressures." USIA's cultural programs were, however, seen by CRS as designed to achieve "tactical foreign policy objectives" while State's cultural programs "stressed the principle of mutuality and long-term 'bridge-building.'" The CRS noted, though, that partly "because of increased congressional criticism of its information programs, USIA has attempted to deemphasize traditional distinctions between information and culture, and to stress longer-term cultural and educational programs."[47] The CRS concluded, then, that "cultural and educational exchange programs do not usually serve short-term foreign policy objectives, but are seen to be in the national interest because of the informal communication which they encourage and the linkages which they foster between individuals and institutions."[48] The CRS consequently recommended combining the State Department's and USIA's cultural programs, and placing them in a new, autonomous agency associated with the State Department or an existing cultural organization. Possible sites: the Smithsonian Institution or the National Endowments for the Arts or the Humanities. This was similar to the Stanton Commission's recommendation made almost simultaneously.

The Congressional Research Service explained its recommendation by stating that "the establishment of cultural relations as the most important component of official U.S. international communication programs and the deemphasis of propaganda which such a move would signal could be taken as a clear indication to the world that the United States is now prepared to listen and learn, as well as to inform."[49]

A lesser-noted section of the CRS study called for a comprehensive American policy in the field of international communications. This had been formally suggested before and many times since 1975, but has yet to be implemented. The CRS study also described the impact of international communications on public diplomacy. The CRS mentioned direct broadcast satellites, computerized data banks, facsimile transmission of printed material, as well as new modes of telephony and television. These among other new technologies hold great potential for magnifying the impact of intellectual exchanges. [See Chapter 13, Recommendations 15 and 16, and by the present author, *Power, the Press and the Technology of Freedom: The Coming Age of ISDN*; Freedom House, 1989–90.]

Seventeen years later, John Richardson, who set the Stanton Commission in motion, had retrospective thoughts.[50] He supported the commission because he felt the information services of the USIA were disconnected fundamentally from the State Department—and shouldn't be. And the components of the cultural program (such as libraries) were managed out of the State Department—and that "seemed odd" to Richardson. These "anomalies" prompted him to reexamine the whole structure. But, he says, "it got out of hand right away." Nobody could control the situation: "You set something going in the world of Washington and it takes on a life of its own." The director of the USIA at the time, Frank Shakespeare, thought most exchange and cultural programs were a waste of money. Richardson was not entirely satisfied with the Stanton report but he was far less pleased with the Carter administration's action, which seemed to him to vitiate the Stanton recommendations and endanger the autonomy of the Fulbright program. He still thinks that USIA's press and public affairs activities should be integrated in the State Department, with educational exchange programs and broadcasting activities located in agencies separate from but reporting to the State Department. However, as years passed, Richardson's views on the present arrangements have mellowed. He believes the USIA, in tension with the FSB and congressional oversight committee, presently keeps the Fulbright program and other cultural matters reasonably free of political pressures. Given also the complex nature of the bureaucracies and the extensive involvement of the academy he regards the Fulbright program as independent as a government sponsored operation is likely to be. He would, however, at least improve the way the United States chooses CAOs. He would recruit scholars for a CAO "cone" in the USIA or, better still, in an autonomous agency under the State Department. He says he is still "high on the USIA— the quality of the people who are attracted to it." It's an interesting career, he says, but would be more so if there were two cones—cultural and informational—"so there would be an equal chance of competing for the top jobs."

Virtually *all* CAOs should come from academia, in the view of James H. Billington, the librarian of Congress.[51] He believes "there should be a program of phasing scholars with regional expertise from academia in and out of these [CAO] positions. Nothing," he says, "would ensure a firmer commitment from the academic community to the Fulbright program—a commitment that is not now there except in a light verbal way— than to have academia responsible for staffing the CAO positions." The USIA in the past had a number of star-quality CAOs.

After President Carter moved the Fulbright and other educational programs from the State Department to the USIA (temporarily called the International Communication Agency, ICA), the controller general of the United States examined the effectiveness of exchange programs conducted under the Fulbright-Hays Act of 1961.[52] The General Accounting Office (GAO) did not make any recommendations. That judgment was attributed to "different conditions [which make] a good practice in one country [become] a bad practice in another." GAO found it "best to rely heavily for judgments as to the adequacy of the practices [on] those in the field most familiar with circumstances in a particular country."

The GAO examined not only the academic exchanges under the USIA but also the Office of Education's [now Department of Education's] Fulbright program. This program is managed by the USED though the FSB routinely approves selections.[53] USED monitors the activities of its grantees. Embassies overseas have little if any relationship with visiting American scholars sent by USED. The GAO found no problems caused by [USED] grantees.[54] Though it may seem more efficient to oversee all Fulbright programs from one agency, the GAO concluded: "Little purpose would be served by attempting to operate the [USED and USIA] programs in any common fashion." The USED program helps American teachers develop expertise in less commonly taught languages and cultures. The USED administers its portion of the Fulbright program to complement its Title VI programs funded by the National Defense Education Act of 1958. Title VI programs are conducted only in the United States, while the USED Fulbright program provides opportunities for study and research abroad. Both endeavor to develop foreign language and area specialists in the less commonly taught languages and cultures in the world. The USED program is designed for Americans, and does not seek funding from abroad. The USIA program stresses "mutuality," engaging non-Americans as well as Americans in the exchanges, and thus encourages foreign financial support through binational commissions. USED sends Americans only to those places where the needed languages are spoken. USIA exchanges with 130 countries are based on broad mutual interests.

On the fortieth anniversary of the original Fulbright Act, two members of the USIA staff writing in the *Foreign Service Journal* said that the Fulbright program "never had a formal list of political objectives."[55] Fears that the program would become politicized after its 1978 move to USIA "have been proven false," the authors stated. They added, there had been generally, through the years, "a growing realization of how useful the Fulbright exchanges have been in promoting long-term national interests." A still larger estimate comes from Senator Fulbright's Oxford tutor, Ronald B. McCallum. He calls his former student "responsible for the largest and most significant movement of scholars across the earth since the Fall of Constantinople in 1453."

For America, the Fulbright program may be the most important legislation affecting the nation's social and political culture since the Morrill

Act of 1862 created the land grant universities and county-agent educationalists. The Fulbright program takes federal support for education a further step. The program supports the internationalizing of American education and enhances America's contribution to education in other countries. By its emphasis on individual scholarship the Fulbright program helps to develop an American civic culture, one of the necessary components for a functioning democratic society.

3

How Do You Get
a Fulbright Grant?

The Graduate Student

Maria Japa, on maternity leave from the *Manila Daily Globe*, applied for
a Fulbright grant in March 1989: "I had just given birth to my son, and
a letter came addressed to my father (among other prominent journalists)
inviting him to apply for a Fulbright. But he had been dead for 10
years!"[1] That's not the whole story. Japa had, indeed, sought a Fulbright
two years after graduation in 1984 but, she says, "I guess I was rejected
because I had little experience then, and was working for a Marcos
newspaper."

Maria reapplied five years later, based on her degree in journalism
from the University of the Philippines and astute political reporting for
a prominent daily newspaper. In May 1989, Japa was informed by the
Philippine-American Educational Foundation that she was one of ten
finalists for four slots in journalism that year. She was interviewed by
a panel of economists and journalism heads.

"They put you down during the interview, asking questions and seem-
ing not to listen to the answers. They asked, 'Why do you think you'll
make it in the United States?' I felt, 'Why do I have to go through this?'
Anyway, I guess I'm just as guilty. As a journalist I ask that kind of
pointed question of politicians. But it's different when you are the one
being grilled."

In July, Japa was notified she would begin three weeks of orientation
at the University of Texas, July 15, 1990, and start classes at New York
University that September.

Considerable preparation and coordination by agencies in the Philippines and the United States had made it possible for Japa to spend a year

earning a graduate degree, and the summer of 1991 as an intern in Washington, D.C. In 1990, Ms. Japa was among 3,015 foreign nationals from 130 countries who received grants from the USIA's Fulbright program. In addition, 1,748 Americans went abroad that year as Fulbrighters in the USIA program. Another 911 Americans went overseas in 1990 on Fulbright awards for the U.S. Department of Education. The complex of interacting agencies for the Fulbright program worldwide includes the following:

The U.S. Information Agency (USIA) is the independent agency in the executive branch responsible for international programs designed to promote understanding of American society, culture, and foreign policy. The agency in association with the State Department oversees some 200 posts in 128 foreign countries. USIA operates the Voice of America as well as programs in education, such as libraries abroad, and visits to the United States from foreign leaders in many fields. The USIA conducts active programs in educational exchange and provides administrative staff for the J. William Fulbright Foreign Scholarship Board, which oversees the Fulbright grant program. The USIA administers teacher exchanges and negotiates agreements covering educational interchange with foreign governments. The agency also provides liaison for the Fulbright program with other U.S. agencies.

The J. William Fulbright Foreign Scholarship Board (FSB) is appointed by the president and serves without salary. It sets policy and approves every listed opening for a Fulbright grant, and every grant made to match the listing—either an opening for a foreign student, scholar, or researcher coming to the United States or an American in these categories going abroad. The FSB operates under the Bureau of Educational and Cultural Affairs (known internally as the "E" bureau) of the USIA. The FSB, says Chairman Charles Dunn, does not control the program's money, personnel, or information about the program. "We are given statutory authority but without any of the three elements that would provide the power to govern: money, personnel or information."[2] The board is a "buffer zone, a balance wheel; we cannot dictate and must cooperate." The FSB co-operates with—"provides the oil that lubricates"—all the other agencies listed in this chapter. When one of those agencies "loses that oil" it's usually because it seeks to act dictatorially. "We are the point guard, to use basketball analogy, that can bring together the various interests," adds Dr. Dunn. He regards Fulbright "as more of an idea than a program: If it becomes more of a program than an idea it will be less successful by being too bureaucratized. Fulbright is the idea that transcends." The FSB staff consists of an executive director, Ralph Vogel; a deputy, Jennifer Newton; and several support staffers.

Also involved is the Binational Commission and the embassy or, in places where no commission exists, the U.S. embassy alone. In Japa's case, the commission is the Philippine-American Education Foundation composed half of Filipino and half of American citizens (including embassy officials and nonofficial resident Americans). The binational commission prepares the list of openings and circulates it at local universities that are prepared to receive American students, scholars, or researchers for specified assignments at named places. The commission also recruits panels of local students and scholars who seek to study or do research in the United States. When the list of American candidates for work in the Philippines is received, the commission approves it.

The Institute of International Education (IIE), a private, nonprofit organization, processes the list of openings for graduate students from and to more than 100 countries—for example, Filipinos coming to the United States, and Americans going to the Philippines—and proceeds over many months to find the best candidates for each of the openings. The IIE was created in 1919 when it supported post-World War I reconstruction of European universities. The IIE is responsible for the Fulbright graduate student or pre-doctoral program, not that part of the Fulbright program servicing junior and senior scholars and researchers. Starting in May of each year to fill slots for Americans sought by universities abroad, the IIE sends publicity to undergraduate and graduate schools around the United States. The IIE also seeks openings in American universities for foreign students accepted by the commission or post abroad, and by the FSB. Often scholarship money for the foreign student will be sought by IIE from the U.S. universities and colleges.

To compile the list of American candidates, the IIE organizes some 1,600 screening committees on large and small campuses across the United States. The competition runs from June 1 to October 31. The committees meet and pass on student applicants at their campuses. Each applicant provides information and IIE compiles a sizable dossier describing course work completed, recommendations, and other information. These are rated by the committee and sent to IIE in New York. IIE then sends these applications to screening committees for the various scholarly disciplines. The screening committee will receive between a dozen and 150 applications. The committee will compose a final list based on the number of openings overseas in the respective discipline. "This process," says Thomas Farrell, IIE's Fulbright director,[3] "is phenomenally complicated. Every member of every national screening committee for the Philippines, for example, must have everyone's dossier. It's daunting."

All committee members are volunteers. Most are former Fulbrighters (like Farrell). The alumni who earned their Fulbright grants as young graduate students "have real ties of affection" for the program, says Farrell.

The following January, IIE sends the recommended applications to posts and commissions abroad. These are shown in rank order as determined by peer reviews. The posts abroad examine the dossiers for acceptability to the local institutions.

The successful students begin arriving overseas a year and a half after their first application. In 1991, some 520 Americans were to receive student-fellow grants for graduate work overseas, and 1,100 foreign graduate students would come to the United States under the Fulbright program.[4]

Foreign students from non-English-speaking countries must demonstrate competence in English by taking the Test of English as a Foreign Language (TOEFL). U.S. universities often require the Graduate Record Examination (GRE) or similar tests for candidates in management, law, and other disciplines. Foreign students are interviewed by the commission or post, and the candidate judged according to the objective of the applicant.[5]

The FSB draws on the services of several agencies with special expertise in regional educational exchanges of students. In selected Middle East countries, the American-Mideast Educational and Training Service (AMIDEAST) arranges study programs for graduate students. University faculty exchanges are arranged through the Latin American Scholarship Program of American Universities (LASPAU), which also assists in the selection of candidates for a special program for Central American undergraduate students.

The Junior or Senior Lecturer or Research Scholar

Alfred Kazin, author-critic and distinguished professor of American literature, says his Fulbright lecturing abroad "meant a very great deal" to him and to American universities as well.[6] He benefited "enormously" from meeting foreign scholars. Some of the best, in turn, contributed to American education. The late Marcus Cunliffe, a British professor of American history, attributed his interest in America to his association with the Fulbright program, says Kazin.

Fulbright scholars moving to or from the United States encounter a process similar to that facing students, with one significant difference. The selection process is operated in the United States by the CIES (see below), not the IIE. The binational commission overseas or, if none exists in the country, the U.S. embassy submits to the FSB in Washington a list of openings for American junior/senior lecturers or researchers. For each opening the list will describe the discipline, other scholarly requirements and place of service. After passing through the FSB, the list will be given to the Council for International Exchange of Scholars (CIES), Washington.

The CIES was created to serve the Fulbright program and, like the IIE, is a private, nonprofit organization. Both are under contract from the USIA, on behalf of the FSB, to provide all selections for Fulbright student and scholar grants. The choice of grantees is restricted to these nongovernmental entities in order to insulate the senior Fulbright program from nonacademic selection pressures, and to ensure that high scholarly standards are maintained. The CIES has been called "the heart of the Fulbright process as the FSB is its head." Final approval for all grants, however, rests by statute with the J. William Fulbright Foreign Scholarship Board. In 45 years, the FSB has rejected only a very few selections by the IIE or the CIES.

The CIES was created soon after the Fulbright Act for the explicit purpose of recruiting and screening scholarly grantees. The CIES is an arm of the American Council of Learned Societies. The CIES has some 80 committees, comprising 350 scholars. Of these, 52 scholars serve on committees of various disciplines, the remainder on foreign-area committees. This considerable voluntary service by scholars across the country contributes tens of thousands of valuable hours at no cost to the government. This service also gives the U.S. academic community a proprietary interest in the Fulbright program. The CIES advertises on college campuses those openings approved by binational commissions and posts overseas, and by the FSB. The 1991–1992 book of CIES offerings, 123 printed pages, includes about 1,000 Fulbright awards in more than 100 countries.

A typical scholar's application goes first to, say, the sociology committee where it is reviewed for the quality of the proposal and the standing of the person. Then, all applications for, say, Germany—in sociology but also chemistry, American literature, etc.—go to the Germany-Austria committee. "We have many people who are very good but do not fit the explicit opening," explains Cassandra Pyle, executive director of the CIES.[7] "You may find someone who is first-rate in American history, but who isn't the Civil War expert they want in Heidelberg. It must be a match." The area committees put together panelists. The CIES nominates the panels but does not make the selection. The FSB, through the USIA, gives final approval.

American candidates for, say, Germany would apply by August. The binational commission in Germany would receive the panels for approval by the end of December and make selections and work out placements as soon as it can. The applicant should have a letter of approval that spring and travel to the German university in the fall. Approximately a year and a half will have elapsed since the application was made. Foreign scholars follow the same process in the opposite direction.

About 70 percent of the American post-doctoral applicants are offered lectureships abroad; some 30 percent, research. Ninety percent of foreign scholars are offered grants for research, and 10 percent for lecturing. In 1990–1991, 53 percent of American scholars stayed abroad for less than six months and the remainder for six or more months. Sixty-one percent of foreign scholars came to the United States for six months or more. Distinguished Senior Scholars, usually chosen to enhance the prestige and programs of commissions or posts abroad, remain for shorter periods.

Foreign lecturers, junior and senior scholars, and researchers are selected after the FSB approves the country proposals coming from the commissions and posts overseas. The selections, based on competitions held by the commissions and posts, are then examined by the CIES for the proper "matches." Final approval is given by the FSB on the basis of the screening made by the CIES.[8]

For lecturers and scholars, the FSB also enlists agencies with expertise in the following regions:

The International Research and Exchanges Board (IREX) conducts an extensive exchange of scholars with the successor states of the Soviet Union and Eastern European countries.

Scholarly exchange programs with China are conducted through the Committee on Scholarly Communication with the People's Republic of China (CSCPRC).

In nearly forty years, the trend favoring grants to lecturers over graduate students has been marked. In 1953, of some 1,275 grants to Americans, 74 percent went to students, 14 percent to lecturers and 12 percent to researchers. In 1989, of 1,780 grants, only 30 percent were awarded to students while 42 percent went to lecturers and 28 percent to researchers.

The Hubert H. Humphrey Fellowships

"The most significant thing about the Humphrey fellowship program," says Erjaz Qureshi, a former fellow from Pakistan, "was that earning a degree was ruled out. Some fellows were opposed to this. They thought that if they came to the United States to study and didn't earn a degree, people back home would think they had been wasting their time. But at our level, a degree would not make that much difference. The Humphrey program gave seasoned professionals the freedom to choose the courses most useful for their own objectives." In Qureshi's case, he left Pakistan in 1981–1982 for a Humphrey year studying management and development economics at Pennsylvania State University. Qureshi has since become Pakistan's trade commissioner responsible for facilitating trade and joint ventures between Canada and Pakistan.

The Hubert H. Humphrey fellowships are another Fulbright program, funded through USIA and managed by the IIE. Humphrey fellows come from developing countries, though Eastern Europe is now included. No Americans receive these fellowships. Their purpose is building leadership for public service. Pissmai Khanobdee, a former Humphrey fellow from Thailand, says that her U.S. academic program and internship prepared her to head the Thai government's policy and planning subdivision. It approves technical assistance projects implemented in every Thai ministry and agency.

Since the Humphrey program began in 1979, more than 1,400 men and women from 107 developing countries completed nondegree programs in planning and resource management, public administration, public health and nutrition, and agriculture. The IIE believes they also became significant resource persons, "strengthening international awareness" in the universities and communities where they studied and worked.

Humphrey fellows are generally nominated by binational commissions or American posts abroad. The IIE creates screening panels to select candidates on the basis of excellence and geographic distribution. "Our screening panels must know the standing of candidates in their countries, and whether the person nominated is qualified or the brother-in-law of somebody influential," says Peggy Blumenthal, vice president of the IIE.[9] The program was designed "as a one-year, mid-career professional-development program for the developing world," says Blumenthal. "At its peak," she recalls, "the Humphrey program welcomed about 150 persons a year. Shrinking budgets have lowered this to 132. But that still admits at least one person from every country in the developing world which nominates an acceptable candidate, and several more from some countries."

The fellows, says Blumenthal, are "a combination of academic and professional—not just professors of public health but someone as well from a national institute of health." The Humphrey program does not send fellows all over the United States, as do the student and scholar Fulbright programs. "We cluster them professionally in twelve universities. All fellows in public health may go to Tulane, and all in urban planning to Hunter." Starting in 1990, the selection of participating campuses has been determined by a regular competition.

The university makes two commitments to a Humphrey fellow: It will provide a solid, nondegree curriculum, and will assist the fellow to secure an appropriate professional placement for one or two months. That may be in a bank or a local community health center. Three times a year all the fellows are brought together for an enrichment program. Shortly after the beginning of the year, all fellows are taken to Washington for an intensive look at how the government works. In midyear, meetings are held at the Tennessee Valley Authority (TVA) for all fellows involved in urban or regional planning, agriculture, or water resources; another at the Center for Disease Control in Atlanta; and a third at the IMF/World Bank in Washington, D.C. At the end of the year, they go to Minnesota—home of the late Vice President Humphrey—to reflect on their experience, and add to the growing worldwide Humphrey-fellow network.

The Teacher Exchange Program

The teacher exchange program (USIA/FSB) sends U.S. teachers—mainly from secondary schools, but also from elementary schools and colleges—to teach in schools abroad. Foreign teachers are matched with the Americans. The similar teachers then exchange places in one another's schools.[10] In 1990, 213 foreign teachers came to the United States and 347 American teachers went abroad. From 1949 to 1990, 19,391 foreign teachers were brought to the United States and 11,416 American teachers went abroad. This exchange is being enlarged as rapidly as teachers can be matched. Special efforts are being made to focus on the liberated countries of Eastern Europe. The largest traditional program has been with the United Kingdom.

Foreign Language and Area Studies for Teachers

An extensive one-way program is operated by the U.S. Department of Education (USED). The CIE of USED runs a $5.8 million Fulbright program under the Fulbright-Hays Act of 1961. (This complements Title VI of the National Defense Education Act of 1958 and Higher Education Act of 1965 which support language and area studies programs conducted within the United States.) The USED-Fulbright programs are designed to meet American needs in education, while the USIA-Fulbright exchanges are two-way tracks to share understanding with other peoples and other governments. "All our [USED] activities focus on less commonly taught languages in the United States, and world areas under-represented in American curricula. We do very little in Western Europe. Most of it is in Africa, Asia, Latin America," says Joseph F. Belmonte, deputy director of the CIE.[11] From 1964 to 1990, the USED program sent 25,619 Americans abroad.

Under the USED's Fulbright-Hays Group Projects Abroad program, Richard Corby, professor of social and behavioral science of the University of Arkansas, took sixteen elementary and secondary school social studies teachers of twelve school districts in southeast Arkansas to Sierra Leone in 1990. The teachers developed curricular products for use in their classrooms. The purpose was to improve the quality of teaching about Africa. One year later, the group met again to assess what had been developed and how useful it had been. Dr. Corby had had a USIA-Fulbright grant in Sierra Leone in 1974–1975 to complete research on his own doctorate. He is planning to lead another USED teachers' project abroad in Cairo.[12]

"A fortuitous experience—unlike any other before or since," is how Dr. Ralph T. Nelson describes his 1990 study/travel seminar to Hungary leading ten master educators (teachers, curricular specialists, supervisors, and administrators) from several states. Dr. Nelson, director of the Columbia Education Center, Portland, Oregon, took the USED group to Hungary at a historic moment in that country's transition from communism. Dr. Nelson had been a USIA-Fulbrighter in Finland in 1963–1965. The 1990 group was escorted through Hungary by the newly appointed Hungarian ambassador to Australia. The seminar met with the president of Hungary and gained insights from the ambassador's political clout, says Dr. Nelson. After their return to the United States Dr. Nelson continues to act as coordinator for the group's new ideas.[13]

Fifteen years ago, the Harvard Middle East Center designed a program in Egypt for Boston-area secondary school teachers. The program was funded by USED. The teachers who went abroad were accompanied by two Harvard professors. Several years later, the center director reported he "couldn't turn those teachers off." They were taking courses at the Harvard Middle East Center (some courses created especially for those teachers), producing a monthly newsletter on the subject, maintaining bibliographies on the Middle East, and keeping in touch with their former hosts abroad. In their classrooms, these teachers used their Middle East experience to enrich several different subject areas.[14]

In Jakarta, this writer met twenty American secondary school teachers and university professors beginning a five-week Fulbright Seminar Abroad program arranged by USED. They had come from a two-day briefing in

San Francisco on the history and current problems of Indonesia. In forty planned lectures in four cities, the group would be introduced to Indonesia and particularly the development issues the country faces: population pressures, family planning, social welfare, environment and natural resources, and tourism as a development program. Macro- and microeconomic problems and strategies were on the agenda. Earlier in their careers, several professors had individual USIA Fulbright grants in Ghana, Uganda, and Jamaica. Others indicated they would apply for individual Fulbright grants in the future. The seminar was planned by Norman Goodman, director in southeast Asia for the IIE.

The schools and colleges represented were diverse, mostly small institutions where the impact by the returning teachers would be considerable. There was also emphasis in this seminar on the use at home of the ideas gleaned abroad—and the planned-for networking of the participants hereafter. Such plans are not built into the USIA system of more individualistic study, research, or lecturing.

A USED officer in mid-1991 proposed a new dimension for the agency's Fulbright program. John C.T. Alexander urged short-term travel abroad grants for American faculty. The purpose was to increase their professional contact with counterparts in Eastern European universities. It was anticipated that this would provide a "quick start" in developing institutional linkages between the United States and Eastern Europe.

The translator for the Dalai Lama on his visits to the United States is a former USED-Fulbright fellow and director of a USED national resource center. Experts tapped by major news media to explain fast-breaking events overseas are often faculty at the USED national resource centers. Articles in popular and scholarly publications on underreported international subjects are frequently based on research supported by the USED-Fulbright program.

The USED-Fulbright program, as part of the (domestic) Department of Education, does not have a visible foreign-policy agenda. As a consequence, scholars funded by that Fulbright program conducted research in China prior to Henry Kissinger's visit, and at least one was in Cuba in 1981. USED's Fulbright scholars were in Ethiopia as the vanguard of Western social policy research after the revolution in 1989, and conducted research in China with Chinese approval after the USIA-funded Fulbright programs were canceled by Beijing. The USIA, however, continued to support U.S. scholars in China even when the Chinese canceled the Fulbright program. The USIA simply supported them under other names and auspices. In 1992, the USIA was mandated by Congress to select thirty Vietnamese students for Fulbright grants, though the United States had not yet opened diplomatic relations with the former enemy.

Says the USED, "The sponsorship by a domestic ministry [USED] and association with academic institutions provide access to human and material resources unavailable to those supported by ministries with foreign policy concerns."[15] USED programs, however, receive funds from the National Defense Education Act.

The USED makes overseas arrangements through the Fulbright binational commissions, or U.S. posts abroad, and with the assistance of IIE and CIES, though some USED-funded schools deal directly with universities overseas. The J. William Fulbright Foreign Scholarship Board also provides approval for Fulbright-funded projects at USED.

This is not an exchange program, however. Only Americans go abroad, individually or in groups. The program provides opportunities for American educators in the humanities, social studies, or social sciences to improve their understanding of other people and cultures through study abroad. Four USED-Fulbright programs do the following:

1. Assist graduate students—present or future teachers or scholars—to engage overseas in full-time Ph.D. dissertation research in modern foreign language and area studies.

2. Provide faculty research abroad from three to twelve months to improve skills in area or language studies not commonly taught in U.S. institutions of higher learning.

3. Enable U.S. institutions of higher education, state departments of education, or private nonprofit educational organizations to conduct overseas group projects. Specialists and facilities overseas are used to integrate international studies into an American institution's curriculum.

4. Create three- to eight-week summer seminars abroad for teachers of undergraduate courses, administrators and curriculum specialists of state and local education agencies at elementary or secondary school level, secondary school teachers of social studies, and teachers of foreign languages at all levels.

The quality of applicants for USED-Fulbright grants today is superior to the levels in the 1960s, says Joseph F. Belmonte. Scholars now have greater opportunity to go overseas. Many receive more than one grant from USED (unlike the USIA-FSB's preference for new applicants). "If a fellow has had extensive experience overseas, that is to his credit in our program," adds Belmonte, "because we're training specialists. The more he is in the host country, the better." All USED students must have teaching as a career goal. A random sample of a recent year's applicants revealed that 85 percent were teaching at institutions of higher education, and had earned their Ph.D.s.

A "concrete example" of USED's Fulbright program and its accomplishments, says John Paul, chief of the advanced training and research branch, is the saga of Walter T. Brown. He first applied for a USED international studies grant 25 years ago. For two successive summers he received Title VI fellowships to study Swahili. In 1967, he went to Tanzania on a Fulbright doctoral dissertation award where he researched his Ph.D. subject. In the mid-1970s, Dr. Brown received two Fulbright curriculum consultant grants for Taiwan (literature) and Japan (economics). In 1980, he participated in India in a Fulbright group-projects-abroad consortium involving Columbia University and the University of Texas. He followed this with an innovative three-year national consortial Title VI project to improve undergraduate area and language studies. Fifty colleges participated in internationalizing their curricula. On a USED-Fulbright in 1981, Dr. Brown undertook research among the Baluchis in Kenya. To continue his Fulbright studies, he was awarded an NEH fellowship for 1983 at Harvard University. In 1985, after co-directing a USED Fulbright group project in Jamaica for K-12/college teachers, Dr. Brown helped secure for Ramapo College, N.J. the largest state-supported award for international education to a state college. He developed in 1990 a group project in Japan for New Jersey college professors. Dr. Brown credits his quarter-century association with the U.S. Department of Education for his success as a classroom teacher and international researcher. The professor has also been elected to the College of the City of New York Hall of Fame for his lacrosse achievements.

There appears to be an uneven system for receiving USED grantees overseas. In Indonesia in June 1991, a group of USED teachers, professors, and administrators arrived from the United States with virtually no advance warning to the American embassy and the local Fulbright foundation. A local representative of IIE had made all the arrangements. On other occasions, the arrangements for instruction of American teachers in the languages of Eastern Java, for example, are made by long-term friends of Indonesian experts—American and Indonesian. The Fulbright foundation has no objection to such collaboration but believes that since it carries the Fulbright name the foundation's credibility is weakened if it cannot even track the USED program. Another criticism is the alleged "wastefulness" of parallel programs of student grants for Americans made by both the USED (DDRAs—doctoral dissertation research abroad) and USIA/IIE (also at the Ph.D. level for research abroad). Both kinds of grantees come for the same time period. The USED provides a somewhat larger stipend than USIA/IIE. Many candidates apply for both, and then take the USED if they are twice successful. One year the Indonesian Foundation decided not to fund any Ph.D. research scholars—but the

USED sent people anyway. In the worst case, a candidate rejected by the Indonesian Foundation would arrive as a DDRA under USED's auspices.

Counseling for Foreign Students Overseas

In 1989–1990, there were 386,851 foreign students at American colleges and universities.[16] More than 200,000 (44 percent) came from Asian countries. Most (57 percent) came to study business and management, engineering, math and computer science, physical and life sciences. Social sciences, fine and applied arts, and humanities attracted 7.7 percent. Overwhelmingly, these students were supported by personal and family funds. Most of these were assisted informally in their home countries by Fulbright offices. They loaned catalogues of most American colleges, and supplied general information about advance testing and application procedures. In Italy, for example, 7 percent of the Fulbright expenditures support this advisory service though none of these students are likely to receive Fulbright grants. In 1990 alone, at least 1,069,197 foreign students were helped in this fashion by the Fulbright program overseas.

4

Fulbright on Fulbright

During a chat in his law office early in 1991, this writer asked J. William Fulbright how he came to create the Fulbright scholarships. The discussion included several related matters such as war and peace and the relationship of education to both. Here are some of his remarks:

What gave you the idea for the Fulbrights?

Basically responsible for it was my own Rhodes scholarship in 1925. Without it, I never would have been here in Washington. I came from [Sumner, Mo.], a little village in the Ozarks. Fayetteville at that time was a town of 5,000, quite remote from the big world. The only way you could get out or in was with the railroad. It was lovely. I liked it. But I didn't know anything else. I hadn't been to places like New York or San Francisco. I played football at the University of Arkansas and we would go to Texas. That's about all. I hadn't seen the world but I never thought I was deprived. We first lived on a farm and then my father moved into town, a little town. I had no history except Fayetteville.

The Rhodes scholarship made all the difference in the world. It was almost like a dream. Everything worked well. I was twenty years old, played football and tennis, and was in pretty good shape. Oxford was made for that. Not every place has the same respect for athletics. In England, in their social credo, they assume if you play athletics you must be a gentleman. In this country it's certainly not that.

But you put no emphasis on sports in the Fulbright scholarships.

I didn't attempt to lay down the details. Rhodes had set three quali-

fications. Leadership was one. Another was sports, and that's the reason
I got it. There were several applicants in my year who had academic
standing as good or better than mine. None of them had the combination
and football!

What made you think of creating academic scholarships?

I was looking for potential political leaders. I was in politics and the
inspiration came from World War II, and the nuclear bombings. The idea
was how to avoid war in the future. No matter what the reason for war,
you've got to settle it some other way. There's no way to survive nuclear
bombs. I don't know what this government is thinking about, buying
more arms. It's stupid: exhausting the country's money, the biggest debt
in the world. It's disgraceful.

To give you an example. Take Alexander Yakovlev, adviser to Mikhail
Gorbachev in the Soviet Union. Yakovlev had a scholarship [at Columbia University in 1959]. There's no doubt he has had an influence on Mr.
Gorbachev. That influence is that the United States, while it challenges
and sounds pretty ominous, and even attacks little countries like Grenada
. . . I'm sure Yakovlev tells Gorbachev, "Oh, yeah, they look big but
they're not going to attack us. They may be stupid, but they're not that
stupid; so you can afford to cut down and change our approach." Which
I think is a substantial reason why Gorbachev changed the approach in
our relationship. I think that's a very concrete result of Mr. Yakovlev's
influence. He's one of the few people who can say to Gorbachev, "Look,
I've lived in that country. They're a peculiar people. They're very con-
ceited and they talk big, but they're not going to attack you." We have
done stupid things but we haven't been so stupid as to attack the Soviet
Union. We got into both World Wars late, we didn't really challenge
anyone, we didn't initiate the wars.

My own experience in the Rhodes scholarship opened my eyes. The
idea that people you meet abroad are somehow different, enemies, is
dissipated. You can't believe they're bad people. I had the same feeling
about Russians. I went out of my way to get acquainted with Anatolyi
P. Dubrynin, the Soviet ambassador. Isolationism may have been a fine
idea for Americans until the invention of radio, the airplane, and nuclear
weapons. We could isolate ourselves from the effects of wars. Young
Americans, and young Russians or Englishmen who come here will be
leaders and will develop a negative attitude toward war. It doesn't mean
you love each other but you know war is no longer the right way to solve

problems. I still think that has validity. I like to think that Mr. Yakovlev
and the others have contributed to that idea.

Did being a college president generate the Fulbrights?

I was a professor and became college president briefly. I was fired by
the governor because he wanted to get back at my mother who ran the
local newspaper. She had attacked the governor. I ran for Congress and
then the Senate against the governor. So I got into politics purely by
accident. Politics is one of the most interesting activities you can have.
You're dealing with people.

How did you use politics to design the Fulbrights?

I introduced the first bill in September 1945, just a few weeks after
we had dropped the bomb over Hiroshima. Going in with this bill was
another opportunity to do something for peace. I had already responded
in my resolution to create the United Nations. There was no opposition
to my bill on the scholarships. They didn't have any idea what it was
about, and they didn't provide any appropriation. The argument I made
was, "Look, for World War I debts you got nothing. In 1933, you just
wrote off those big debts. Now, we can at least get something. They
could at least take our students and let them go to their schools." And
that's all the bill provided, just authority to use credits. Appropriations
came later, after the scheme proved itself and people could see it was a
good thing.

You didn't mention your peace motive, or even "mutual understanding"?

I was very conscious of both. But Congress was very sensitive and I
was advised to get the bill through without getting it bogged down in a
lot of controversy. The administration sent up a bill proposing ways to
dispose of leftover U.S. wartime properties in Europe. I simply attached
my amendment to it. President Truman's attention wasn't focused on my
bill. I wouldn't know what was in his mind. I brought the bill out at five
o'clock under the unanimous-consent procedure. Normally both parties
have just a few members present. If nobody opposes a bill it passes without
objection. If I had not been very careful the bill might have been de-
stroyed in a controversy. In 1945 we were a very isolationist country. Six
months later, in the hall one day I saw old man [Kenneth] McKellar,
senator from Tennessee, who was chairman of the Appropriations Committee. He looked upon me as an upstart. "Young man," he said, "that

measure you had is a very dangerous bill. If I'd a-known about it I would have opposed that." He said, "Don't you know it's very dangerous to send our fine young boys and girls abroad, and expose them to those foreign isms?"

Did the program proceed as you had envisioned?

It did, until 1965. Then Lyndon Johnson fell out with me over the Vietnam War and—I can't say whether he called attention—anyway they cut back the Fulbright program severely, from about 6,000 grants a year to about 2,000. And the appropriation then was still very small. I can't help but think he said, "Oh well, that's Fulbright's—no good anyway." He wasn't particularly interested in the program.

Where do you see the program going now?

It may be revived, if we have any sense, and try to focus on all Eastern European countries and the Soviet Union. It's a great opportunity if the administration has got enough sense to take it. Their students would welcome an opportunity to come and study here. The original idea, which is still sound, I think, is to take your best American graduate students, not their families. Give them the opportunity to live abroad a year or two—people who will probably be leaders in their communities or in business or education—to influence the way their communities think about international relations. I've protested the way the program is administered today. Too much is spent on sending professors and their families over. I also testified against putting the program in the U.S. Information Agency. I thought that gave the program a feeling of being in a propaganda agency trying to "sell" the United States. That was not my idea. It was to enable those people to make their own judgments about America and themselves. I want it to be a nonpolitical program. Prior to Jimmy Carter's putting it in USIA, is the way I want it. Previously, when the program was in the State Department, it really took no interest in the scholarships. And the original chairman of the Board of Foreign Scholarships was that wonderful, talented Commissioner of Education of the State of New York [Francis Spaulding]. The program went beautifully until Lyndon Johnson cut it back. It could stand that all right, but when Jimmy Carter put it into the USIA I was afraid it would be ruined.

If the program is nonpolitical, is it in the national interest?

Yes, it's in the long-term national interest, not in the immediate national interest to influence our policies today with the [former] Soviet Union or anybody else. That's why it's so difficult to explain to congressmen, because they are properly interested in the current situation of a country. They can't afford to be concerned about what it's going to be like ten, twenty years from now. You see the program is more than forty years old and you're just beginning to see an effect; just now do I recognize people like Yakovlev. It takes so long. But I still regard the program as political. It has political influence. It will enable people to find a way to avoid war. That's its main purpose. When I was young I had a little car and used to drive some students who were in the ROTC (Reserve Officers Training Corps). That impressed me very much, the future of warfare—I didn't like it—friends could get killed, you know. In the long run there are political implications in educating bright, young people that war is not an alterative.

How do you feel about "Fulbright" becoming a common noun?

I've gotten used to it. In politics you are subjected to all kinds of criticism as well as praise. And after you've been in politics for thirty years these personal things don't affect you one way or the other. But, yes, I like to be associated with this sort of thing—that's true.

Summing up, in a letter to this writer after the interview, Senator Fulbright wrote:

> In short, my original idea was not a general education program for all needy people but a program designed to influence political matters through the intelligent leadership of the important countries. This has been accused of being elitist, however with the very small amount of money available for this activity it certainly can't be considered a general education program. . . .

5

Who Are the Fulbrighters?

Before the Declaration of Independence, Benjamin Franklin and Thomas Jefferson engaged the *philosophes* of France in informal exchanges on political and social theory. Surely they must have shared this intelligence with George Washington, who later wrote the following:

> It should be the highest ambition of every American to extend his views beyond himself, and bear in mind that his conduct will not only affect himself, his country and his immediate posterity, but that its influences may be coextensive with the world, and stamp political happiness or misery on ages yet unborn.

With little change, George Washington's counsel could define the Fulbright scholarships. Today, we would couple "her" with "his," and perceive "views" (as George Washington probably intended) to mean both Americans' perception of people and affairs abroad, and the transmission overseas of American culture. Presumably, it would be George Washington's "highest ambition" to foster exchanges of ideas. This president, who warned on leaving office of "entangling alliances" abroad, nevertheless spoke of "political happiness" in universal terms.

From the program's inception to the present, some 180,000 Fulbrighters have extended their views in this manner. This statistic (see Appendix C) is impressive enough but behind it are the dramatic personal histories of intellectual travelers whose Fulbright grants influenced their lives, nations, and "ages yet unborn."

Particularly dramatic are the graduate students—the young men and women whose minds and careers are wide open, both still stretching. A prominent American editor, forty years after taking his Fulbright at

59

Cambridge, still feels enriched by the college founded in the fourteenth century, where he attended the chapel of Kings College built by Henry VIII, and was moved by the "bust of an alumnus—Chaucer."

A current Fulbrighter is Zdenka Gabalova, an ascetic-appearing Czech with a doctorate in art history from Charles University, Prague. Her husband is political adviser to President Václav Havel. She and a Polish colleague stormed through 200 New York studios, early in 1991, selecting works of American artists for a well-publicized exhibit at a Queens museum. The show is a metaphor for the discovery of America by formerly trapped citizens of communism. Gabalova and her associate, said one reviewer hailing the show, "come bearing their opinions of America."[1] More than that, Gabalova told this writer, "I'm discovering many layers in the art world here I had no idea about before."[2] At New York's New School for Social Research where she taught, she also learned. "I can see how the institution was built and how it functions, because we have to build in Czechoslovakia. We still have the old system of institutions that does not really function. It runs as it did for forty years under the communists." When she returns home, says Gabalova, "I will certainly try to change the art mafias. The old Ministry of Culture is still intact except for the new minister and people at the top. But it will take time for private enterprise to develop." Wrote the reviewer, "Expect the new decade to be marked by more of these tentative and formerly forbidden exchanges [between the former communist countries and the United States]."

A recent Lebanese Fulbright scholar describes the impact of America on an alert citizen of a Third World "police state."[3] Imad Khachchan grew up in Syria because of the turmoil in Lebanon. He is completing graduate work on a New York University scholarship. His intellectual transformation peaked when he participated in three days of frank discussions in December 1989 at—of all places—the U.S. Military Academy at West Point. Khachchan went to the academy with other foreign Fulbrighters studying in the New York metropolitan area.[4] He says he was reluctant to go to West Point, just as he hesitated at first to come to the United States. "It was fear, I think, fear despite one's desire, fear of this big establishment. Fear that these would be political discussions with which I would not agree," he said. "I did not grow up in the tradition of speaking freely to the State, inside the State to the people, or to the army. I didn't have the fear a friend had—that our rooms in the hotel were bugged. But I was concerned that somebody was keeping an eye on us."

What happened once Khachchan arrived at West Point? "The opposite of what I thought, in all ways," he said. Great differences of opinion were aired on all sides. The subject was terrorism, and combating it. Coming from Lebanon, Khachchan was regarded as a specialist on this subject. He did not offer platitudes. "I spoke often. I felt self-confident. I didn't find the defiance I had anticipated. My views surprised the cadets. I didn't try to play politics and say what they may have wanted to hear. I said that Americans are isolated here, but their country is involved overseas. To my surprise, the cadets' attitudes about terrorism and its causes changed very much." Khachchan managed during the sessions to question directly Admiral William J. Crowe Jr., former chairman of the Joint Chiefs of Staff, and Admiral Stansfield Turner, former director of the Central Intelligence Agency. Some time later, the commander of the West Point conference wrote that "Mr. Khachchan did an outstanding job [discussing] the problems of terrorism in the world. Mr. Khachchan participated vigorously throughout the conference and it was noted that he consistently provided differing views because of his nationality. This gave the American students a side that they would not have otherwise seen."[5]

Not all Fulbrighters experience such rapid change as Khachchan. Indeed, most common are longer term values generated by the relatively brief Fulbright experiences.

Joseph Lelyveld was named managing editor of the *New York Times* in 1990. Thirty years earlier, as a 23-year-old graduate student, he was a Fulbrighter in Burma. "It was a wonderful year in my life," he now says.[6] "Why Burma? I had a number of answers, some academic, others in terms of a career I could dimly see ahead. I have felt good about Burma ever since . . . My avowed aim was to study political attitudes."[7] But he gained much more. Lelyveld wrote that one extended trip deep into Burma was "the most memorable seven weeks of my life. Every day still stands out distinct."[8] He served as a stringer for the *Times*—the beginning of his writing career at a world-class newspaper. Lelyveld "traveled hard" on his Fulbright award in Burma and "had a very rich experience, which was formative for my subsequent experience as a foreign correspondent." He adds, "That was the most intense experience of a foreign culture I probably ever had."[9] As the Fulbright year ended, Lelyveld "traveled slowly through India, which had a lot to do with my later becoming a correspondent in India." This, says Lelyveld, "was really a crucial year, and in terms of Burma it mattered too. I'm probably the only person in American journalism who cares about Burma." He returned there as a correspondent whenever it was possible to enter the country. The Fulbright program was shut down in 1962 "by the terrible Ne Win regime." Lelyveld, who wrote an honored book on South Africa when he was *Times* correspondent there, says, "If I had been just a

correspondent who had not had the [Fulbright] experience of really coming
to terms with foreign culture in a grassroots kind of way, but had just
sailed in under the banner of the *New York Times*, I would have had much
more superficial experience in the countries in which I lived." He adds,
"I really struggled, maybe in a naive and youthful way, to understand
what it meant to be an American in the world, and what my responsibilities were as an American in the world."

A non-American Fulbrighter studied here, became a citizen of the
world, and continues to be grateful for his youthful experience in the
United States. He is Hans Janitschek, now with the U.N. Population Fund.
As secretary-general of the Socialist International he helped prominent
European leaders compete for power, some successfully. "I thought in
1953 I would gain and learn enough in America to help my country,
Austria, which was still half under Russian occupation."[10] Janitschek not
only earned a degree at Haverford. He traveled across America. He met
Jackie Robinson, Pearl Buck, Enrico Fermi, and Vice President Nixon.
He played Viennese songs on his guitar and auditioned at the Blue Angel
in New York. He felt America's "generosity of spirit," he says, even
though Washington policies often did not coincide with the Socialist
International's. "Here I can *be*," says Janitschek. He spent fourteen years
representing the Austrian government in the United States. He says he
was chosen to play a major role in French President François Mitter-
rand's career: "My supporters thought I was okay because I had the
Fulbright scholarship, and therefore wasn't a KGB agent!" At special
college events today Haverford students sing "Haverford, My Haverford."
An asterisk beside the title credits "Hans Janitschek, Fulbright exchange
student from Austria."

The Fulbright imprimatur decisively changed the lives of Americans
prominent in diverse careers. Their own assessments are convincing.

A "triple hitter" on the Fulbright scoreboard is Robin Winks, Yale
historian and ex-Master of Berkeley College. He was a Fulbright graduate student in New Zealand in 1952, a Fulbright professor in Malaysia
in 1962, and Cultural Affairs Officer in the London embassy where he
chaired the Fulbright Binational Commission from 1969 to 1971. As did
seven other Fulbrighters at the time, Winks married a New Zealander
and maintains permanent ties with the country and his former Fulbright
colleagues. That student year was "a transforming experience for me,"
Winks recalls.[11] He maintains a scholarly interest in New Zealand and
uses "anthropological insights in history," an approach developed in
studying the Maori civilization in New Zealand. He also discovered "we
can better understand ourselves through a foreign experience, and so I
remind people—congressmen, binational commissions, and others—that
the Fulbright program isn't some form of aid or cultural imperialism or

carrying American expertise to a foreign country (though it does that too), but it's also setting up a large body of people who have acquired not only knowledge about this foreign country to which they go, but far deeper knowledge about our own country, to return here to teach or do research."

One Fulbrighter, on the basis of her sojourn overseas, returned to New York to establish a new form of daily journalism. Ada-Louise Huxtable went to Italy in 1950 and 1952 as a graduate student in art and architectural history. "It changed my life," she says.[12] "Whole worlds opened. We [Fulbrighters] were to see things in an entirely different way. It was scholarship's gain, the country's gain, personal gain." In Huxtable's case it was also journalism's gain. She began to write architectural criticism. That led Huxtable to the *New York Times*. It created the first regular architectural beat on any newspaper. Under her byline appeared professional descriptions of buildings and other environments, coupled with aesthetic criticism and pragmatic analysis of the work's usefulness. Her columns tracked American consciousness about the environment before the word environmentalism was created. She cherishes her Fulbright years because they enabled her to discover that architecture is not only a complex art, but an international one. "You've got to understand social background, history, culture, why we're doing these things and the economics of it." A building which is a work of art, she says, "must take its place in our lives and in history in a way that's natural." Opening Fulbright recipients' eyes to such understanding, says Huxtable, "is one of the most constructive programs this country has ever had."

Robert Brustein, director of the American Repertory Theatre at Harvard, spent 1953 and 1955 as a Fulbright student at the universities of Nottingham and Oxford. Brustein began his distinguished career in the theatre by directing undergraduate drama at Nottingham. Years later, Brustein returned as a Fulbright lecturer. "So I look at the Fulbright program both from the senior and junior point of view, and I have nothing but praise for it," Brustein says.[13] "I don't think there's anything like it. It has brought Americans into the twentieth century and into the international arena in a way that nothing else has." Brustein adds: "It was probably the most valuable thing that happened to me in scholarly life. Everything cohered, coalesced in those two special years." The program, says Brustein, "was created by a civilized man, Senator Fulbright, and was one of the very few programs in this country that paid homage to the notion of civilization—that our country could be a civilization as well as a society. As a result we bring civilization back with us, once we broaden ourselves, and (I hope) are able to pass that on to our students as opposed to the same dull teaching."

The civilized essayist one sees regularly on television and whose essays grace *Life* magazine says his Fulbright year in Ireland in 1965–1966 was "one of the great events of my life."[14] Roger Rosenblatt still remembers details of the initial Fulbright interview, and his decision to pursue his specialty in Irish literature. Until he became a Fulbrighter, "all my knowledge of Europe was through writers. I had no sense of people, no sense of geography, very little sense of politics." These were his first memories of another culture. "For Americans, one of the pleasures [of a Fulbright grant], of going to Europe, was going back to a world of sensibility and a world of reference that you got only through the conversations of your parents and grandparents." The most valuable part of the year for the essayist-to-be was not the formal study but "the people, the experience of talking about their lives, the folk stories," and the young traveler's learning to speak Gaelic. He did this by hauling water and going to mass with the villagers of Conomorra. This, Rosenblatt calls promoting "glorious irrelevancy" along with scholarship.

Derek Bok, president of Harvard (1971–1991), not only developed a scholarly monograph during his Fulbright year in France, but also met his Swedish wife-to-be. Her father, a leader of the European Economic Community, and the young Bok's earlier interest in the EEC "had a lot to do with the future shape of my life."[15] Together, "that was decisive in turning my career toward the university as opposed to the practice of law. It solidified a lifelong interest in international matters." Indeed, says Bok, "if we needed a Fulbright program years ago, I don't see how anybody would deny that we need it even more now because our connections with the rest of the world are more intimate than they were at that period."

The Fulbright experience included marriage along with scholarly pursuits for some, and a new nationality for a few: Alberto Vitale, recently named chairman of Random House, America's largest book publisher, applied for a Fulbright in 1967 as a citizen of Turin, Italy. The Wharton School at the University of Pennsylvania "opened up a whole series of opportunities," he says.[16] The key to any scholarly program, says Vitale, "is an opportunity through academia to get to know the United States." During one spring break Vitale rode a bus across the country, staying overnight with the families of a truckdriver, an engineer, and others. At another break Vitale wrote to the controllers of two dozen major corporations such as Ford, IBM, and Lockheed, and asked to visit them. All but one were "terribly forthcoming." This "tremendous experience" became "a new set of assets when I went back to Italy to work for Olivetti," he says. The company returned Vitale to the United States to visit the financial people he had met on the Fulbright. "One thing leads to another," Vitale recalls, "and it's a vast opportunity." He regards the Fulbright program as "one of the most enlightened initiatives that the United States has undertaken in the field of education and international relations." Today, he says, the nations of the world are great at trading with one another, but when it comes to communicating beyond trade there is much room for improvement. "Indeed, most of the major problems that the West has been facing are in large part related to a lack of understanding of our own respective cultural differences."

The exchanging of cultures is dramatically attested by Hsi-Huey Liang, chair of the history department at Vassar. Liang in 1953 was a student in Berlin of Jay H. Cerf, an American Fulbrighter preparing his doctoral thesis on the East German youth organization, Freie Deutsche Jugend (FDJ). That year, 1953–1954, writes Liang, "was when I became a historian." To Jay Cerf and his wife, Carol, Liang writes, "I owe both a lifelong debt for their friendship [and instruction] during that year."[17] The teacher and student entered East Berlin several times under great tension to interview and take photographs in the communist sector. Cerf eventually stopped conducting interviews there because the Soviets were said to be seeking a hostage to trade for a Russian consular officer who had defected in Tokyo. Among the interviews Cerf conducted was with a boy from the Aktionsquipe Freie Deutsche Jugend.[18] This group of ex-FDJ members sought to shake the faith of FDJ leaders in communist doctrine. They broadcast songs and mailed pamphlets to the Soviet zone. Cerf became a specialist in international trade and briefly served in the Kennedy administration. He died in 1974 at the age of 51. But his early teaching still influences Hsi-Huey Liang. In 1990, he published *Berlin Before the Wall: A Foreign Student's Diary*. It is an account written in 1953-1954 as Liang researched working-class life in Berlin. The Cerfs appear repeatedly in Liang's account of his academic and personal life.

"I certainly lived out the Fulbright dream," says Georgie Anne Geyer, widely syndicated columnist, television panelist, and author.[19] She has interviewed Fidel Castro, Ayatollah Khomeini, Saddam Hussein, and other far more heroic actors on the world scene. Her career was shaped by her Fulbright assignment to the University of Vienna. It was the year after the Four Powers left Austria. Everything was still in chaos, and the university was disorganized. She learned German, studied Spanish, "and three weeks after I got there the Hungarian revolution broke out. So I worked with the students at the border." It was, says Geyer, "a very tragic and exciting time for a 21-year-old from Chicago." That year, she says, "was just extraordinarily joyous, tremendously free and intellectually exciting." Says Geyer, "I read, studied my journalism, got to know all kinds of Austrians, began working as a journalist and have been writing ever since about other cultures." That, she adds, "is what I really do. As a foreign correspondent and columnist I write completely on international affairs, what other cultures are like. That's what my books are." The Fulbright gave her writing "so much form and was a very maturing thing for me." She went to Vienna "still a young girl and came back a young woman." She sums up her experience: "The Fulbright program contributes immensely to the national interest. For that purpose, it's probably the cheapest one we can ever have."

Another writer, Norman Podhoretz, editor of *Commentary* magazine, earned a degree during three years at Cambridge starting in 1950. (He combined a Kellett fellowship with his Fulbright.) He visited the "international network" of Fulbrighters in France and Italy during vacations. The scholarly experience had "an enormous effect on me," Podhoretz says.[20] "It's unthinkable that I would be the person I am without that experience—certainly one of two or three most important experiences in my life." Not solely because of the chance to study at a great British university and live the life of a Cambridge "young gentleman," but "living in a foreign country." Podhoretz says he was "lucky to get the last whiff of the old England." Some lifelong friends he made at Cambridge were from South Africa, Australia, India, Pakistan, and Africa. It was a very exciting time, he says, and a "good time to be an American and to be studying abroad." He found "a lot of anti-Americanism" during the oppressive McCarthy era, and saw himself "becoming more of a patriot . . . discovering that meant something, being an American." Podhoretz recalls he was "more or less on the left in those years—but some of the really radical left-wing Fulbrighters reacted negatively to attacks on America. It was amusing because [several Fulbrighters] at Cambridge were communists—I use the word strictly, not loosely. We had always thought there was some sort of security check involved in the award of a Fulbright. If so, it was obviously very inefficient. One student spent most of his money mimeographing anti-American propaganda. I would use him as a case in point in arguing with anti-American English leftists who said McCarthyism made America fascist. No fascist state would have given this guy a scholarship and let him come to Europe to do what he was doing!" There was, Podhoretz says, this paradoxical dual development. "On the one hand, one found oneself becoming more American in one's sense of oneself and, on the other hand, much less provincial and parochial because one was living in a foreign country." Podhoretz's first published writing appeared in the distinguished Cambridge literary review, *Scrutiny*. The "enormous amount" of political reading stayed with him. "Years later," he recalls, "when I broke ranks with the left I found that a lot of the stuff I read at Cambridge [was immensely pertinent]. I have nothing but gratitude for that experience."

The present librarian of Congress, and former chairman of the Fulbright Board, James Billington, spent his Fulbright year in Finland researching Finnish-Soviet history. This was a time when an American researcher could not work in the Soviet Union. Many Finns who held Fulbrights rose high in their government. "You cannot overestimate that influence, after they came to understand us," Billington says.[21] "They were not always friends, but at least they understood us." The present Finnish ambassador to the United States was not a Fulbrighter, but both his wife and his mother were.

Senior lecturers and researchers in the Fulbright program make an important though different contribution from the graduate students, and also receive valuable career and life-influencing rewards.

Moments before Prime Minister Rajiv Gandhi was assassinated in May 1991, Barbara Crossette, the *New York Times* correspondent in India, moved to the back seat of his car. She interviewed him on the forthcoming election. Five minutes later, he left the car, walked ten yards and was killed instantly by an assassin's bomb. Years earlier, Crossette had rushed to India from Bangladesh just after his mother, Prime Minister Indira Gandhi, was assassinated. In both tragedies, terrorist Sikhs were suspected. Because of her experience as a Fulbright lecturer at Punjab University in 1980–1981, Crossette was suited to cover both stories with exceptional insight. She has particularly broad contacts with Sikhs. After Mrs. Gandhi was killed, Crossette went into Sikh areas where she saw widespread acts of vengeful slaughter, including scalping of Sikhs on trains. The Fulbright lectureship, says Crossette, helped prepare her for four years of *Times* reporting in India and elsewhere on the continent from 1988 to 1991. During her Fulbright year, she lectured at many Indian universities, and was surprised at the heavily academic style of teaching journalism. There were few typewriters, no editorial supplies except those she purchased, and no hands-on practice of journalism. Today, she says, the journalism curriculum is known as "communications" and most graduates go into public relations or marketing. The Fulbright year introduced her to India "like a necklace," she says, "one bead led to another." The experience magnified her knowledge of the vast country, including its language and its people, and broadened her own reportage. When she returned to Washington, Crossette served on a Council for International Exchange Scholars (CIES) selection committee. And when across-the-board financial cuts struck the United States Information Agency (USIA) in 1981, threatening to close down the Fulbright scholarships, Crossette wrote admiringly of the program in the *New York Times*. Then USIA director Charles Z. Wick relented, and targeted cuts elsewhere. Her January 29, 1992 report described the creation of 30 Fulbright scholarships in the United States for Vietnamese students—the first arrivals since before the Vietnam War.

Another recent American Fulbrighter was in Tiananmen Square on June 4, 1989 when the Chinese military massacred student demonstrators. Michael J. Berlin arrived in China in August 1988 to teach journalism at the Chinese Academy of Social Sciences and the China School of Journalism. Both train reporters for Xinhua News Agency, China's international wire service, and the English-language *China Daily*. This was an important assignment for a Fulbrighter, particularly since the news media were becoming more liberal, even feisty. "Most Chinese reporters I met," said Berlin, "took pride in the fact that they were actively, if gingerly, pushing at the frontiers of press freedom."[22] Fulbrighter Berlin was a professional partner at that heady moment. When the military beat the students, he says, "it transformed the protest movement and turned press freedom into one of its prime goals." Berlin left China a month after the massacre. By then, his Chinese journalist friends were "publicly compliant, privately defiant . . . ready to encourage any further movement toward the liberating world of 'true facts.'"[23]

Daniel Boorstin, well before becoming librarian of Congress (now emeritus), was a Fulbright lecturer in Rome. "It was the greatest experience of my life, and the life of my family," he now says.[24] "It came at an important point in our lives." Such experience is not quantifiable, Boorstin says, but it can help create a broader, more sophisticated scholarship, which America needs in the years ahead.

A similar view is held by Alfred Kazin, prize-winning author-professor. He lectured on a Fulbright grant at Cambridge in 1952 and, he says, "benefited enormously."[25] The scholarship "gave me a chance to see the European scene myself, and especially to meet foreign scholars." Such contacts resulted in great benefit to American universities, Kazin says. He is especially interested in European scholars coming to the United States. "It is an important asset of the Fulbright program." Some of his students abroad suspected that the Fulbright was "a propaganda thing," Kazin recalls. "After I gave a lecture on F. Scott Fitzgerald, a French woman whose English may have been defective thanked me for 'defending American policy so well.'"

Nathan Glazer, the Harvard sociologist, went abroad as a Fulbright lecturer six times and served two terms on the Board of Foreign Scholarships. He visited programs in Morocco, Egypt, Pakistan, and India and lectured in India and Australia. He believes the Fulbright program has to be "sharply focused and have a few specific functions."[26] The primary objective, he says, should be "spreading knowledge of the American culture: history, politics, and so on, like the British Council's function."

He calls this: "American civilization presents itself." This has a surprisingly small role in the program, Professor Glazer maintains. "People from the developing world come here and study business, journalism, and how to run a TV station. They don't want to study American culture. Many Americans who go abroad don't want to deal with American culture either. Many are engaged in self-improvement." Dr. Glazer calls for spelling out more sharply and more limitedly the ways to come here and go abroad—and what are the U.S. national interests in this process.

Two Fulbright lectureships brought secrets of the Dead Sea Scrolls to Rome and Melbourne. Theodor H. Gaster was master of 29 languages, many of them ancient tongues of the Middle East. He was among the first in the 1940s to decipher the scrolls of ancient Judaism found by a peasant boy in the desert sands. Gaster, who died in 1992, humanized the myths of many old sects and religions. He sought to make the ideas of early history and beyond understandable to modern students. He placed them in their natural lifestyles. Gaster combined immense scholarship with great wit. He enchanted lay as well as scholarly audiences, abroad and at home. He fills a special niche for this writer: My wife, Marianne, and I first met in Theodor Gaster's living room in 1958.

In May 1991, a team of high-level Soviet economists met with counterparts at Harvard to draw up a plan they hoped could save the Soviet economy. Marshall E. Goldman, deputy director of the Russian Research Center at Harvard, was skeptical about the success of the meeting, absent strong governmental reforms at home. He gave the visitors "credit for trying." Fourteen years earlier, in the fall of 1977, Goldman became the first American economist to lecture in the Soviet Union. His Fulbright award had "an impact on me," he says.[27] "It was a kind of midlife lift and in my mind my life was very different afterward. It was the longest period I'd ever spent in the Soviet Union, and it helped improve my Russian. It gave me the opportunity to discuss American economic issues with Soviet young people. But I was also invited [outside class]—even at a time when it was not the thing to do—to give lectures on the Soviet economy. So that brought in a very important perspective. To many of the people in attendance it was as if the Messiah had come. That's how they treated me. A lady in a dormitory, who had heard my pretaped broadcast for the Voice of America, wanted to know if I was the man from outer space! Some people who came to class got into trouble because they had heard about [my closed-session lectures] but came nevertheless." The visit gave Goldman credibility as a Sovietologist as well as an economist. Now, says Goldman, the former Soviets "are more eager than ever to be accommodating because it provides them with the scholarship they need." Hence, one may assume, the hurried Russian economists' visit to Harvard.

Fulbrighters seem to be everywhere, even on the moon, and at every level of accomplishment.

"The valley has been less altered by being explored than have been the explorers,"[28] Astronaut Harrison H. Schmitt declared after spending three days on the moon in 1968. The valley on the moon that he described may be a metaphor for the Fulbright experience. It, too, may change the traveler more than the host. Schmitt was a student Fulbrighter in Norway in 1957 when the Soviet's Sputnik circled the earth. He describes his Fulbright experience as "a year-long adventure in education, science, and politics, an adventure which brought new thoughts that ultimately changed the course of my life." The young geologist would explore space himself, share his reflections with young people, and—more widely—when he was elected to the U.S. Senate.

In New York, the curtain rises on a play starring Jacqueline Brookes. The *Playbill* says she is a graduate of the Royal Academy of Dramatic Arts, which she attended as a Fulbright scholar. The year that Gorbachev's adviser Alexander Yakovlev discovered America on a scholarship (1959), Thomas R. Pickering, U.S. Ambassador to the United Nations during the Persian Gulf War, was a Fulbrighter in Melbourne. Yakovlev's colleague, Yevgeny Primakov, who also studied in the United States, directed the influential Institute of Oriental Studies in Moscow, and in 1991 was the intermediary in Iraq trying to end the Persian Gulf War and advance the Mideast peace talks.

College presidents, in addition to Harvard's Bok, earlier in their careers, have been Fulbrighters: Mortimer Appleby, Clark University (Germany, 1973–1974); Edward Bloustein, Rutgers University (United Kingdom, 1950–1951); Hanna H. Gray, University of Chicago (United Kingdom, 1950–1952); John W. Oswald, Pennsylvania State University (the Netherlands, 1953–1954); Frank H. T. Rhodes, Cornell University (United Kingdom scholar in the United States, 1950–1951); and John R. Silber, Boston University (Germany, 1959–1960).

Journalists, in addition to Crossette, Geyer, Podhoretz, and Rosenblatt, included Fox Butterfield, *New York Times* (Taiwan, 1961–1962); Frederick Graham, CBS News (United Kingdom, 1959–1960); Margaret Greenfield, *Washington Post* (United Kingdom, 1952–1953); and Hedrick Smith (United Kingdom, 1955–1956).

Scientists included Hans Bethe, physics (United Kingdom, 1955–1956; Nobel Prize, 1967); Joshua Lederberg, medicine (Australia, 1957–1958; Nobel Prize, 1958); Emilio Segre, physics (Italy, 1950–1951; Nobel Prize, 1959); Charles Townes, physics (France, 1955–1956, Japan, 1956–1957, lectures in Europe, 1972–1973; Nobel Prize, 1964); James Watson, medicine (Argentina, 1986; Nobel Prize, 1962); and Roslyn Yalow, medicine (Portugal, 1979; Nobel Prize, 1977).

Historians, in addition to Billington, Boorstin, Handlin, Katz, Winks, and Woodward, included Henry Steele Commager, Amherst College (France, 1957–1958); John Hope Franklin, National Humanities Center, North Carolina (Australia, 1960–1961; lectures in Latin America, Asia, 1972–1973); Leon F. Litwack, University of California-Berkeley (Soviet Union, 1980); and William McNeill, University of Chicago (United Kingdom, 1950–1951).

Economists, in addition to Goldman, were Andrew Brimmer, former member, Federal Reserve Board (India, 1951–1952); Martin Feldstein, Harvard University (United Kingdom, 1961–1962); Milton Friedman, Hoover Institution (United Kingdom, 1953–1954; Nobel Prize, 1976); Wassily Leontief, New York University (United Kingdom, 1951, Federal Republic of Germany, 1961; Nobel Prize, 1973); Franco Modigliani, Massachusetts Institute of Technology (Italy, 1955; Nobel Prize, 1985); Paul Samuelson, Massachusetts Institute of Technology (lectures in Asia, 1972–1973; Nobel Prize, 1976); and James M. Buchanan, George Mason University (Italy, 1955; United Kingdom, 1961; Nobel Prize 1986).

Other scholars, in addition to those mentioned in the text, included Peter Berger, Boston University (Germany, 1964); Seymour Martin Lipset, George Mason University, (Japan, 1963, United Kingdom, 1965; lecturer, Chile, 1987, Canada, 1990); William H. Whyte (Peru, 1961); Daniel Aaron, Harvard University (United Kingdom, 1968–1969); Walter Berns, American Enterprise Institute (France, 1965); Ernest Boyer, president, Carnegie Foundation for the Advancement of Teaching (India, 1984); Morris Janowitz, University of Chicago (Germany, 1952–1953); Leo Marx, Massachusetts Institute of Technology (United Kingdom, 1956, France, 1965); Peter Viereck, Mount Holyoke College (Italy, 1955); Aaron Wildavsky, University of California-Berkeley (Australia, 1954–1955); and Helen Vendler, Harvard University (Belgium, 1954–1955).

Writers, in addition to Kazin, were Renata Adler (France, 1960–1961); John Ashbery (France, 1955–1957); Robert Bly (Norway, 1956–1957); Paul Fussell (Germany, 1957–1958); Joseph Heller (United Kingdom, 1949–1950); Galway Kinnell (France, 1955–1957); Scott Momaday (Soviet Union, 1973–1974); Wallace Stegner (Greece, 1963); Peter Taylor (France, 1955); John Updike (lectures in Africa, 1972–1973); and Eudora Welty (United Kingdom, 1954).

The arts, in addition to Huxtable, were represented by musical composers Dominick Argento (Italy, 1951–1952); Aaron Copland (Italy, 1949); George Crumb (Germany, 1955–1956); Philip Glass (France, 1964–

1965); George Rochberg (Italy, 1950–1951); Ned Rorem (France, 1951–1952); Roger Sessions (Italy, 1951–1952); and Virgil Thomson (France, 1960–1961). From the theatre, in addition to Brustein, went Michael Moriarty, actor (United Kingdom, 1963–1964); Stacy Keach, actor (United Kingdom, 1964–1965); John Lithgow, actor (United Kingdom, 1967–1969); Israel Horovitz, playwright (France, 1975–1976); William Ball, director, American Conservatory Theatre, San Francisco (United Kingdom, 1953–1954); and Arvin Brown, director, Long Wharf Theatre, New Haven (United Kingdom, 1961–1962). From the graphic arts went Dale Chihuly, glassmaker (Italy, 1968–1969); Milton Glaser, graphic designer (Italy, 1952–1953); Nancy Graves, painter (France, 1964–1965); Peter Marzio, director, Houston Museum of Fine Arts (Italy, 1973–1974); Philip Pearlstein, painter (Italy, 1958–1959); and Richard Serra, sculptor (Italy, 1965–1966).

Eleven Fulbrighters, later in their careers, received Nobel Prizes—a favorable commentary on the foresight of the Fulbright selectors.

Many Fulbrighters have gone on to high office in other countries. In 1986, on the fortieth anniversary of the Fulbrights, among the former recipients were the then prime minister of Sweden, Ingvar Carlsson, dozens of former and current cabinet ministers, including the minister of defense in Belgium and the minister of finance of Colombia, at least forty former and current members of various parliaments, ten current Supreme Court justices, and dozens of former and current ambassadors, including the New Zealand ambassador to the United States, a former prime minister of his country.[29] In 1990, the Moroccan minister of cultural affairs, a well-placed counselor in the royal palace, the rector of a university, and numerous department heads throughout the country were all Fulbright alumni. That same year, Japanese alumni included the presidents of the universities of Tokyo and Kyoto, several justices of the Supreme Court, the minister of health and welfare, heads of major corporate and banking institutions, and leading journalists. In Spain, the minister of education and a number of university rectors and ambassadors are former Fulbrighters.[30] In Uruguay, a senator, a former senator, two former deans, a former president of the Central Bank, chairmen of several state entities, directors of institutes, and the director of the National School of the Dance were Fulbright grantees.

Students, researchers, lecturers and senior scholars have gone to or come from 130 different countries under the Fulbright banner. The listing above is vastly incomplete. Some country-examples suggest the degree of influence returning Fulbrighters have had in their homelands.

One of the newest binational commissions is in Mexico. This step coincides with the significant free-trade discussions between the United

States and its southern neighbor. Numerous high-ranking positions in Mexican public life have been occupied during the past two years by former Fulbright grantees. Pedro Aspe, Mexico's finance secretary, earned his doctorate in economics at the Massachusetts Institute of Technology in 1978 under Fulbright auspices. Herminio Blanco, deputy secretary of commerce for free trade; Jaime Zabludowsky, coordinator of the commerce ministry's free-trade negotiating unit; and Aslan Cohen, assistant coordinator for free trade, are among the Fulbrighters involved in the U.S.-Mexico trade talks. Fulbright alumni among prominent Mexican scholars include Silvia Ortega Salazar, rector, Metropolitan University, Mexico City; Leon R. Olive Morett, director, Institute of Philosophic Research, National Autonomous University of Mexico; Carlos Ornelas, adviser on educational policy, Secretariat of Education; Carlos Bazdresch, president, Center for Economic Research (CIDE); and Enrique Cardenas, rector, University of the Americas, Puebla. These "important players in the policy scene in Mexico," according to the U.S. embassy there, "reflect the high esteem and respect Fulbright grantees command in this country."[31]

In Ecuador, a large number of Fulbright alumni have held high positions, including the vice president, minister of energy and mines, minister of finance and president of the World Bank, undersecretary of finance, undersecretary of industries, national directors of energy consortia, director of the Institute for Statistics and the Census, and the president of the National Association of University Professors.[32]

Since before World War II, exchanges with Latin America have not equaled the number of scholars traveling to or from Western Europe or Japan. A special U.S. student program was initiated in 1963 by the Board of Foreign Scholarships to attract qualified graduating seniors to receive Fulbright awards in Latin American institutions. The program required foreign-language proficiency. Twenty-five years later, Edward Purcell analyzed the value of a special Fulbright program to inspire Americans to study in Latin America.[33] Purcell, a USIA foreign service officer, had coordinated the original program. After one year, the project had seemed so successful that the FSB eliminated the distinction between special and regular programs in Latin America. The 1990 survey attempted to capture the perspective that 400 former grantees have on their Fulbright experience in Latin America.

Almost a third of those who responded teach Spanish, Latin American history, or related subjects at the university level. Eleven teach related subjects in high school or elementary school. Twenty-two work in the international field in government, in international banks, and in such agencies as the Agency for International Development (AID) and Catholic Relief Services. One became president of the Inter American Press Association. All said there was a "clear link between their Fulbright grant and their choice of career."[34] Business, commerce, and industry account for the careers of thirty-one of the respondents; twelve are in medicine or health services; ten practice law, one as a federal judge. Other grantees include homemakers, urban planners, naval officers, a nutritionist, a film producer, a nun, a radio announcer, and a theater critic. Even those whose careers seem not to be related to their Fulbrights say they trace their career direction to that Fulbright year. Respondents also cited "their own increased ability to contribute in the United States to making informed policy and decisions on Latin America, as ordinary citizens, voters, and policymakers in a wide range of fields."

Australia and New Zealand are active binational exchanges. The 2,400 Australian Fulbrighters include Sir Zelman Cowen, former governor-general of Australia and later provost of Oriel College, Oxford. Sir Zelman spent his Fulbright year at Harvard Law School in 1953 and was visiting professor there in 1963–1964. He has taught at many U.S. universities. "I have known of no one who has visited America under the auspices of the Fulbright scheme who has not returned to Australia greatly enriched and vastly stimulated by the experience," says Sir Zelman. He calls the Fulbright program "an outstanding act of statesmanship."[35] Other Australians awarded Fulbrights include Nick Greiner, former premier of New South Wales; Gordon Reid, former governor of Western Australia; Justice Robert Nicholson, Supreme Court of Western Australia; a dozen directors-general of education in various states; prominent professors, researchers, and administrators in various academic disciplines; and chief executive officers in industrial organizations. Coralie Hinkley went from Sydney to New York for graduate study in modern dance. Fulbright, she says, "uplifted my life." She studied with Martha Graham and at the Julliard School of Music, and returned home "to give back as much as I could." Hinkley created modern dance programs for students and teachers at several leading Australian institutions. Several Fulbrighters from Australia were featured in the Queen's 1990 Birthday Honors List.

More than 1,600 Fulbrighters who went to or from New Zealand in 40 years were asked about their experience.[36] Some 662 responded to questions about the aims and benefits of the program. More than four-fifths reported gaining new ideas that they were able to develop and subsequently apply in their careers. One New Zealander reported that "every research project I have carried out since, has incorporated something of what I learned. Many of these ideas have still not reached New Zealand." Another wrote, "My return to New Zealand was a real let-down. Opportunity to really use experience came thirteen years later and became the basis of post-graduate nursing education in New Zealand." An American exchange teacher wrote, "The children in Shawmuk Hills school in Grand Rapids, Michigan, knew considerably more about New Zealand and the Maori than most Americans would ever have." Dame Marie Clay, a Fulbright graduate student in 1951, wrote that "as a young adult this award made me more sensitive to my own society. It has allowed me to move easily between the two countries throughout a whole career, to teach, hold office, publish, and consult as readily in the United States of America as in New Zealand."

A New Zealand teacher describes the early Fulbright application procedure as "daunting." Says Alison Hanham, "We had to be fingerprinted, solemnly swear not to overthrow the government of the United States by force or live by prostitution (what a hope!) and attest that we did not approve of communism. There was a space on the form for one's police record, which was filled by a stamped ambiguous statement 'police report not available.'"

Helen Hughes, who became parliamentary commissioner for the environment, attributes her successful career directly to the Fulbright award that took her to Vassar College in 1952. Though the legal systems in New Zealand and the United States differ, R. O. McGechan studied the teaching of law in the United States on a Fulbright grant in 1950. He returned to change the entire method of teaching law in New Zealand. Students once learned law by rote. McGechan, later dean of the faculty of law at Victoria University in Wellington, introduced the American-style case method. In the continuing flow of ideas, the American Joseph Jaudon came to New Zealand on a Fulbright in 1986. The litigation skills program that resulted was due primarily to Jaudon's visit. Sir Wallace Rowling likes to say he has twice been an ambassador for New Zealand—once as Fulbright exchange teacher (1955) and the second time as his country's ambassador to the United States (1985–1988). He also has been prime minister of New Zealand. He is one of many Fulbright grantees who later occupied high positions in their own countries. Some examples:

- Argentina: Eduardo Rabossi, secretary for human rights
- Brazil: Fernando Henrique Cardoso, federal senator
- China: Some prodemocracy demonstrators in Tiananmen Square in 1989 were Fulbrighters returned from America
- Colombia: Enrique Low Mutra, justice of the Supreme Court
- Cyprus: Andreas N. Philippou, minister of education
- Greece: Andreas Papandreou, prime minister
- Hungary: Geza Veszenszky, minister of foreign affairs

- India: S. M. Krishna, minister of state for industries
- Israel: Magen Broshi, curator of the Dead Sea Scrolls Museum
- Ivory Coast: M. Bakary Toure, rector, University of Abidjan
- Korea, South: Hyun Jae Lee, prime minister
- Malaysia: Datuk Elyas bin Omar, mayor, Kuala Lumpur
- Nicaragua: Silvio de Franco, minister of finance
- Nigeria: J. H. K. Nketia, historian and educator
- Norway: Gro Harlem-Brundtland, prime minister
- Philippines: Marcelo B. Fernan, chief justice, Supreme Court
- Poland: Marcin Swiecicki, minister for foreign economic cooperation
- Sri Lanka: Lalith Athulathmudali, minister of education and higher education
- Turkey: Arif Caglar, rector, First University; National Commission for Higher Education
- Yugoslavia: Dimitri Rupel, minister for foreign relations of Slovenia

An American abroad discovered Chaucer as a college alumnus; many foreign Fulbrighters in America were introduced to Jefferson and Whitman. One discovery was unique. Gordon F. Ferris, world-renowned entomologist, during his Fulbright year in China in 1948 came upon a previously unknown gall-forming insect. He named it *Fulbrightia gallicola* "to commemorate the Fulbright Act . . . and in honor of Senator Fulbright."[37]

6

Is the Program Effective?

James M. Chang, while a student in Taiwan in 1973, was deeply impressed by the American civilization he discovered at the U.S. Cultural Center in Taipei. In August 1991, on behalf of his government, Chang opened the Chinese Information and Culture Center in New York City. At the ceremony he declared that the U.S. center in Taiwan had been responsible for one million Taiwanese studying in the United States and billions of dollars of trade with America.

- Is cultural exchange effective?
- Is the Fulbright program effective?

How does one judge its value? Should the criterion be cost-effectiveness? How much is a Fulbright grant worth in dollars, francs, yen, or rubles? To the recipient? To his or her institution? To the nation? To a foreign country? To peace? When is effectiveness best measured? During the next budget-writing cycle? A decade later? Forty-five years later? Or beyond?

One is reminded of a premature estimate of one professor's research. Samuel Pierpont Langley was advised by a *New York Times* editorial, December 10, 1903, to stop putting "his substantial greatness as a scientist in further peril by continuing to waste his time, and the money involved." Langley was convinced he could create "a flying machine." The *Times* said "life is short, and [Langley] is capable of services to humanity incomparably greater than can be expected to result from trying to fly." Sagely, said the *Times*, "(T)here are more useful employments."

Today, almost 100 years later, how does one estimate Professor Langley's effectiveness? By airline income grosses worldwide? By the replacement value of railroad and steamship travel? By air power incapacitating the enemy in the Persian Gulf War?

In October 1973, challenged by the need he saw to conceptualize the diversity of exchange-of-persons programs so as to provide policy leadership in Washington and the embassies abroad, John Richardson, then an assistant secretary of state, directed this formulation for the nation's educational and cultural affairs: "Programs [including Fulbright] are designed to strengthen patterns of informal communication in ways that favorably influence the environment within which U.S. foreign policy is carried out and help build the human foundations of the structure of peace." The program sought to do this by (1) enlarging the circle of those able to serve as influential interpreters between this and other nations, (2) stimulating institutional developments which favor mutual comprehension, and (3) reducing structural and technical impediments to the exchange of ideas and information [from the "CU Program Concept," October 1, 1973].

How then must one assess the Fulbrighters? One by one, to discover what changes were wrought, and what these changes produce. Such an assessment is bound to be partially subjective. This writer sensed this in interviewing scores of Fulbright grantees, past and present. Even those whose Fulbright experience was 40 years earlier still reveal that certain brightening of the eyes, a glow along the smile lines, and rapid-fire recollection of what it was like, what it meant then, and subsequently, how the "Fulbright grant changed my life." Repeated over and over, were these personal assessments.

How does one translate such assessments into gains of productivity? Negotiators of trade-union contracts quantify labor costs used to produce a product. How does one value research completed for a dissertation? Or the subsequent use of that new doctoral skill in curricular design? Or the use of that curriculum by scores of teachers, in many times that number of schools, influencing countless students? Try another kind of assessment. Numerous Mexican scholars in recent years completed Fulbright studies in the United States. They returned home and many rose to high positions in their government. In 1991, Presidents Bush and Salinas de Gortari signed a historic mutual trade pact. Most of the Mexicans who prepared the way in the economics, labor, and other ministries had been Fulbrighters in the United States. What is the value to either country or to their capacity for cooperation of this considerable Fulbright impact on bilateral diplomacy?

The International Monetary Fund (IMF) told one United States Information Agency (USIA) official that prior to the change of government in 1989, the Polish economists they could really work with constructively were those who had come to the United States on Fulbright grants.

Such influential contacts can have an affective as well as cognitive value. These exchanges built across boundary lines increase empathy and influence behavior. The Fulbright alumni become a worldwide community. This is what concord is all about.

Years ago, Charles Frankel, who headed CU, then the State Department's bureau for educational and cultural affairs, understood the need to insulate cultural programs from the grosser pressures for "evidence of effectiveness." Such "evidence" he described as "quick political or economic benefits."[1] He understood, but still was restive under the cumbersome bureaucratic arrangements for Fulbright grant making. Frankel preferred the Swedish model. Its government votes cultural-affairs money to the privately run Swedish Institute. It is removed from the bureaucracy and Parliament, though answerable to the government.

In America, there will always be clamor from Congress, the administration, or the bureaucracy for "evidence of effectiveness." The issue must be addressed. Effectiveness can be viewed as a current response to an immediate need, say, for favorable publicity for an administration or the Fulbright program itself. Frankel tried to understand how instant effectiveness worked. "One of CU's most effective programs," he had been told, "was its sponsorship of tours by American folksingers, who went into the boondocks to entertain Indian peasants or African villagers." Frankel queried his associates for proof that the villagers liked the folksingers: "What was gained? What were the objectives we were trying to accomplish?" Frankel was told that if the peasants liked American folksingers, they would like America. He doubted this would generate a lasting effect on the villagers' farming more efficiently, voting better, or even taking more pleasure in music. Finally, Frankel was told that President Johnson himself had noticed the work of these groups and had invited its members to the White House, where he had poured praise on them. At this point, Frankel relates, "I realized I had tracked the quarry down: folksingers were 'effective' because they called the president's attention to CU's programs and CU could use that kind of support." Frankel comments, "As a test of the effectiveness of a government policy, it seemed to me equivalent to testing the effectiveness of a surgical operation by taking the surgeon's blood pressure after the operation's completion."

No folksingers have traveled under the Fulbright program, but assessing effectiveness on short-term values remains a temptation.

The Spanish and Portuguese democratizations in the 1970s, the revolutions of 1989 in Eastern Europe, and similar changes in the Soviet

Union since 1985, if not earlier, are more evolutionary than revolutionary. Cultural communication and then political changes worked their way through these societies over many years. In each place, once the authoritarian figure passed from the scene the old political infrastructure crumbled. We can never know how large a role cultural diplomacy played in each case. We do know it was a factor. Slowly, quietly, American scholars and researchers went inside these countries during their dark periods. Even then, professionals and scholars from each of these lands came to the United States. One of the most underreported and undervalued aspects of the intellectual exchanges with the Soviet Union is the impact Soviet scholars made on their society after studying and researching in the United States. One highly publicized visiting scholar, Alexander Yakovlev, undoubtedly had an enormous effect on the development of Mikhail Gorbachev's perestroika-and-glasnost, and the USSR's more relaxed foreign policies.

But perhaps no less important, over the long term, were the scores of other Soviet specialists who came to America from 1957 to the end of the 1980s. I recall lunching with a Soviet minister in Paris in the late 1980s. He discussed world affairs with the same assurance and moderation as his Western European colleagues. He was fluent in many languages, and was comfortable discussing human rights abuses, frankly and optimistically. He was in his late sixties. I could not help wondering how he had developed such a worldview in as closed a society as was the Soviet Union during most of his lifetime.

We now may know part of the answer. Hundreds of Soviet scholars visited the United States on academic grants.[2] They returned home and remained in contact with one another during the still dark days. These intellectuals formed a "cell," the traditional communist term for infiltrating into another society. Only this cell remained *inside* the Soviet Union. Its objective: to introduce reforms that would alter Soviet society, make it more productive, more responsive to citizen needs, and far less under authoritarian direction. This was *not* directed by Americans for American purposes. It was rather the creation of Soviet intellectuals who sought to bring their motherland into the twentieth century and prepare it for the twenty-first.

It is clear that what was done in Eastern Europe and the Soviet Union through programs such as the Fulbright program and its associate, the International Research and Exchanges Board (IREX), was to create "a set of underground establishments which exerted a tremendous amount of, and in some cases decisive, influence in overthrowing the old order"—the words of Allen Kassof, long-time director of IREX. As early as the 1960s, Kassof recalls, cadres were created in the USSR to secure

American exposure. At first, they were reasonably convinced of the soundness of the future of their own system. "Year after year, particularly when we saw the same people, including the seniors, you could see the corrosion taking place," Kassof says. "So we provided them with a deep sense of dissatisfaction with what was going on, part of that generated by the situation in the Soviet Union itself, but part of it was embarrassment. As one Soviet alumnus put it, "the exchange provided two standards of comparison of the two systems, and on every score the American would come out ahead." The exchange did more than have an enormous corrosive effect. It also provided a set of conceptual vocabularies that then formed the basis for what the Soviet scholars *did*. This, Kassof adds, influenced all who came to biology, physics, or other disciplines. They would leave with a different idea of how you did things organizationally—what a university is like. "American universities," Kassof concludes, "had an enormous influence. They are a national treasure, not duplicated anywhere else in the world." Yet, ironically, the IREX program was attacked in the United States for giving away technology and allowing communists to influence Americans. The Soviet scholars were, indeed, carefully chosen elites but in the end, says Kassof, they constituted the Soviet underground establishments. The events of 1989 and August 1991 came in a great flood. These relatively small programs, costing a few million dollars a year, had enormous consequences. Cost-effective? In a similar way, Francisco Franco was said to understand that following his death there would not be a deluge—but democracy. He is reported to have told an American official in the early 1970s that "after my death [Spain] will turn democratic." Franco added, "For a democracy to exist, a country must have a middle class. I have built a middle class in Spain."[3] In the former Soviet Union, the intelligencia is the middle class. Whether it can create or sustain a democratic society is still unclear. But the process is vital for citizens of the world. Cultural diplomacy played a significant role in the USSR with a paltry budget and only a few thousand scholarly exchanges.

Some tests of effectiveness are still more difficult to assess. How does one value the work of a single American researcher overseas or a foreign researcher in the United States? Historian John Hope Franklin's answer: Evaluate the publication record of a researcher whose work has been passed by peer review. One may examine the individual's product or his or her career attainments. That we have done in this and other chapters. It is also useful to evaluate the findings of one study of Fulbright awards in nine midwestern states.[4] Of 803 Fulbrighters who responded, 49 have to their credit 64 published books or monographs or documentary films. Some 284 have published 519 articles and book reviews or produced filmstrips on their specialties. At least 147 Fulbrighters read 274 papers to professional meetings or gave speeches relevant to their professional careers. Eighty-seven completed theses and dissertations on their Fulbrights. Other accomplishments resulting from the Fulbright awards were 53 new courses introduced; 73 paintings, works of sculpture, or musical compositions; 150 concerts, recitals, and exhibits; and many more works of writing and musical composition then in process.   It is less mechanical—and somewhat more difficult—to judge the effectiveness of university teaching across cultures. Pamela George, a Fulbright professor from North Carolina who served on the faculty of education of Chiang Mai University in Thailand, set down some "lessons from U.S. Fulbrighters in Southeast Asia and their colleagues in Thailand."[5] Dr. George lists some of the "myriads of tasks" U.S. Fulbright professors perform:

- participating in the organization (and even having major responsibilities) for national or international conferences;
- hosting foreign visitors on campus;
- consulting on research projects with faculties, departments, and universities;
- writing graduate research manuals and models;
- developing computer software and programs;
- editing English texts, reports, speeches, theses abstracts, handbooks, articles and applications for colleagues;
- participating in many "honoring parties" for guests and groups from the university;
- giving workshops for staff development within departments, for all new faculty members in a university, for teacher-training colleges, as part of international organizational work;
- participating in lecture tours to visiting campuses;
- counseling disturbed students;
- supervising graduate student research;
- ordering books and other supplies from foreign vendors;
- simplifying reading material and texts for colleagues using English reading materials in their classes;
- typing in English;
- consulting with faculty members who want help, references, direction for continued education in the West;
- writing Thai colleagues' lectures or speeches;
- teaching colleagues or students to use computers; and
- serving in ambassadorial capacities for departments, faculties, and universities when events, seminars, and ceremonies are held.

How does one judge the effectiveness of such diverse activities—all performed as an American university teacher in a land abroad? Perhaps we should not seek evaluations of individual performance. Instead, we should turn for guidance to the initial objective of the Fulbright program: "to promote mutual understanding."

Does all this teaching in classroom and, perhaps more importantly, outside, and all this research and publication enhance mutual understanding of Americans and foreign nationals in each of the 130 countries in which there are Fulbright programs?

The question is particularly important in this post-cold war world. Despite the melding of the European Community, the successful merchandising of technology by Japan, and the coalescing of regional self-awareness in the Asia-Pacific area and Latin America, the United States will play the most prominent single role in improving the world system. However one defines a "new world order" the opportunity to build one will continue for no one can say how long. Just as immediately after World War II, when the Fulbright program emerged, there is need for American idealism mixed with economic and political pragmatism. That opportunity, once again, can excite young people. The Fulbright program can magnify the life-changing experience of individuals.

"If the great percentage of our foreign aid were given as grants such as Fulbright," suggests Georgie Anne Geyer, the Fulbrighter who writes syndicated columns and books, "we'd have a much better world." She acknowledges the need for economic and military assistance abroad, but would stress "bringing foreigners to American universities because they go back home and change things." It is, she adds, "a tremendously practical program. No pie in the sky at all. It is cunning and practical, amazingly cost-effective, wonderfully so." Such programs may even reduce losses from "so much of our economic and military aid that has just been thrown away," Geyer adds.

Some leavening of this highly favorable assessment is provided by two Americans who examined the impact of U.S. higher education on Brazilian students who were Fulbright grantees.[6] "It was striking, indeed almost startling," the investigators report, "that throughout our conversations we did not meet a single person who expressed regret at having studied in the United States." Many, however, experienced alienation once they returned to Brazil. Their American experience made them "forward-looking," rather than seeking instant gratification as did their locally trained cohorts. The U.S. experience also provided a standard for "local appraisal" which tended to set them apart. One student said he learned in the States to protest abuses of human rights and sexism. The authors comment, "From one perspective this could be seen as destructive alienation. From another, it was sowing the seeds of political change!"7 One graduate said, "To be taught the power of reason and to be denied the opportunity to use it is profoundly disturbing." Respondents reported they had better access to information sources as a consequence of their study abroad, and a more sophisticated understanding of their own economy as well as international forces.[8] For those Brazilians seeking technical careers, advanced training in the United States was seen as the "fast track" to success. Many returning students were turned off, however, by the prospect of working in state-owned enterprises. Some interviewed spoke in patriotic terms: "It is valuable to Brazil that I studied abroad. I know English, I know many top people in my field, I know advanced techniques of analysis. With many others like me, Brazil is bound to benefit. It is a form of technology transfer for which we are most grateful."

Few cited the acquisition of new facts or new tools as their most important gain. As one scientist put it, the most valuable benefits were "a challenging atmosphere, stimulating colleagues, and excellent support facilities."[9] Many had never been asked to express their reactions before, and "in several cases they were quite moved to have to do so."

Several spoke of American graduate education as a "collective experience." For social scientists, this communal spirit was their collective participation in the public policy process and public debate, which they now fashioned after the careers of their mentors in America. This participation included movement into and out of government, the media, and the universities, Washington style. What these respondents shared, said one, was "an awareness of the inevitability of complexity and faith in the process of compromise, negotiation, flexibility, and equilibration." One observer of the Brazilian scene who did not have an American background told the investigators that "the American-trained Brazilians, with their academic rigor and seriousness of purpose, have great influence already and are destined to have much more."

Another assessment of a special Fulbright project was made in 1989. Four years earlier, Henry Kissinger and the National Bi-Partisan Commission on Central America—in the heat of controversies over the insurgency in El Salvador and the Marxist government in Nicaragua—had concluded that a large student exchange with these countries would be a useful response to violence and the recruiting of students for courses in the then Soviet Union. The Central American Program of Undergraduate Scholarships (CAMPUS) was established as a pilot effort.

The 1989 assessment by Development Associates, Inc. under contract to the USIA concluded the following:

- CAMPUS largely fulfilled its principal goals. Many graduates who were exposed to an American university education were now in key professions, and expanded their intellectual horizons. Most earned a certificate or degree that enhanced their stature back home. They also gained a better understanding of the United States.
- Ninety-seven percent of the participants completed the program.
- The first year of CAMPUS fulfilled the program's objective of offering scholarship "to lower socioeconomic groups."
- In most instances, CAMPUS scholars were placed in appropriate academic programs at U.S. institutions. They contributed to the reduction of skill shortages in their respective countries.
- CAMPUS developed leadership links between the United States and Central America. Returned CAMPUS scholars established a Fulbright alumni association in Panama and Costa Rica. Salvadoran students developed an exchange program with the University of Wisconsin-Eau Claire.

Here are some of the individual accomplishments: Virtually all 154 students in the 1986–1988 class earned bachelor's degrees, half with double majors and/or substantive minors. Forty percent made the dean's list or earned other scholastic honors. One was valedictorian, others graduated summa, magna, or cum laude—though few could speak or write English at the outset. There were top-ranked departmental graduates in education, geology, journalism, mathematics, psychology, rhetoric, and sociology. One was an intern at the Smithsonian Institution, and another at the American Philosophical Association. The group attended twelve different colleges at a cost of $4,600,000. By 1993 there will be approximately 315 more student participants at an estimated cost of $12.5 million. One question raised by CAMPUS, successful though it has been, is whether this experience is in the founding spirit of the Fulbrights. "Student" initially meant graduate student, not undergraduate. Yet the concept was clearly in favor of the younger participant who has a long life and full career ahead. One Fulbright representative overseas favors the junior-year-abroad approach for American Fulbrighters. Why not freshman-to-senior-year abroad for foreign students? But what about American undergraduates? Should their most formative college years be spent abroad? It is unlikely such an arrangement can be made to fit the strict Western European systems. And it is less likely that Third World colleges would satisfy the stringent objectives of either American parents or Fulbright placement specialists. CAMPUS, however, may be a pilot not only for Central America but for congressionally mandated undergraduate programs in Eastern Europe and countries formerly part of the Soviet Union. Similarly, Congress in 1992 mandated scholarships for thirty Vietnamese students. The geopolitical purpose: "to further economic liberalization now underway in the Socialist Republic of Vietnam, helping to foster additional economic and political changes." The students would take courses in economics and commercial law. The $600,000 in over two fiscal years would presumably be taken from other Fulbright programs. Sometimes "effectiveness" is an ephemeral, almost spiritual gleaning. Such was Kiyohiko Tsuboi's experience. The professor in the Department of English at Okayama University School of Letters, Japan, writes:

> In one of the simple and austere rooms of the special collections [at Princeton] we sat at a desk with [F.Scott] Fitzgerald's handwritten papers spread before us. The next moment it seemed that I was talking directly to him. Reading his delicate handwriting in pencil on yellowing paper, some words erased and rewritten with colored crayon, I almost spoke to him aloud. Here you are! I have been looking forward to this moment for a long time. Then I thought I saw his sad smiling face, with his arm stretched out to the "green light." "I saw him. I was him." There his naked soul was beating on "against the current, borne back ceaselessly into the past." His unfulfilled desire, his never-ceasing quest for the meaning of life, and his unhesitant commitment to the truth under the cover of "the greatest, gaudiest spree," all of Fitzgerald was before me. I felt as if I stood on the top of a high mountain face to face with the man I had long sought.[10]

That Fulbright experience was expressed poetically. There are other ways. But, clearly, not best by quantification. All education becomes an ambiguous storehouse for future use. International education and cultural exchange is little different. One must regard its promise as a matter of trust. "Truth is," remarks Robin Winks, one of the Fulbright program's most committed practitioners, "as most educators know, one cannot prove the effectiveness of education, of cultural programs, or of Mozart in soothing the savage beast." Writes Winks, "We either believe the Burkean idea that education pays because it leads to a stake in society, or we do not, for we certainly cannot prove it."

Yet in retrospect, we can make certain judgments. There is an "exponential" advantage from Fulbrighters who pass on their benefits to others, remarks Robert Brustein, the Harvard drama specialist. "Jesus had only twelve disciples," he notes wryly, "and two thousand years later half of this world is Christian!" People who are passionate about what they believe pass it on to other people, Brustein says, and they become passionate too and pass the belief on to other people. "It propagates itself,"

Brustein declares, "but if you begin with the assumption that everything has to be totally planned and representational you're going to debase the notion of truth and the notion of culture."

That said, how do we judge the effectiveness of the Fulbright program, past, present, or future? There are no guarantees that persuasion will result from cultural exchanges. When Joseph Lelyveld was a Fulbrighter in Burma he spent hours conversing with U Thaung, a prominent Burmese editor and anti-American. The U.S. embassy had given up making him "see the light." Lelyveld talked to U Thaung gravely and quietly about Burma. "Our conversations took the shape of a hill, which we climbed from opposite sides, hoping to reach the top together."

Daniel Boorstin, the Fulbrighter who became librarian of Congress, regards a major achievement of the Fulbrights "the cosmopolitizing of the U.S. faculty."[12] Or, as Harvard President Derek Bok puts it: "Who would you like to negotiate an oil agreement with—Sheik Yamani, who was at Harvard for a year or the Ayatollah Khomeini?[13] Sure, Yamani will represent his country actively, and he may be shrewder for having been here, but we all benefit from having shared common experiences, common spirits."

Speak to regional directors of cultural affairs at USIA desks in Washington and you will hear mixed professional estimates of Fulbright operations abroad. These men and women have served at posts overseas, and some are Fulbright alumni. The universities in one country would not have any status without its local scholars who secured their doctorates on the Fulbright program. Americans going abroad bring back a similar resource, but their universities often ignore that resource, one director says. In the Middle East, there is no real two-way exchange. It's a one-way street for Arabs going to the United States for undergraduate and postgraduate training. Today, Americans, mostly of Arab descent, are hired mainly for their ability to speak Arabic, or as instructors in technical fields. More American graduate students should be encouraged to go to these countries as researchers or lecturers in other disciplines. Nepal can absorb only one or two American lecturers but Nepalese graduate students come to the United States in large numbers and return to teach. In some countries, American lecturers arrive not well briefed. Great flexibility is required in some places. Classes may not meet as anticipated. The language level of students may be lower than would have been accepted at the American's university. The syllabus may change before the visiting professor arrives. The foreign university may expect more development-oriented instruction than the visitor expected to provide. And, of course, living conditions may be quite different than promised.

The highly visible achievements are there: The first Fulbright generation occupies positions of leadership in countries around the world. They reflect a "capital of good will." American studies are now taught in nearly all Western European countries and have spread East and South. University chairs in American history have been established in many countries. Reciprocally, writes John Hope Franklin, "I invited a Dutch historian to come to Brooklyn [College] and to teach for a year . . . I need not tell you that Brooklyn has never been the same since. That would be true of the students, their parents, and the community in general, for they got an entirely new perspective as they began to view their country through the prism of Dutch insight and perception."[14]

Double this impact by adding the element of exchange, magnify it still further to account for all the individual "life-changing" experiences, and you arrive at the initial Fulbright objective: mutual understanding among peoples. The Fulbright program may thus be seen by educators as an effective educational instrument—by policy makers and diplomats as a foreign policy asset. Because the program never had stated long- or short-term political goals, this asset of cultural diplomacy satisfies an initial objective. The program, however, does not serve partisan interests, or even the policy interests of an administration. The Fulbright operation is too well buffered from political influence, and the selection process too long to provide rapid response to short-term geopolitical interests.

Yet the program helps improve the quality of public policy debate in the United States and abroad, and the quality of foreign scholarship addressing the culture, history, and government of the United States. The foreign-language and area studies run by the Department of Education have provided more than 15,000 U.S. citizens with the opportunity to improve their skills. And another 50,000 Fulbrighters have studied or taught abroad. Paralleling the emphasis on foreign area studies in the United States are American-studies programs in more than 100 countries abroad. This is reciprocity, toward mutual understanding.

The Hubert Humphrey fellowships in thirteen years have more than 1,400 alumni in 109 countries. Cost-sharing on the twelve U.S. campuses contributes an average of $7,600 per fellow. The fellowship provides mid-career professionals from developing countries a year's nondegree program and a short working internship.

Further, the Fulbrights have expanded the receptivity abroad for the American university model. The U.S. style of organization and administration of levels of higher education and interdisciplinary cooperation now appears in many places overseas for the first time. American ideas and methods in the social sciences have been particularly adapted abroad.

Perhaps least heralded as an asset of foreign relations is the Fulbright program's commitment to serving the long-term national interest. This factor, in itself, tends to remove whatever uncertainty may result abroad from some U.S. policy of the moment. The Fulbright course is, at least, consistent. It reflects the diversity of America and its educational system. That consistency reflects fundamental values, whatever the policy position today.

"The Fulbright program is a model of investment in long-term national interests," declares the U.S. Advisory Commission on Public Diplomacy.[15] "By building good will and trust among scholars around the world, it has created a constituency of leaders and opinion-makers dedicated to international understanding."

All that America can ask of this vital constituency is that such leaders and opinion makers help build the human foundations for cooperation and community that are crucial to a more just and peaceful "new world order."

7

Problems: Tensions in Policy, Performance, and Support

The Fulbright program is many things to many people. "The person in my position," acknowledges one of the program's overseers,[1] "is supposed to provide a synoptic view of all the piecemeal parts, so that if someone asks, 'What are your priorities worldwide?' they will get the answer at this point." This director can tell a great deal about local or regional programs. But, he adds, "there is no mechanism even conceivable for a global perspective." There is instead "an aggregate and then rationalization of many partial objectives." Parts of the program "grow like Topsy and what passes for planning is really rationalization of how we got to where we are, by looking abstractly." So, he concludes, "there is a lot of ersatz historian in anyone who wants to be a planner."

The Fulbright board, according to its former chairman, Walter A. Rosenblith,[2] former provost of the Massachusetts Institute of Technology, is "too much of a rubber stamp—not because of political reasons but because there is too much to be done." Thousands of grantees are involved each year, and once the independent screening committee has made its choices, "there is nothing much the board can do," the former chairman says. He believes the binational commissions are a "weakness" of the program because they are not composed of highly qualified academics who understand the complexities of the academy nearly as well as they know business or politics. The program, he adds, "is not easily spelled out" by the board, which itself does not always include prominent scholars. The FSB, says Rosenblith, rarely has current intellectual issues on the agenda. Yet the Fulbright board is held in a vise not of its creation. It faces problems without the power to enforce change. It can, however, if it grasps the nettle, cut the bureaucratic maze and recom-

91

mend policies that can alert all the disparate Fulbright operators. That
was the accomplishment of the FSB's 1991 White Paper (see Appendix
B).

A U.S. Information Agency (USIA) executive who observes the Fulbright program finds that it is overly field driven. Sometimes posts will
ask for a highly specialized person to fill a local development need. Yet
if the academy were the sole selector, he feels that 70 percent of the
grants would go to Western Europe. One director of a USIA overseas
region, however, regards the White Paper as oriented to the American
academy, projecting the Fulbright program as an "entitlement program
for American academics." The program, he believes, should be dedicated primarily to expanding mutual understanding among other countries
and the United States. He believes that in some countries "the Fulbright
program seems to pursue irrelevance as if it were a mark of intellectual
integrity."

He cites a country with a murderous insurgency that requested a scholar
who could help display America's interest in easing the political crisis.
"If we leave it to the academic community itself to decide its priorities
[in that embattled country] and the decision is that the one remaining
lectureship be given to someone whose own scholarly interest will produce additional understanding of the architecture of Christopher Wren,
rather than someone who is not a tenured professor at a major university
but who might feel free to come to the beleaguered country and create
some better feeling—I say there has to be room in the program to admit
that." In brief, "we should try to get someone into this country's university because it has an important American purpose. Other countries are
more frank about the political nature of their [educational] activities.
They don't understand why we act as we do. Our moral 'purity' is in
some ways admirable. To others, it is naive."

The FSB White Paper raises the issue of regionalism—not automatically seeking exchanges from every country every year, but filling only
the most essential slots with only the best candidates and doing this on
a regional basis. This would tend to raise the quality of Fulbrighters and
address the financial stress by reducing the number of grantees. The U.S.
embassy in China expressed its professional opposition to regionalization. "Fluctuations in funding would undermine Fulbright's purpose here,"
the Beijing embassy cabled.[3] Its purpose: "To build American studies at
key Chinese universities." In 1991, there was no Fulbrighter at Beida,
the leading university in China. The cable quoted an Americanist on the
faculty pleading for "top-flight American academics—nothing less." To
attract them, he said, they must be recruited for only a semester, not
longer, as the FSB White Paper recommended. The embassy supported

this plea and said that "adding a short-term component will help recruit more and better scholars." There was no mention of the American absence as a response to the killings of students in Beijing two years earlier.

Back in Washington, four USIA cultural coordinators representing as many regions, chided the FSB for not paying sufficient attention in its 1991 White Paper to the perspectives of foreign scholars. They pointed out that binational commissions must be satisfied as well as non-American academics, though the validity of this is seriously questioned by a former FSB chairman, Walter Rosenblith, as noted earlier. The four favored lecturers rather than students because the former, it is alleged, "promote linkage among institutions and may help strengthen curriculums," and thereby have a long-term effect—"more than research or student grants." The four also implicitly rejected regionalization. They said the Fulbright program "should maintain its presence worldwide"—determined by "long-term U.S. government and international exchange goals," not the specific interests of the American academic community. The four agreed, however, that grants should be made on a one-year term, but said this was often not possible and so the balance between long- and short-term grants should be studied carefully in each country.

Another problem for the Fulbright program is the earmarking of its funds for special projects determined outside the Fulbright process. "Earmarking," FSB Chairman Charles Dunn told a subcommittee of the House, August 1, 1990, "sometimes follows fads and inhibits flexibility." He cited the arrangement announced at the Malta Summit by Presidents Bush and Gorbachev. They planned an exchange of 1,000 American and 1,000 Soviet students. The FSB unanimously resolved that no funds should be taken from Fulbright programs in Western Europe or other areas of the world to support these new initiatives in Eastern Europe. That project, however, is likely to grow from the 200 undergraduates now involved so that resources that would be much more effectively used at the graduate level are now being absorbed unproductively at the undergraduate level.[4]

The Fulbright program is subject to many tugs from the academic world as well as government officials. To rationalize legitimate influences from many directions in the Fulbright maze, the program—sometimes unplanned like Topsy—operates in this way: USIA, through its E-Bureau ("E" for educational and cultural affairs), houses the J. William Fulbright Foreign Scholarship Board. The FSB, presumably, directs the entire Fulbright program. There is, however, a Fulbright program run by the U.S. Department of Education (USED). The USED's grants, however, must be approved, if not constructed or conducted, by the FSB. The FSB has no operational responsibility even within the USIA's orbit. The

USIA's field staffs (known overseas as USIS—"S" for service) mix in-formational and cultural programs. USIS staffs, however, operate in Amer-ican embassies run by the Department of State. Normally, a USIS person, known as the cultural affairs officer (CAO), reports to the public affairs officer, the PAO of USIA. Yet in forty-eight countries, active binational commissions must accommodate two nations' governmental and academic goals. In another ninety countries without binational commissions the agenda of the U.S. embassy more directly influences the Fulbright pro-cess. The post or commission overseas screens, interviews, and nomi-nates foreign students and scholars to the FSB, and scrutinizes American Fulbrighters to be. The screening process in the United States is operated by two main contractors, the Institute of International Education (IIE), for graduate students, and the Council for International Exchange of Scholars (CIES), for junior and senior lecturers and research scholars. The 100 USIA personnel who run the Fulbright program and all other cultural programs (roughly 16 percent of the agency's $1 billion budget) would have greater responsibilities and probably more colleagues if the CIES and IIE did not handle grant screening.[5] But would the program then be perceived as fulfilling political objectives? Presently, programs in the field would be far smaller were it not for the contributed time of U.S. academics through CIES and, to some extent, IIE, and the volun-teers of Fulbright commissions and posts overseas. No similar contribu-tions are received from any other source in one U.S. administrative mechanism.

Many Fulbright candidates to or from the Middle East and North Africa pass through the nongovernmental America-Mideast Educational and Training Services (AMIDEAST). Exchanges with Latin Amerian coun-tries for training university faculty are conducted through the Latin American Scholarship Program of American Universities (LASPAU). Fulbright and other funding for research in non-Fulbright-commission countries of Eastern Europe and the Soviet Union's successor states goes to the International Research and Exchanges Board (IREX) (though not all Fulbrighters in the Soviet Union were IREX grantees, and not all IREX recipients are Fulbrighters). There are also special scholarship programs for Tibetan refugees, Burmese refugees, and the committee for scholarly exchange with the People's Republic of China. The procedural maze aside, the main power thrusts are the political (with academic interests) of the governmental establishment, and the academic (with political interests) of the university establishment.

Is that madcap organization? Or does it lead to a remarkably success-ful amelioration of adversarial objectives and conflicting interests? So successful, that real contradictions, real problems, somehow are overcome by the very idealism of most actors, and the diversity of the global exercise? The conflicts and problems highlighted in this chapter should lead to some answers, and additional questions.

The failure of the Fulbright program's overseer to produce priorities on a global scale is no different than America's usual inability to develop a workable vision for some new world order. That is not solely America's failing. Democracies generally are weak in ordering their future, let alone their present. And the U.S. government is the world's finest (or worst) example of a polity that has created checks and balances to guard against checks and balances.

Indeed, there is a neat parallelism between the functioning of the full Washington establishment and the organization (if that is what it is) of the Fulbright establishment. Fulbright, like the larger government, exudes power at least sufficiently to operate a vast program, if not maintain a standing army. And, like the government, that power comes from, and goes to, many directions. The FSB, like the CAO, is, in Charles Frankel's words, "the man in the middle." Just as states in the United States can assert rights against the federal government, and vice versa; Congress against the President, and vice versa, the courts against both, and ultimately the legislatures against the courts, so the Fulbright program has its structural tensions both in the United States and overseas. Those tensions force constant examination of the criteria and procedures for selecting Fulbright grantees and placing them in appropriate places for defensible purposes. As with the checks and balances of the U.S. government, the Fulbright structure and procedure seem overly cumbersome; for an outside observer, almost impossible to fathom. Yet again, as with the American system generally, complexity, when properly conceived and intelligently employed, is a guardian of democracy. Complexity growing out of structural tensions is often a sign of a healthy democracy. No less, can it signify a successful foreign exchange program. Provided the signs of real differences, real problems are not ignored until they lead to dysfunction.

The tensions in the Fulbright process help define the objectives and procedures as well as the problems. The main tensions are as follows:

Nationalism vs. Internationalism

Basic Fulbright legislation clearly places the objectives of the program in the American national interest, with strong emphasis on "mutual understanding"—internationalism—an active part of national interest. Bilaterally administered and funded Fulbright programs, moreover, must blend foreign academic goals with American objectives. Third World countries, for example, favor developmental disciplines. Upwardly mobile nations prefer business and management slots rather than the humanities.

Statism vs. Individualism

Does the Fulbright program serve primarily the government(s) or the scholar? Although the legislation clearly stipulates the U.S. government's objective, it just as clearly makes individual scholars the means of achieving both the national objective and enhancing the academic's contribution to his or her own career and—no less important—the Fulbright grant's possibilities for broadening human understanding. Foreign scholars reflect not only their country's traditions but often its current politico-economic mission. The U.S. scholar may reflect the currently favored vogue of the American academy. Consequently, in choosing disciplines, projects, and scholars, the grant makers must assess the purposes of both nations in the exchange, as well as the goals of individual scholars.

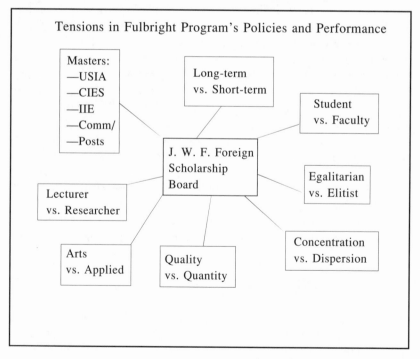

Tensions in Fulbright Program's Policies and Performance

Masters:
—USIA
—CIES
—IIE
—Comm/
—Posts

Long-term vs. Short-term

Student vs. Faculty

J. W. F. Foreign Scholarship Board

Egalitarian vs. Elitist

Lecturer vs. Researcher

Arts vs. Applied

Quality vs. Quantity

Concentration vs. Dispersion

from a design by Charles W. Dunn

Concentration vs. Universalism

Fulbrighters go to or from 130 countries. This is the only two-way academic exchange of this dimension ever in history. During forty-five years, every part of the globe has been served by the Fulbright program. Maintaining so diverse and far-reaching an academic enterprise, aiming constantly for high scholarly standards, requires far greater funding and professional skills than concentrating on certain geographic or geopolitical areas. Selecting areas of operation can be a major concern of the managers. This tension came sharply into focus with the perceived need in 1991 to assist the opening or reopening of universities in post-revolutionary Eastern Europe. Should cuts be made in Western European scholarship, the heartland of modern, not just Western, civilization? Should Third World exchanges be sharply reduced though Americans were ill prepared through lack of advance study for crises in Iran, Iraq, Central America, and most developments in Africa? The next crisis will most likely erupt in a developing country, but who knows where and will scholars be able to warn and advise?

Short Term vs. Long Term

Some scholars and their disciplines emphasize today's problems. Some governments, American or foreign, now or at different times, expect rapid payouts for investment in academic exchanges; economic or political goals drive academic undertakings. Others—scholars or bureaucrats—recognize that some disciplines and some academic modes generate long-term change, indeed evolutionary progress in human values and experience, that, in fact, mutual understanding, the primary objective of Fulbrights, is seldom realized in the short term.

Humanities/social sciences vs. Science/technology

Favoring the humanities and social sciences rather than physical sciences or technology is the interdisciplinary counterpart of the concentration vs. universalistic dichotomy. Fulbright should be all-inclusive, in this as in geography, some argue. To favor the humanities is to undervalue scientific and management skills, which developing countries and some rapidly advancing developed nations demand. To do so, also reduces the perception of progress in the short term. Success in the humanities, moreover, is less verifiable even in the long term—unless one values

highly the study of human personality, individual interactions, the struc-
turing and performance of societies, and literature, language and the
arts. It is argued, moreover, that there are many sources of grants for
physical science and management, but steadily fewer in the humanities/
social science.

Education vs. Propaganda

At the heart of this debate is the feared politicizaton of the Fulbright
program. This is a many-sided controversy that arose with greatest fer-
vor in 1978 when the Fulbright program (along with other cultural works)
was moved from the State Department to the USIA (then briefly known
as the International Communications Agency).The USIA expresses
American political policies through global broadcasts over the Voice of
America, pamphleteering, book production and distribution, invitations
to foreign political and social leaders to visit the United States, and
displays and performances abroad of American themes and productions.
All of these carry policy implications, often subtle but seldom oriented
primarily to other-nation or universalist interests; yet the USIA's pro-
gramming probably has been less blatantly "propagandistic" than any
other nation's public diplomacy. Still, the transfer of the Fulbright program nettled some in the American academy and in CU, the State Department's designation for cultural affairs before they were transferred.
In the program's early years at CU, the chairman of the binational Fulbright commission was generally the cultural affairs officer, who may
have been a prestigious academic on brief assignment. Senior USIA
officers, at home or overseas, paid little attention to CU and its operation. With the transfer to USIA, the fear of "politicization" arose with
some in the academy, while it is, of course, heatedly denied at posts
overseas and in the USIA.[6]

There are other forms of presumed politicization. President Lyndon
Johnson, the Democrat, drastically cut Fulbright budgets in the mid-1960s.
Senator Fulbright attributes this to Johnson's anger at Fulbright's personal stand against the Vietnam War and the American academy's general opposition to that struggle. President Ronald Reagan, the Republican, appointed mainly "conservative" members to the Fulbright Foreign
Scholarship Board. The Bush administration, involved in the Gulf War
and committed to bolstering nascent democracy in Eastern Europe, debated concentrating substantial Fulbright resources to those two regions
to the detriment of areas of less immediate political concern. Yet the
grant screening process is virtually in the hands of the academy—which,

it has been argued, has its own political agendas, favoring "liberal" as opposed to "conservative" projects for research or lecture themes, or "liberal" researchers and lecturers. The associate director of USIA, William P. Glade, says he sees no evidence of a partisan type of politicization in grant selection by either the academic or the government agencies.[7] Political criteria, however, have clearly driven the allocation of funds by countries and regions. Political objectives may well color the structure of opportunities presented by the Fulbright program in particular countries, especially those without a Fulbright commission.

Whether on academic or political grounds, the CIES and IIE are sometimes perceived by CAOs abroad as arbitrarily determining grantees without the approval or even knowledge of the binational commission, though there is no reason to think that political criteria are employed by either organization. Similarly, Fulbright scholars or teachers chosen by the USED may appear at American embassies abroad with little or no advance information given the post. The CAOs and commissions withhold their ire and serve USED scholars the same as USIA Fulbrighters. Finally, governmental exchange programs, by whomever devised, are by definition intergovernmental—another name for politics. And politics, in the term's best sense, is the interacting of competing forces. What else is the mathematics of a democratic society?

Researchers vs. Lecturers

American diplomatic missions abroad generally would rather receive senior lecturers than research scholars. Lecturers, particularly prestigious seniors, "show the flag" with greater ease. They generate publicity, readily signal American attention to local concerns, and can help the PAO or CAO meet high-level officials who might not be as easily accessible. Lecturers, moreover, address large numbers of students. Local officials, particularly education ministers, prefer star lecturers for similar reasons, and are wary of some research scholars who may investigate subjects that prove too sensitive by domestic political or social standards. The American academy, however, is believed to favor sending abroad more researchers than local posts and commissions want. American scholars going to a foreign country often want to pursue research based on their established individual academic objectives. Some regard lecturing as an interference with their research project. Yet a 1989 Carnegie survey found that 70 percent of faculty indicated that their primary interest lay in teaching rather than research. The senior researcher, when committed to the Fulbright mission, however, is more than an egocentric specialist. He or she removes the sense of strangeness from events or people in another country. The economic, social, political, or psychological wellsprings of another society are connected to a larger world. A high percentage of Fulbright awards now go to lecturers, although American researchers going abroad can provide scholarly insights and research techniques that will enhance the work of foreign colleagues and students. That, too, leads to academic progress and long-term relationships.

Small vs. Large Universities

The first impulse of many foreign graduate students is to enroll in the most prestigious American universities, and foreign universities often seek lecturers and researchers from the same small set of institutions. The FSB, however, asks CIES and IIE to encourage small as well as large institutions in every region of the United States to welcome appropriate foreign candidates and provide American nominees for Fulbright grants. Fairness to all candidates is not the only reason. A Fulbright objective remains the heightening of Americans' understanding of the rest of the world, and foreign students' experience of more of America than the elite educational centers of New York, Boston, Chicago, and Berkeley-Stanford. The Fulbright selection process thus enables all members of Congress to see the program operating truly nationwide in every congressional district. This position, however, also rests on the conviction that, thanks to the mammoth social investment in graduate education since World War II, scholars of excellent quality are now to be found in schools all around the country, not just in the handful of the most prestigious institutions.

Students vs. Faculty

Just as PAOs and CAOs abroad tend to disfavor American researchers, the selectors overseas often would choose established lecturers over graduate students or junior scholars. Younger academicians do not provide name recognition and generally require much more personal attention. During the past twenty-five years, student grants dropped from 57 to 31 percent of all American Fulbright beneficiaries. In 1990, the Fulbright Board of Foreign Scholarship concluded that "we do not sacrifice quality and clear potential when recruiting graduating seniors, although one-on-one, an advanced graduate student's file will occasionaly look more impressive to a screening committee." The board's overall goal is to make awards to the brightest, most promising American students before they formulate career plans. The very highest ranked American students are not going on to doctoral programs in the percentages they were twenty years ago, the board noted. Consequently, such students are not touched by the life-changing Fulbright experience of earlier generations. And, too, while senior grantees transmit overseas the wisdom of their longer experience, the young students have ahead a full career and lifetime in which to influence American as well as foreign societies—that mission, once again, of enhancing mutual understanding. It is generally assumed at posts abroad that the Fulbright program suffers today from having too few academic stars. Nostalgia clouds such recollections. Today's stars were not all that prominent when they held Fulbright grants decades ago. The stars of yesteryear, moreover, were not necessarily the best teachers; they had celebrity status, some because they ventured out of academia into politics, others because they supported popular political or ideological causes, in or out of academia. They had much to offer, but lesser-known scholars, then or now, may be at least as good "lecturers."

Seek the Best and Brightest or What?

This is a discussion of academic "quality" as the principal criterion for selecting Fulbrighters. James Billington, librarian of Congress and former Fulbright board chairman, makes an eloquent case for a program that seeks the best minds and lets them follow their own curiosities. A program that supports individual inquiry, he says, is also a compelling projection of American values. But what are the implications? How does one determine "the best and brightest" in widely diverse disciplines? How would that criterion affect foreign candidates? Would it harm binational and private sector cost-sharing? Would some traditional categories of Fulbright awards be undercut by favoring grants to area specialists? Would such a program be perceived, particularly by Congress, as serving the national interest?

The CIES, through peer reviews in each scholarly discipline, rates every candidate on a scale of "1" to "4," 1 being most qualified by academic attainments. Yet a scholar graded "1" may be a poor teacher despite an impressive dossier for research and publication. A "2" may be a good teacher with solid research and publication, but little experience in the country seeking a lecturer. Some 3s and 4s may have excellent potentials, if not lengthy histories of academic achievement. Many 3s and 4s today are in nontraditional academic careers, some in administration or in applied fields such as engineering. Many, too, are in American studies or work in unusual foreign languages. Many, says CIES, are "good people" who are rated highly effective after their overseas tours end. In weighing "quality," then, CIES selectors must also consider (1) the size of the stipend (will it attract the high-quality person?), (2) the duration of the grant (will a "star" academic leave home base for longer than a three-month stint?), (3) the nature of the assignment (will the candidate fill the precise description of the country's demand and will the nominee actually be allowed to perform abroad as anticipated?), and (4) has the country asked CIES to fill a slot for which, even after some recruiting, it cannot find a suitable candidate? This suggests that the quality`of the academic opening overseas should be more rigidly inspected by the binational groups or U.S. posts abroad. This is difficult in countries that provide cost-sharing and want specific assistance for academic projects. All Fulbright grant making, then, is based not solely on "quality," certainly only rarely on "star" quality, but almost always on trade-offs involving, at the outset, academic qualifications and, then, other factors such as those described above. It should be understood that dissatisfaction with Fulbrighters' quality is not an isolated phenomenon. Rather, this questioning reflects the need for national policy making in all fields of education. The quality of American education generally is highly controversial, as it should be. Finally, the Fulbright program is sometimes thought to be ready to fill all academic needs, everywhere, which is patently impossible. It is still less possible if academic "quality" must be demonstrated in every selection. Yet PAOs and CAOs abroad complain of deteriorating quality, while joining foreign demands for unfillable or difficult to fill slots. For example, if there is only one candidate for an esoteric teaching subject or one at a relatively undesirable location, a single applicant may be given the grant, despite a relatively low peer-group grading. Foreign nationals, in most places, however, still regard the Fulbright program as highly prestigious. Caroline Yang, executive director of the program in Japan, maintains that the Fulbright process, through its unique system of administration, melds excellence with practical goals far better than might be apparent on a day-to-day basis. Although there are built-in tensions among the broad, diverse constituency, the bilateral programs combine pure scholarship and short-term practical goals.

Selection: In the United States or Abroad?

The IIE and CIES were contracted from the start to direct the Fulbright screening process. But the binational commissions also play major roles, so major that some USIA-State Department bureaucrats prefer not to create new commissions and instead run Fulbright programs through American posts where no second government shares the selection process. To what degree, however, should the commission or post overseas, or indeed the foreign university, have the right to make the de facto selection of applicants from among candidates already screened by CIES or IIE? The commission/post, together with the foreign university, claims the right of approval before the FSB acts. In theory, and often in practice, it works that way. There is probably no better formula. But anomalies exist. One director of a commission in southeast Asia with decades of experience in the region says the scholar-in-residence program makes the commission "little more than a post office." The CIES cables the commission to invite a particular scholar to the United States, and if that one is not available to try the second on the CIES list, and so on. The scholar-in-residence is a regional program run by the USIA through CIES and often responds fairly directly to the preferences of the U.S. academic community. Regional programs are disliked by binational commissions because they prefer to have direct control of the resources themselves.

To offset pressure from the United States to fill overseas slots with researchers, the commission director in Thailand has assigned all but one of eleven Americans coming overseas to a consultancy-researcher-lecturer combination. The Thai university will use the Americans to assist graduate-level teachers or develop social science research methodology. This is not exactly developing U.S. research capabilities, which is what American researchers want. CIES, however, will provide these Fulbrighters under a regional research grant that is not charged to the Thai commission. This trade-off presumably satisfies the Thai commission, the individual researchers and the Thai university. But this does not meet another criticism of the CIES process. Its procedure does not include a personal interview with the candidate in the United States. If quality is to suffer anywhere, says one commission director, it suffers for lack of a personal meeting: "With six people looking at a person and talking, you get a sense of that person and how he's going to react." American students are scrutinized on their campus, and foreign senior scholars are thoroughly interviewed abroad. Only American seniors are not interviewed in the United States. Moreover, says this commission director, the applications are not only too long and complex, but too country-specific. Many times a scholar is not placed in a country in which he has an immediate interest. When proposed to another country where he could readily serve, his candidacy is prejudiced because the application forces him into a particular national groove: "Why should we take him in Thailand when everything indicates he wants to go to Singapore?"

Mutual Understanding: American Studies and Foreign-Area Studies

Whether or not one thinks that the Fulbright program should "sell" America, there is no question but that it should incorporate opportunities abroad to teach American studies,[8] just as it enables American foreign-area specialists and others to renew and refine their expertise by a period of work abroad. Both are essential if the program is to enhance mutual understanding. In the nature of the case, however, most overseas American studies positions will be lectureships rather than research opportunities (there being seldom any local Americana materials for a researcher to use), which means that it is often hard for the Americanist to secure the necessary supplementary funding from his or her university. Moreover, some of the most important opportunities for lecturing (at the undergraduate level) require fluency in the local language. That is not a normal part of an Americanist's professorial function. How this dilemma is to be overcome is increasingly problematic.

These widely diverse problems and tensions faced by the Fulbright program are inevitable, given its fundamental dilemma, voiced by Senator Fulbright: "It is a modest program with an immodest aim."

By 1995, the proportion of the U.S. government's contribution to the Fulbright program may be considerably reduced. Other governments, foundations, corporations (foreign and domestic), and universities may seek increasingly to influence the objectives as well as the procedures and selections of the Fulbright program they support. So far, the binational commissions operate with a high degree of independence but that could change as the funding comes increasingly from sources other than the U.S. government.

The struggle for control of the Fulbright program within the United States has resumed. There was a hiatus after the program was moved from the State Department to the USIA in 1978. The struggle is still between academia and government officals over which constituency should control the program. At the urging of the academy, several years ago, Senator Claiborne Pell suggested moving the program to the Smithsonian Institution. There have been recommendations to take it to the Library of Congress. The prevailing view, so far, has been to keep the program close to the foreign service establishment.

These two different approaches—placing Fulbright under the academic or the USIA-State umbrella—raise a fundamental issue: What best serves the initial Fulbright objective of stressing mutual understanding of peoples in this and other countries? Does that objective require operational ties to other governments, particularly through binational commissions?

If so, is not the USIA-State site the best for this purpose? But what of the accompanying Fulbright commitment to favor academic control of scholarly and project selection and improve Americans' understanding of the rest of the world? Does that objective require operational ties to the academy such as can be found in the Smithsonian Institution and the Library of Congress?

Can both objectives be served in the same agency as at present? Or are the two objectives mutually exclusive? If so, should the Fulbright program be divided between the academy and the foreign affairs establishment? Should American scholars be selected and sent abroad through the Smithsonian's apparatus, and foreign scholars chosen and brought here by the USIA-State? Under such a division should both programs be known as Fulbright scholarships? Under such a division, the academically oriented institution would still need the active assistance of the State Department's posts abroad in selecting university assignments for Americans, just as private U.S. grant makers now enlist embassies overseas to make their assignments.

Are there added values to having the academy dominate the selection and assignment of Americans going abroad? To what purpose? There already are academy-run foreign scholarship programs without connecting the American end of Fulbright to that agenda. And how would USIA-State select foreign scholars and approve projects acceptable to U.S. universities without some academy linkage such as the present service provided by CIES and IIE? Or should USIA retain the Fulbright program but be reorganized into two distinct and equal career ladders— information and culture—with a strong, internationally distinguished cultural leader heading the culture cone, and assured of equal bureaucratic power?

All aspects of the Fulbright program—domestic and foreign, academics and diplomatists—may conceivably need one another. What has been debilitating is the struggle of one or the other to dominate the full program. Yet, as the relative scarcity of resources for both informational and cultural/academic activities increases, the struggle seems destined to continue until some new consensus can be reached—if it is, indeed, attainable—or new funds can be secured for both sides of the program.

8

Who Pays and for What?

Two basic questions are put to the Fulbright program:

1. How much does it cost and who pays the bills? This chapter answers that question.

2. Is the Fulbright program cost-effective? That is the wrong question. It should read, Can the United States afford *not* to have a Fulbright program? That is a subject for a different chapter because that raises a question of fundamental public policy; call it public diplomacy, cultural diplomacy or, as I prefer, national cultural policy.

Don't worry about money! That is the official advice given the grantee by the Fulbright management handbook: "The objective of this grant is to permit the student to concentrate on this project without undue concern for financing."[1] Again, "The financial aspects of a Fulbright award are, to a considerable degree, incidental."[2] Yet financing a Fulbright experience nowadays is of considerable concern to the student or scholar, foreign or American. The grantor, moreover, becomes a master magician juggling seen and unseen financing pots and schedules. By late spring, placement officers speak of burnouts from the pressure of matching qualified candidates to advertised openings, but with inadequate funding to make the match work. Financing Fulbright grants hardly is "incidental" or of "undue concern."

If the organization of the worldwide Fulbright program is a bureaucratic maze partially so designed to prevent the politicization and loss of academic integrity, the financing of the program is even more difficult to examine in all its parts.

Senator Fulbright at the outset conceived the program as a cost-free enterprise. His brief amendment in 1946 arranged barter-like expenditures for academic exchanges. That would pay costs of foreign and American students coming and going. They would use credits accumulated from foreign governments by their surplus property sales (trucks, foodstuffs, and clothing) after World War II. These funds paid the transportation costs of foreign students, which carriers accepted in foreign currencies, and the transportation and maintenance costs abroad of American students, also paid in foreign currencies. U.S. universities provided scholarships for foreign students.

The too-well-kept secret of Fulbright funding, especially in recent years, has been the considerable financial assistance the program has received from private American colleges and universities, to say nothing of the family savings of the grantees themselves. This funding factor has never been totaled. Yet sources of support other than the federal treasury should be amply recognized. Not simply to provide them with proper acknowledgment—universities and scholars, after all, supply this funding to enhance their own scholarly endeavors—but to reassure Congress that the Fulbright program, first, is a major national asset, and second, that it is so important that considerable private sector money has been provided, along with growing foreign governmental funding.

The universities provide scholarships and other aids for the best and brightest foreign students. The universities, to be sure, earn considerable income from other foreign students whose studies are paid for. Some 386,851 foreign students were in America in one year (1989) because it is said to house two-thirds of the best universities in the world. U.S. higher education is, therefore, a highly successful "export industry."

More than 500 American institutions must be queried to determine how much each has contributed to Fulbright exchanges through the years. They waive tuition fees, wholly or in part, for foreign students. They provide housing without charge or at low cost and, in many cases, stipends for student teaching or other purposes. Foreign scholars receive teaching salaries and other emoluments from universities. In forty-five years, 117,518 foreign Fulbrighters have come to the United States. A complete accounting of the funding and value of in-kind assistance provided to Fulbright grantees (students and scholars, foreign and American) by colleges and universities is beyond the scope of this book. Some rough estimate can be made. New York University, with an annual population of 50 foreign Fulbrighters, is about average among the large U.S. universities. NYU reports it contributes between $20,000 and $25,000 per Fulbrighter per year. This estimated contribution is based on waiving tuition and housing, and allocating costs for research; scholarly, office and clerical support; and library privileges. Over the years, roughly estimated, NYU has contributed some $15 million to the Fulbright program. Other universities, such as Harvard and the University of California, have undoubtedly contributed more. A rough estimate by the Institute for International Education (IIE) forecast at least $30 million contributed to Fulbright students by the American university community in 1991-1992.[3] This includes support for students who remain in the United States to pursue graduate degrees as well as those who come on one-year Fulbright grants under Institute for International Education (IIE) auspices. Those who arranged their own placement probably received another $2 million in funding from the universities. In addition, the universities support Hubert H. Humphrey fellowships by providing $7,600 per fellow, or about $4 million over the span of the program so far.

The senior-scholar and research programs of the Council for the International Exchange of Scholars (CIES) estimates that during 1991 private-sector contributions to the Fulbright scholars will have totaled $4.4 million. This will include waiver of $2.1 million in university fees for visiting scholars, $356,000 in host support for the scholar-in-residence program (an average of $10,480 per scholar), $256,000 for enhancements including honoraria, $950,000 ascribed to the feeless service of the CIES board and peer review, and $752,000 for feeless service of campus workshops and distribution of Fulbright materials. Over the lifetime of the Fulbright program, the CIES programs for scholars may have generated some $132 million in nongovernmental support. Finally, several student/scholar exchange groups that operate in particular regions of the world generate additional assistance for Fulbrighters from American universities.

Foreign governments increasingly provide cost-sharing for Fulbright exchanges. In 1990, other governments contributed $20.6 million through direct contributions to binational commissions. Spain allocated $7.6 million while Washington added only $412,000 to that binational exchange. Germany contributed $4.6 million and the United States provided $1.8 million. Japan gave $2.5 million to the American government's $1.5 million. The Scandinavian countries shared costs with the United States almost equally. Developing countries, with or without binational commissions, provided in-kind contributions totaling at least $11.6 million. In-kind gifts were in the form of housing, airline tickets, salary continuations, stipend supplements or tuition waivers. Three developing countries also made grants to the Fulbright program of $355,000. In some countries, private donations also came from corporations, foundations, and Fulbright alumni. Altogether, over the 45 years, about $1 billion has been contributed mainly by American universities and some foreign contributions to the Fulbright program. The U.S. government spent $1,350 million from 1947 through 1990. Non-U.S. government funding thus added some 71 percent to the Fulbright operation.

The federal government provided the initial impetus with authorization to use blocked funds overseas. As these funds ran out in each country, Congressional appropriations stabilized the Fulbright program. In the 1950s about $10 to 12 million a year was appropriated. In the 1960s, as new countries joined the exchange, funding increased to $18 to 27 million a year. In the late 1960s, Fulbright funding was cut about 50 percent. Congressional funding rose to $37 million in 1980, $77 million in 1985 and $91 million in 1990. The U.S. Department of Education (USED) receives another $5.8 million for its Fulbright programs. Other governments contribute about $32 million. The program's direct governmental cost, then, is about $140 million, of which the U.S. government contributes $91 million. About $12 million of this is for American-side administrative costs. Of the $12 million, $10 million goes to CIES and IIE to run the grantee screening operation for scholars and graduate students. Another $1 million is spent for screening processes at several smaller institutions concentrating on the Middle East, China, Latin America, Eastern Europe and successor states to the Soviet Union. These figures do not include any charges against the time spent on Fulbright matters by CAOs and PAOs in the embassies overseas. Significantly, on any given day about 1,200 people work on the Fulbright program worldwide—paid and volunteer, part-time and full-time personnel, in the U.S. government, commissions abroad, selector agencies, and universities.[4]

Expressed in 1970 constant dollars, however, there has been little fluctuation in federal funding from 1950 through 1990. In that earlier year, government support was $24 million; in 1990, it was $27 million in 1970 dollars. Yet the number of countries and individuals served has increased dramatically. In 1949, the Fulbright program operated in ten countries; today, it works in 130 nations, on every continent. The variety of scholarships, moreover, is greatly enhanced.

These figures too easily give the impression that Fulbright managers have worked miracles. They seem to have received less and less money per grantee, but provided more and more—and more diversified— service. Logic, as well as simple economics, indicates otherwise. The value of each grant has greatly diminished. Excellent foreign students are asked not to go to a top American graduate school that has accepted them, in favor of a less prestigious one that provides financial aid. Other bright foreign students may be offered no more than a "travel grant"—an airline ticket to the United States—as their Fulbright award. "Increasingly," the FSB acknowledges, "Fulbright is only a part, sometimes an inconsequential part, of a financial package, rather than an award of excellence." America's "star" academics going overseas turn to other scholarly grant makers who provide larger stipends in support of research projects with funds for research assistance, computer use, and other amenities. The following is excerpted from an unsolicited letter received in June 1991 by the Foreign Scholarship Board (FSB):

> Thank you very much for your letter informing me of my acceptance as a Fulbright scholar in Hungary for the academic year 1991–1992. Unfortunately, I have decided to decline the award. As a senior scholar with a family to support I cannot afford to live in Hungary and cover ongoing expenses here, given the size of the stipend. I have also received a research grant [from another donor] whose stipends are based on the salary participants receive in the United States. The dollar allowance is far more generous for someone of my rank, and so I have accepted the [other] grant.
>
> I use this opportunity to express my concerns regarding the Fulbright program if it continues to be funded at current levels. Fulbright exchanges are an extremely well-regarded program both here in the United States and abroad. Competition for grants normally is quite stiff, and it is a very prestigious award to hold; indeed, I decline with great regret. One of the main reasons, however, that the program is so highly regarded is its ability to attract top-rate scholars from both the United States and exchange partners who participate. I do not think the program will be able to continue to attract people of such caliber if it begins to impose a financial cost on their participation. To expect [scholars] like myself to take a drop in salary from over $60,000 a year to under $20,000 a year to go to a country with a thirty percent rate of inflation and a fixed exchange rate is asking a bit too much.
>
> [The writer made several other recommendations for funding language training and budgeting for computerized equipment.]
>
> Sincerely,
> (signature)
> University of California—San Diego

The Fulbright reputation, indeed, has developed a momentum that carries it abroad. Once the program is introduced in a country, it is difficult for the local selectors not to hold an annual competition for grants. The program's prestige—still high worldwide—inspires most American diplomatic missions to participate in the process. To continue the Fulbright name in some countries, however, candidates are recruited for some awards. Rarely, some are accepted no matter what their qualifications. So far, except for problems of physical safety in-country, the program is open-ended. This means there is little control over the wide geographic dispersion of exchanges. Every participating country, of course, follows an approved budget. There is as yet no plan, however, to concentrate Fulbright exchanges either by limiting the number of countries served each year, or operating exchanges in some countries only once in several years. Insufficient financial support for the present scope of the program is a major handicap. Clearly, the Fulbright program is now too many things to too many people. To recover the unmatched prestige the program had for American scholars in its first four decades— and retain that same prestige it still enjoys abroad—serious financial decisions must be made now:

- Should the Fulbright program be cut back?
- Should it receive far greater financial support?
- Is there a third course?

Some alternatives, which affect funding as well as the objectives and structure of academic exchange, are discussed in Chapter 13.

9

Country Model: Japan

The face of Kenichi Takemura is the best recognized on Japanese television. His radio voice is better known than the Emperor's. He has been called "a demigod of the Japanese airwaves." He is Japan's leading critic and commentator on all public issues. Takemura sits in a low armchair in his downtown Tokyo free-lance studio. The floor is covered by stacks of paper: manuscripts he's writing and reading for his literary mill. Above him, on floor-to-ceiling stacks, are single copies of 260 diverse books he has written. So many, they are catalogued by years of publication. Takemura, writing in Japanese, often about English and its uses or America and its values, is more prolific than Isaac Asimov.

In 1953, Kenichi Takemura gave up cub reporting on *Mainichi Daily News* to face a severe culture shock: visiting America on a Fulbright. "It was like winning first prize in a lottery. I didn't study much," he now says, "but that year there gave me a lot to think about."[1] Formally, he completed orientation at Yale and two semesters at Syracuse University's School of Journalism. "That influenced my whole career. The bigger thing: I never doubt the goodness of the American people, whatever their government does. That's ingrained in them."

In return, "One aim of the Fulbright program has been quite well achieved in me. I am considered one of the staunchest allies of the United States. The people see this because I'm constantly on radio and television." Takemura reciprocates in other ways. "I invite American Fulbrighters to my villa to spend nice days, just as I had been invited to American homes in the States." This, he says, is more than reciprocity. "It's indebtedness. The Japanese are of the character to respond when someone shows us kindness." The Fulbright program encouraged the younger generation

113

of Japanese, he says, "when it seemed there was little hope for the future." Now, says Takemura, "It's our turn to do the same thing for other countries." He acknowledges that the Japanese are aloof by nature but says "we must reflect on our behavior. Otherwise Japan will be excluded by others in international society."

At the moment, far from aloofness, the Fulbright program in Japan reflects the profound indebtedness that Takemura describes. As with Fulbrighters everywhere, today's students and scholars are frequent travelers and prepared for, if not inured to, culture shock. The changing program of the Japan-U.S. Education Commission is directed largely by pioneer Fulbrighters of the 1950s and 1960s. They acknowledge that the Fulbright program strongly influenced their top-ranking careers. But they ask, Can the program perform the same for today's students and scholars?

Justice Akira Fujishima of Japan's Supreme Court had a Fulbright grant in 1958 at Michigan University's Law School. He studied American case law for the first time. To this day, he says, when deciding a case on Japan's highest court he ponders how American law, though different, can contribute.[2] It provides another way of dealing with criminal issues. Justice Fujishima, like most Japanese Fulbrighters of his generation, could not have afforded an academic year in the United States. They returned home, not only grateful but successful in their fields: judiciary, government, business, and university. They still come together, as Fulbrighters, to discuss their experiences and those "good old days."

Yuji Tsushima is a prominent member of the Japanese Diet, and a former finance minister. His Fulbright in business administration at Syracuse University (1955–1956) helped prepare him for roles in international finance. He also made "loyal friendships" in America, and retains strong ties with Japanese Fulbrighters. "I did my very best," he says, "to get the Japanese contribution to the Fulbright program increased. I appealed directly to the prime minister. I sincerely believe that, given the present financial situation, the Japanese government should contribute more to the Fulbright program."[3] The Japanese now cover about 60 percent of the cost of the binational program. But this does not fully satisfy Tsushima. He believes Fulbright "is very profitable" for Japanese society. His countrymen are fully attached to their homeland, he believes. They return to Japan bringing information and techniques secured in America.

Any weekday after 11 A.M., in the small offices of Japan's Fulbright commission, you can see the student caravan to America forming. It's an unpublicized, significant phenomenon—the study-abroad boom. In 1989–1990, 29,840 Japanese students were enrolled in American universities.

As many as forty young students an hour, their numbers replenished throughout the day, squeeze around one table in the Fulbright office to examine 2,500 American university catalogues. These young men and women will not apply for Fulbrights. They are prepared to arrange their own travel to the United States and cover tuition and expenses. This minimal service provided by the Fulbright commission once was offered by the U.S. embassy until it bestowed the project to the Fulbright program. There is little if any money in the Fulbright budget for what is euphemistically called "student counseling" by the Educational Information Service. Fact is, most students are not counseled in Japan. Students may take catalogues from the shelves and return them to their place. Fulbright operations in other countries attempt some personal and group counseling.

On a busy corner in downtown Tokyo, outside the Kentucky Fried Chicken licensee, scores of Japanese teenagers display a passion for America besides chicken. Their T-shirts tell of past and future travel to the United States. Eighteen percent of the students going on their own to the United States seek business and management studies. Humanities and social sciences attract another 18 percent. Others choose mainly technology- or science-related courses. Remembered with pride is one "office lady"—a young then-liberated woman who completed school, worked in an office, but confronted the "glass ceiling" for woman workers. She came to the Fulbright office about ten years ago asking about secretarial schools in the United States. A Fulbright staffer told her there was something called an MBA program. She took catalogues from the shelves, decided to apply to Harvard—and was accepted. This "office lady," now "thirtysomething," is director of Morgan Stanley in Tokyo and the pride of the underfunded counseling service.

Although nearly 30,000 Japanese are enrolled in American institutions of higher education, fewer than 1,000 Americans are studying in Japanese colleges and universities. "That," says an American official, "is as serious as the U.S.-Japanese trade imbalance. Over a long term it could be very serious." For the Japanese, says Representative Tsushima, "this is very profitable, costwise." He concludes, "While you have always sent more Japanese to America than the number of Americans who came to Japan, this must be reversed." Japan must spend more for American students and scholars to come to this country. But even that view is not wholly altruistic, given the perceived need to educate more American opinion leaders about Japan, "I have many friends in the American Congress—senators and representatives. In my view there is a striking gap between the politicians and opinion leaders who know Japan well, and those who do not. That gap of misinformation can easily spread to the grassroots"—the same stratum of American society that TV critic Takemura remembers for its "goodness."

Pragmatism increasingly influences Japanese-American academic exchanges as it does trade and high-tech competition between the two countries. This is not surprising. In both the short and long terms, academic exchanges directly and indirectly influence binational economic and political relations. The Japanese realized this from the beginning of the Fulbright exchanges in the 1950s. Dr. Yasunori Nishijima, president of Kyoto University, cites his own experience and projects it into the future. He went on a Fulbright award to the only place in the world then specializing in his field of polymer science. For three years at Polytechnic Institute in Brooklyn, he collaborated with scientists from all over the world. "They shared the excitement of research. I still have a strong impression of a global academic community having been created—friends I still maintain all over the world. It was an important factor for Japan, too—this global network—for Japan was struggling to find a new way to live in the world."[4]

President Nishijima lectured last year at a fortieth Fulbright anniversary in Norway. Fulbrighters from all over Europe agreed, he says, that the program has far more than an educational effect. "Its members are like a brotherhood—more and more important in this drastically changing world." That networking factor "is not so apparent," he adds, "but the activity is important." Indeed, he concludes, "the effects of the Fulbright program are probably far greater than Fulbright himself could have anticipated. The short-term effect can be seen by the individual scholar, but the long-term effect is hidden."

How can the pragmatism of Japanese society and the idealism of the Fulbright program be blended in the new era?

A red-brick school across from the Mexican embassy, high on a back street of Tokyo, held two classmates in the 1950s. One became a cabinet minister, Yuji Tsushima; the other a major businessman. They remain good friends and great supporters of the Fulbright program. The government leader increased Japan's funding for Fulbright activities. The businessman heads the Japan-U.S. Commission, and is raising substantial private funds for the program. He is also on the board of the IIE in New York. The industrialist Shigekuni Kawamura, president of Dai-Nippon Ink Chemical, Inc., responds out of his own Fulbright experience. He was a child in America before World War II, but his memories come mainly from his Fulbright year after the war. He found no antagonism toward Japanese. Mainly, he was "astonished" by the financial markets and the U.S. economy. The Fulbright grant strongly influenced his career: "Having been a Fulbrighter is very prestigious in Japan, far more valuable than graduating from Tokyo University [an evaluation put rather differently by Ryuichi Hirano, former president of the University of Tokyo. He takes pride in his university, and also in his own experience as a young Fulbrighter!]. Even more important is being a member of the Fulbright alumni. They're all first-class people. That human network is very valuable."[5] But times have changed in some ways. Today, says Kawamura, for those working for banks and corporations, "it is a disadvantage to get a Fulbright grant." Corporations send their staffs to study abroad to improve their skills and cement business ties. Such visits on company business count toward advancement. But Fulbright recipients are not regarded as company trainees, and get no credit toward advancement. Kawamura would focus the Fulbright program hereafter on academic rather than corporate grantees, and on fields in the humanities rather than business and technology.

Yuji Tsushima's plea for "more Americans" to come to Japan as Fulbrighters—partly to fulfill what Kanichi Takemura calls Japan's "sense of indebtedness to America"—has foundered on the realities of academic work in Japan. No one casually becomes interested in Japan as an academic specialty, or even a serious research subject. "You pay an enormous price in learning that difficult language and penetrating this difficult society," an American resident declares. Consequently, over the years, few other than long-term Japan scholars have come here to do serious work. But that is changing. The study of Japan has broadened beyond Japan area studies to other disciplines. Such opportunities are regarded with less awe by younger American students. The new pre-Ph.D. program is a step in this direction. Some would like to see it get below the bachelor-degree level and become a kind of junior-year-abroad. Some 300 high schools in the United States teach Japanese, and it's becoming popular in the universities. Before more Americans can study in Japan, then, the bottleneck must be broken in Japan, not the United States. The academic atmosphere, with the exception of several universities, is not "welcoming," according to an American observer. There is little support for the visiting American. The Japanese must first invest in infrastructure—language tutoring, textbook translations, interpreters, and a more hospitable social setting.

To expand Japanese-American academic exchanges, the Japanese government recently created the Global Partnership Fund. This major fund will move past the usual Japanese-American controversies to support global studies such as environmental protection and refugee problems. The intention is to remind Americans that their relationship with Japan goes beyond trade, with its obvious frictions, and can include various positive and cooperative relationships. The enormous funding of this program could be used to build the infrastructure needed to expand all academic exchanges in Japan, including the Fulbrights.

If this can be done, says Rob Nevitt, public affairs officer at the American embassy, the "extraordinary Fulbright alumni, with their loyalty and energy," will help.[6] They reflect more than the traditional Japanese feeling of obligation, he says.

> In the immediate postwar period they were very poor, still uncertain about the attitude of their former adversary, and unsure what the world had in store for them.. But one of the things it turned out to have provided was a fairly munificent occupier who said, "We want to send your best to the United States to help rebuild your country." So off they went, leaving behind the rubble in Japan, entering the '50s with euphoria—dazzled—grateful—and with great profit. Some were scholars. Others went into business and politics. That generation has an overpowering feeling of loyalty and support for the Fulbright program. They raise an enormous amount of money, earning enough yen in their Osaka golf tournament to fund two Fulbright grants a year. We worry, however, how that legacy is passed on because the attitude of successor generations of Fulbrighters is not quite the same. One hopes it may be contagious, to some extent.

In the Japan-U.S. commission, as in others, Nevitt, in his capacity, rotates with the Japanese government's representative as chairman of the binational commission. Yet the commission is legally independent of both governments. In Japan, as elsewhere, this body flourishes despite the too-easy criticism that a binational commission, by definition, will inevitably politicize the academic exercise. The cultural affairs officer (CAO), whose job is fostering cultural diplomacy, sees the Fulbright program little differently than his superior, the public affairs officer (PAO), whose job is politically oriented. Nevitt, we were told, "has very, very strong views about the importance of the Fulbright program being academically credible." Yet, my embassy informant adds, "to say the Fulbright program works in a political vacuum would be naive."

The Fulbright budget process itself is an intergovernmental matter. The proportion each government provides requires political negotiation. Both sides see the real utility of the Fulbright program as its prestige, tradition, and high standards. "Monkey with those," says our informant, "and you're on a counterproductive road. That's self-evident." There are, of course, different national interests reflected in academic choices that must be mediated by the Fulbright commission. The Japanese want to include far more management, technical, scientific, and engineering studies. Americans favor the humanities and social sciences—a cultural and intellectual rather than a technical exchange. Is this academic bartering, politicization? Or is it an expectable negotiation over the conceptualization of an academic program that serves two vastly different cultures?

Nevitt responds from the PAO's perspective: "Everyday I spend a lot of energy on issues that may have a week's lifespan: What is the American response to the Japanese view on the rice issue? That occupies my time. But my satisfaction as a professional is in the things that manifest themselves years later. And the Fulbright program is an investment in the future."

Perhaps in Japan the fear of politicization is overcome somewhat by Caroline Yang, the strong and energetic executive director of the commission. She is responsible for motivating the prominent alumni, arranging competitions for Japanese going to the United States, and placement of Americans coming to Japan. Every four or five years Yang conducts a retreat for intellectuals, journalists, and others to examine the Fulbright program, and consider new directions it should take. She drafts the annual plan for the commission's approval. By February, 15,000 copies go to universities, schools and other places that attract potential candidates for Fulbright grants. Students apply directly to American universities on the basis of the commission's printed announcement. Only after the student has found a receptive American university does the commission notify IIE to complete the paperwork and formalize the grant. The quality of Japanese students may be gleaned from the fact that many receive substantial financial support from American universities, in addition to Fulbright assistance.

The Japanese commission, moreover, recently began requiring all students and junior scholars going to the United States to take at least one or two courses in American society or history. The secretariat reminds grantees that the Fulbright stipend is not just to support their individual studies but, through academic exchange, to enhance mutual understanding of the two peoples. Fulbrighters are expected to report to the commission when they return home. Then they are encouraged to become active members of the Fulbright alumni—a prestigious company, still. The chairman of Japan's celebration of the fortieth anniversary of Fulbright exchanges, not accidentally, is Toru Hashimoto, president of Fuji Bank.

10

Country Model: Indonesia

Indonesia, the fifth most populous country in the world, is a major political force in southeast Asia. This archipelago of 13,500 islands extends about 3,000 miles. Indonesia is also developing its economic power. The Philippines, Malaysia, Singapore, and other nations of ASEAN (headquartered in Jakarta) look to Indonesia to approve major new initiatives. While promising Indonesians democratization, the government still exerts strong control over the political, economic, and educational systems. In Indonesian fashion, these controls are often whispered, cast in traditional cultural modes. Yet, Indonesian educational leaders recognize that intellectual development is essential to economic development. They recall that on independence day in 1945 there were only 300 college graduates in Indonesia, and most of these were doctors or lawyers. The Fulbright program has significantly helped Indonesia change and expand its system of higher education. That system, in turn, influences secondary education. The reforms have also helped Indonesia establish a sense of national identity. Fulbright, however, maintains an image separate from that of a development program. It is committed to excellence in the exchange of ideas.

At the end of the 1960s, Harsja W. Bachtiar, head of the education ministry's research and development, first approached the Fulbright program for help. "My main interest was the Indonesian nation itself," he now says.[1] "That was primary. Second was the relationship between Indonesia and the United States." He utilized the program to alter the entire concept of his country's system of higher education. "We had inherited the tradition of Dutch universities where education tends to be compartmentalized. Students concentrated on a single discipline. In the

121

States students were given the opportunity to examine their horizons, scope, interest, and knowledge, and then cover a variety of disciplines and fields of study. That was liberal education as I saw it when I studied in the United States."

At a conference of Indonesian educators in 1968, a psychologist suggested that every student, regardless of his faculty, be required to take four basic courses in natural science and four courses in the humanities. Bachtiar welcomed the recommendation but realized it could not be implemented for lack of trained academics in these fields. "We could not expect our senior academics to design these courses," says Bachtiar, "because they had to provide leadership for the development of higher education, and for the political field."

Bachtiar turned to the Fulbright program for help. Ten junior Indonesian academics were sent on Fulbrights to the University of California-Berkeley and six to the University of Hawaii. They expanded their own knowledge, Bachtiar recalls, and designed interdisciplinary courses in basic social science and the humanities. They were also in a better position to assess the full Indonesian curriculum. Soon they became leading figures in Indonesian education, so valuable, Bachtiar partly regrets, that they became ranking bureaucrats rather than full-time teachers. But they did, indeed, produce the courses required of all Indonesian university students since the beginning of the 1970s. "That," says Bachtiar, "could not have happened without the assistance of the Fulbright program."

In the 1980s, as Indonesia developed natural resources and expanded middle-class consumerism, education favored the technologies, science, and agriculture. It was easy to get education grants for short-term development but, Bachtiar says, "far more difficult to get fellowships for history, political science, literature, philosophy, and the so-called soft sciences. But life in society does not only consist of economics! We must, therefore, develop all aspects of human endeavor. The Fulbright fellowships helped by sending Indonesian junior scholars to the States."

The development of American studies, moreover, was a natural accompaniment of other assistance. Despite the prevalence of American films and television, Bachtiar says, "there was still a lack of knowledge about American high culture—philosophy, literature, the arts—the most important part of a nation. Intellectual products tend to be transmitted through high culture. We didn't have experts on America, so the development of American studies was very important. We need American specialists who can interpret developments in the United States and inform the general public as well as decision-makers here. The establishment of the American studies program, which seeps down into the secondary schools through teacher-training schools, could not have been accomplished without the Fulbright program."

American studies are taught in widely separate parts of Indonesia. In some places, they teach American history through its literature. One rector has opened a modest "American corner" on the campus. It is maintained by a former Fulbrighter. Returnees have created an American resource collection in West Sumatra. The Fulbright returnees asked for a videotape player to continue their interest in U.S. affairs. USIS supplies the tapes.

In Indonesian fashion, the Fulbright program has been directed not by a binational commission, or by the American embassy directly, but by a nongovernmental Indonesian foundation with binational representation. The American Indonesian Exchange Foundation (AMINEF) is composed of prominent Indonesian citizens and government people, and their American counterparts. The executive director has been an American.

Since 1989, however, AMINEF has been in transition. The two governments have agreed to convert AMINEF into a binational commission. That would formalize the commitment of both countries to academic exchanges. The treaty would lock-in American financial support but it would also commit Indonesia to some cost-sharing, perhaps in the range of 10 percent at the outset. Indonesia, presently, is a unique model of Fulbright relationships. AMINEF as an operational mode has been halfway between the embassy-controlled model and the commission model. Draft treaties to govern Fulbright exchanges have been rewritten several times. The near-final version is being analyzed in five or six Indonesian ministries, including foreign affairs and national security. This new binational concept generates great caution among usually cautious Indonesian bureaucrats. But signals suggest that by 1992 there will be a formal birthing of the binational commission in Indonesia.

The outgoing executive director complains, however, that AMINEF "has been relieved of control over who gets U.S.grants."[2] Ann vB. Lewis says "more and more regional grants" made in the United States "erode the role of the local board and its binational program, hurting the credibility of the Fulbright program." It is "mystifying" for Indonesian board members, she says, when after they discuss at great length the coming of great researchers, they are told only one of them will get a grant. After AMINEF had made a selection, the U.S.-based screeners rejected without explanation some candidates they had already informed Jakarta they rated highly.

Will there then be greater conflict between academic and political interests? The big money—the World Bank, USAID, and the local mass-education program (run by a former Fulbrighter)—provides $30 to $40

million for development education, and generates obvious political interest. "We get $1 million for Fulbright," notes Michael M. Yaki, public
affairs officer at the U.S. embassy, "for the kinds of things we do."[3]
There is, he adds, "a place for excellence, and we should not get buried
under the other programs. As long as we're able to assure that short-term
political interests are never imposed on the program, we're fine. And as
long as my counterparts understand that our short-term political interests
may be best served by carrying out our long-term plans, then we have
no problem."

Meanwhile, the Fulbright program continues. In mid-1991, ten Indonesian students from as many disciplines were selected for Fulbrights in
the United States. Three others were named Humphrey fellows and six
were selected as Fulbright research scholars. Six Americans arrived in
Indonesia as Fulbright lecturers in 1991, from as many disciplines, joined
by twelve U.S. Department of Education (USED) doctoral dissertation
research (Fulbright) grantees.

The impact of such exchanges, over the years, differs markedly in the
two countries. This was visible amid the skyscrapers of New York in
mid-June 1991. Forty-five Indonesian dancers performed an ancient Hindu
epic, the Ramayana, before an overflow audience of 1,200. With the
Hudson River as backdrop and the World Trade Towers shadowing the
wings, the outdoor expanse of the World Financial Center served as
theater. The world-class dancer who performed as Hanoman, the legend-
ary monkey-king, was also the impresario who arranged this and similar
events in Europe, Asia, and elsewhere in the United States. He is I. Made
Bandem who danced with Martha Graham and for a decade has been a
selector of Fulbrighters from Bali. The Fulbright contribution of Indonesians in America has been strongly in the arts.

In 1980, Dr. Bandem earned his doctorate in ethnomusicology at
Wesleyan University. That Connecticut campus, since the 1970s, has been
well known in Bali for the parade of Balinese artists, many of them
Fulbrighters, who have studied and performed under Professor Fredrik E.
deBoer. He coauthored a book on Balinese dance with Dr. Bandem and
is working on another with Fulbrighter, Nyowan Sumandhi. He brought
a traditional shadow puppet show to the Metropolitan Museum of Art in
New York. Wesleyan also houses, year-round, a *gamelan* orchestra composed of many-sized gongs, drums, and other percussions. Fulbright artists
under deBoer's direction filter through Wesleyan.[4] He provides the academic framework that enables the Indonesians to gain international
stature and interact with the network of scholars in many countries who
are interested in Bali. This is a classic Fulbright "exchange."

Bandem told me that the greatest value of his going to the United
States was to acquire the methodology for dance and musicology—to

learn to discuss, analyze, and improve traditional arts.[5] That, he says, blends the East with the West. He reminds us that the United States has already integrated many European as well as Asian forms into its own culture. That exchange continues through the Fulbright program with one unusual example: Andrew F. Toth, an American, had a 1974 Fulbright grant to teach musicology in Indonesia. After several years, he joined the Foreign Service. He is now U.S consul in Bali where he's also visiting professor at Dr. Bandem's Indonesian School of the Arts. Full circle.

Putu Widjaja, short-story writer, filmmaker, and magazine editor, is also part of the Wesleyan-Fulbright alumni. He went to the university in 1985 as an artist-in-residence sharing experience in Indonesian theater and literature. "I taught, but also learned there to perform with a script," he says. "That was new for me and for the students. They were used only to Western methods of drama. I brought them Eastern methods—process-oriented drama."[6] That is, performance without advance planning and precise rehearsal. "I didn't expect to have influence, but I got it. I encouraged students to stop thinking only about product-oriented drama, but also process-oriented theater. I learned, too, to sit around a table and talk first, before going straight to the stage, as we do here. I came back home and didn't realize how I had been influenced to think and analyze ahead. People knew me before I went to America, but *about* me after I returned."

Widjaja received not only broad praise in *New York* magazine, but in America in three years managed to write one hundred short stories, six dramas, and five novels. "It was wonderful," he says. "In writing, three years in the United States equals fifteen years for me in Indonesia." In film, he says, it's easy to practice product-oriented creation because film is expensive and planning is necessary. But in theater, he now combines the two styles.

What about the content of Widjaja's work? "To see my country from far away made me love it more," he responds. "It was hard to say what I thought of America. It's even hard to say what is Indonesia, though I was born here. It's hard to judge even the thing you know well. But the years in America made me feel more open. I realized you never know everything. You learn every day. Even if you are sure now, maybe the next minute will change. That affected my writing a lot. It made it more wise; some might say more obscure, more open-ended, allowing for more interpretation." His writing, he acknowledges, is not easily communicated. "My work on stage is also experimental. Students in America responded, though my writing was not Western. So I concluded I'm on the right track." That "track" is important to Widjaja. "Many people in Indonesia think they are Indonesians because they were born here. But they learned so much from Western radio and television that they are not really Indonesian anymore. When you present something based on their Indonesian roots and traditions—which they no longer understand—you seem strange to them. I was uncertain until I got confidence, and for that my travel to the United States was very important. I have to keep on that track." Drawn from the Fulbright experience, then, was change in structure, more emphasis on the product, and some change in form, with the content remaining deeply Indonesian. He drew on Western technique to evoke the Indonesian tradition. Moreover, says Widjaja, "I don't want to speak only to my own people. I want to use the international idiom to speak to the world. And the Fulbright contributed to that importantly."

Another prominent Indonesian profited from a Fulbright year at Stanford University. "But that was not exactly by my design," says Aristides Katoppo.[7] In 1973, he was exiled (originally) for five years for newspaper writing that displeased top officials. He had previously been invited to study abroad. When the president of Indonesia, the minister of information, and the chief of security decided—not by court decision or formal action—he would be better advised to leave the country, Katoppo accepted the Fulbright award. This writer first met Katoppo in Kyoto, Japan, in 1974 and protested his banning and exile. That was the first of several bannings of Katoppo. The latest is still in force. He sits in his old office in Jakarta but his name has been removed from the masthead. "I've been beheaded," he says. He can enter the newsroom and consult with writers and editors; they visit him for advice. "But," he says, "I'm a ghost."

Perhaps. Nevertheless, Katoppo's influence on Indonesian journalism has been considerable, particularly after his exile in the United States. That experience altered his conception of journalism. He introduced it to Indonesia where it flourished—until Katoppo was banned again. Stanford gave him the opportunity to do more focused reading and exchange views in many disciplines with knowledgeable people. After fifteen years in journalism, he says, "one's knowledge tends to become fragmented, with too much emphasis on what is important today, though that may be quite insignificant tomorrow." The intellectual climate, "despite my skepticism then, led me to explain 'what it means.'" In addition to learning, Katoppo also lectured and counseled students in the journalism school.

About that time rioting erupted in the streets of Jakarta, as his paper had predicted. Friends cabled him not to come home yet. He recalls that a member of the Indonesian military told him, in New York, "Lucky you are here. I would have arrested you." The man later became chief of intelligence and security. Katoppo then spent a year at the Center for International Affairs at Harvard. Then, after two years, Katoppo "just walked back in" to his old paper. He said he had absorbed as much as he could from the American academic community. He was ready to try new ideas in Indonesian journalism. After three years, Katoppo revived a failing magazine. He built its circulation from 20,000 to 200,000 by a different approach to what is news. He covered crime, for example, not in isolation but by examining trends and recounting the "process" behind events. The authorities decried vandalism and rebellion among the youth. Katoppo arranged and publicized meetings for young people to discuss problems on equal terms with adults and officials. He sought to change a basic aspect of Indonesian journalism. Many stories have one source, the minister of information. "Good journalism," he says, "should reverse that—one story with many sources." Indonesia, he adds, "is a pluralistic, multicultural society. We needed to cover a broad spectrum, not a one-sided view."

Circulation soared, but the paper was banned in 1978 and again in 1986. Katoppo was "beheaded," on the threat that the paper would lose its license to publish if he remained on the masthead. "They banned me but I banned them," Katoppo says wryly. "I refused to publish pictures of the top three officials—in one, two, three order—as they appeared each night on state television—and as they once did in the Soviet press. No more ceremonial pictures. Only photos of real life: developments in the marketplace or on the bus. It's a different concept of news. We print it not only because the minister speaks, but we reverse it. Because we print it, the minister must speak out, and answer."

Katoppo's colleagues say he's too advanced for his time. He doesn't deny that prudence is the better part of valor. He finds a certain advantage in being a ghost: "I'm not really here formally, so the minister can't fire me again."

In a country where press freedom is not yet assured, the Fulbright program has helped prepare several brilliant journalists for the day when they can practice their craft and thus contribute to that mutual understanding the program is pledged to generate.

11

Country Model: India

Soon after Rajiv Gandhi was assassinated in 1991, the new prime minister announced a revolutionary change in Indian politico-economic policies.[1] He sent his finance minister to Washington to seek help from the International Monetary Fund. Most important, that step would be based on India's turning significantly toward—not, as in the past, away from—a market economy. Major Indian newspapers hailed this radical step as long overdue. Clearly, this action was triggered by world events: the failure of command economies in the Soviet Union and Eastern Europe, and four decades of abysmal economic consequences in other Third World countries that did not embrace functioning market systems. India, a major developing-country model, has made some successful strides. Food production has increased significantly. New manufacturing and industrial centers are operating. But the government had not educated the public to the responsibilities, opportunities, and indeed, problems of a market economy. This educational necessity is on the minds of Indians who have had Fulbright scholarships and those Americans who help manage the binational exchange program today.

Academic exchanges with India, increasingly, are under pressure from the pragmatic needs of economic development. The humanities and even the social sciences—which can address India's severe sociopolitical problems, but are suspect for domestic political reasons—vie, not always successfully, with more job-oriented disciplines. India's academic exchanges, then, are a more typical Third World model than Indonesia's. There, despite similar straining toward economic development, the cultural contributions of Indonesia and the United States receive greater emphasis.

One of India's early Fulbright successes is now being recognized. Dr. Jagjit Singh, whose grant took him to the University of Nebraska in 1959, returned home to establish the Institute of Marketing and Management. He insists that the Fulbright program has never acted as a political force. But, he says, "it has broadened the minds of people, particularly those who have been to the United States and have seen that free society in action." Yet, he adds, "many of us at the macro level have made contributions: The marketing revolution here, I can tell you, has been carved out of the Institute of Marketing. When we set up the institute, government officials didn't even want to hear the word 'marketing.' Today, they not only use the word, but they practice it. They have adopted the policy which our institute calls 'marketology'—the macro marketing idea which is now accepted in the Planning Commission." The commission is India's major economic instrument.

The micro approach of many of today's economists returning from the United States is criticized by one of India's leading economists. Professor A. M. Khusro is columnist and resident editor of the *Indian Express* and *Financial Express*, prominent financial papers, and chairman of the Aga Khan Foundation.[2] On leave from the University of New Delhi in 1965, he had a senior Fulbright fellowship at Massachusetts Institute of Technology, attended a seminar at Harvard, and also taught at Tufts University—all during the same semester. "Giving and receiving went on all the time," he says. He did research on food policies and land reform in India. "That rich academic life became a permanent asset for me," he now says. "I used it to build up my writings in later stages of my life. Some part of the Fulbright impact was instrumental in my assignment as India's ambassador to West Germany."

The Fulbright name has always had great prestige in India, Khusro acknowledges, but he has concerns about younger economists returning home. "In economics, as in all fields, there is now a great deal of emphasis on the technology of research: econometrics, statistics, emphasis on the technique of analysis. As more and more such economists arrived, they became a group unto themselves. Their papers became highly technical. Techniques rather than content were discussed 90 percent of the time. One must keep up with new techniques, but the process has gotten out of balance. The techniques have become the subject of discussion, not the phenomenon. As a result, policy makers in government and in private corporations turn away from this kind of economics and approach. So compared to the earlier generation, from the 1950s through the 1970s, present-day economists are cut off from policy makers and are in a world by themselves. Their impact on policy is much less felt."

Khusro believes that the negative aspect of Indian economics may be a "transitory matter." Most of his colleagues, he says, "have turned a little sick of the command nature of the Indian economy. What we studied in the United States was not allowed to function in a constrained situation. Now all this is changing. India always had some experience with a market economy, unlike the Soviet Union. So relevance of training in the United States, the world's foremost market economy, is going to be much more sought after, unlike the past twenty years."

Echoing Khusro's criticism, one American observer in India believes that some American Fulbrighters in other disciplines are also too esoteric: "Imagine! Thirty intensive days when an ethnomusicologist goes to one village in the middle of Gudjira to record songs he excitedly reports are sung only at a certain time of the year. That's true of 'Jingle Bells' too!" This observer asks: "Are the right people coming? Is the program structured for pure academic exercise, in that esoteric sense? Is mutual understanding—subjects of broader interest to both national constituencies—still a criterion?"

That observer believes that "if you have a long-term commitment to academic exchange, maybe we're in a down period for a decade. And if you're thinking of an America for another one or two centuries ahead, that doesn't matter as much. But it *does* matter, because we do not know whether the Congress—or we—have the staying power to say we're going to be an empire for the next 200 years; and it is in our long-term interest that academic exchanges are something we do. Or are we going to pull back, and become isolationist?"

What is the moral? That observer asks the Foreign Service overseas to express the needs of host countries. "Yes, posts have to work with some programs that get quicker results than the Fulbright program. But posts have a good sense of what kind of exchanges are working, institutions you can work with, and which fields are of interest to the host country. American scholars should have greater sensitivity to what host countries need, and to what posts overseas say is the need."

That observer suggests that Indian and American scholars and government officials be invited to a conference to devise a ten-year plan. Such a meeting was held in New Delhi in 1974. Its recommendations still form the basis for the Fulbright commission's activities. The criterion should be—says that critic—"not which American scholars want to come here, but what the local scene needs."

That 1974 conference was strongly supported by Professor R. K. Chhabra, former executive secretary of the influential University Grants Commission, and a member for more than a decade of the U.S. Educational Foundation in India (USEFI), the Fulbright commission.[3] He acknowledges that over forty years there have been "ups and downs in the

Fulbright program due to the political situation in the two countries." At one stage, he recalls, "there was difficulty in bringing researchers here in certain fields. Even Indian researchers were limited. So in 1974 we called together academics on both sides to make clear what we want to do. This removed much of the discord. That's what we can do today."

That Indo-American Conference on Academic Collaboration agreed that "wherever possible collaborative research and training programs in both countries would be the favored means for promoting [academic] interaction and, where appropriate, interdisciplinary research should be encouraged." The conference set forth twelve areas for further research in the social sciences and humanities. These included Indian and American civilization and culture, including language and literature; quantitative methods and techniques in social sciences; international trade and finance; urban studies and planning; comparative political and legal processes; comparative social structures; library management; educational technology and teaching materials; museology; musicology; linguistics; and social ecology.

This agenda was sufficiently extensive to fuel the binational exchange in the ensuing years. But the recommendation to arrange collaborative research is unfulfilled, and remains on Professor Chhabra's agenda. He would encourage teams of Americans and Indians—students, juniors and seniors on each team, and representing different disciplines—to collaborate on a single research project, in one or both countries. The project should be designed to cover two or three years, he believes. Scholars may not be expected to devote full time to the project, though they should be accessible to colleagues. There are obvious difficulties in designing the project, and in staffing it. But the idea remains.

American researchers still face some restrictions. For years, India would not allow political scientists to examine the operation of the Congress Party. Certain geographic areas such as disputed territory or places of ethnic insurgency are closed to researchers. Exceptions may be made for scholars of tribal cultures. Some young American researchers, frustrated at having their projects rejected, go elsewhere. Someone must be intensely interested in India to persist. American embassy officials argue that if Indians want Americans to understand their country and have a better perception of it, the world's largest democracy is going to have to be more open.

India's Ministry of Human Resources Development, through S. G. Mankad,who also sits on the Fulbright commission, says he considers the Fulbright university exchange "important."[4] He says he's pleased that the number of Indian scholars going to America has been increasing. He regrets that fewer Americans appear in Indian universities. But, he adds, "we do get very good researchers and scholars from America." He suspects that fewer American scholars come because there is more interest in China and Japan. He insists that restrictions are minimal and are enforced mainly to protect the safety of researchers in troubled areas. Though Indian scholars may go wherever they please, Mankad asserts, few go to sensitive areas such as Assam or Punjab or to the Andamans, distant islands in the Indian Ocean. "What is heartening," says Mankad, "is now you are getting scholars to work on more modern subjects—-like environment, urban management, and areas of that nature."

Mankad insists his government does not influence the selection of Fulbright grantees—Indian or American—or the subjects they will pursue as students, lecturers, or researchers. "Leave it to the academics," he declares. "The selection committees keep the needs for a particular subject in mind. The government doesn't lay down any policy. After all, we have a very large system with only about fifty Indian scholars going to America each year."

Leonard J. Baldyga, minister counselor for public affairs (PAO) at the U.S. embassy, confirms that in the three years he has been on the Fulbright commission the Indian government's representatives do not seem to have an agenda for selecting grantees.[5] "In fact," he says, "they've been very helpful in advising us how to get certain proposals through the bureaucracy; matters such as visa clearance, and sensitivity with certain areas of study and research." For a democratic country, extra sensitivities remain. Apparently, though, if study objectives are carefully phrased most projects will be approved. An American official sitting on the binational board also is under some restraint. "You've got to maintain the sanctity of the academic-qualification process and the binational process in terms of the needs of scholarship," says Baldyga. "We cannot impose our views. It would backfire."

The larger problem is selecting Indians from all parts of that large nation, and enabling Americans to study, lecture, or do research in the full range of Indian universities. From commission offices across the country, there is extensive recruiting to secure Indian candidates. But some limitations arise for Americans. "We deal not only with elite [Indian] institutions but with all the geographic areas we can get into," a member of the commission states. "But we must ask, 'Is it unthinkable for us to refuse to send somebody to an institution that is not really in condition to accept that professor or lecturer because of inadequate facilities?'" The problem cuts two ways. The quality of Indian Fulbrighters is "quite high," the member says, "but the problem sometimes is the quality of Americans coming in." He repeats the litany: Different kinds of people apply for Fulbrights now. The program doesn't always meet an

American's concern with securing tenure, or demands to publish or lecture at elite U.S. institutions, or receive a higher stipend than Fulbright can offer.

Today's elite Indian scholars often are Fulbright alumni. At a meeting arranged for me I asked a dozen prominent alumni to describe the impact of the grant on their careers and suggest ways to improve the exchanges. Some responses:

Dr. M. S. Rajan, the first Fulbright professor to go to America from India: Two years at Columbia University (1950) in international affairs radically changed my life and aspirations. Like so many young men in this country who don't get what they want, I was a round peg in a square hole. The Fulbright changed my outlook. I have a deep sense of fulfillment. But there are exaggerated expectations of what a small, modest program can achieve. This is the second most populous nation in the world, and the number of Fulbrighters must be a few thousand. And it is an ancient civilization in which you can't do much as an individual—individual fulfillment, yes—but so many things you learn in the American experience you can't carry out here. I've tried some modest things and always face resistance. But do not judge the Fulbright program by conventional criteria of the numbers who have risen high. The program has a far-reaching impact on all individuals in a subtle way. The kinds of things that legislators would like to see as evidence, you will not find. But it has done a lot of good for this country and, I hope in the long run, for the United States.

Dr. D. Raj Mahajan, cardiac surgeon to the president of India, consultant to U.S. and Indian hospitals: The Fulbright program has contributed immensely to research in medicine. When I left India on a Fulbright we performed only limited surgery in my specialty, cardiac surgery. I had experience in Cornell Medical Center and Memorial Sloan-Kettering Institute in New York. I'm proud to say I was instrumental in developing two programs of open-heart surgery in New York. I did the first aortic transplant in the American literature. I also developed a cardiac distribution system. Now, we are doing in India all the open-heart procedures, including very highly sophisticated, high-technology procedures being done in the best centers of the United States, United Kingdom and Europe. And our results are as good as theirs. I work in three hospitals. The majority of my teams are American-trained. Some are Fulbrighters and we are very proud of that. Fulbrighters everywhere, I have found, develop leadership qualities. We never discuss politics but there is no doubt that our intellectuals influence the thinking of our country. And we do have our say.

G. K. Kapoor, principal, Birla Vidya Niketan, New Delhi: I visited the United States in 1969–1970 and taught senior students physics and mathematics in a senior high school in southern Missouri. I introduced a new course originated by MIT professors. It helped me become a better teacher, and for the past ten years principal of a large school here. The aim of the Fulbright program—increasing understanding between nations and strengthening their relationship—has given me a mature view of the relationship between the United States and India. I understand the United States better, and I understand my own country better. Mature people can make a greater contribution if there is a binational program to strengthen this relationship. It is useful to explain the United States all around India and, in the States, to explain India in a more mature way.

Rajiv Kumar, producer, news and current affairs, Doordarshan (TV) News, Delhi: I went as a practicing journalist in mid-career for exposure to the American media. We have only [state-run broadcasting] in this country but the United States has thirty to forty cable channels. As soon as the Syracuse University semester was over, I went on my own initiative to NBC-News in New York, with Tom Brokaw, and CNN in Atlanta. I went to understand the philosophy of broadcasting in America; in effect, the very nature of freedom of expression. Very important. Media can influence all aspects of life. Through CNN I was able to strike a deal with the government network in India. I became coordinator of CNN in India. Practically every week, I now talk about India or America on worldwide television. Where India was not known, or was known mainly for disasters or communal strife—there is a negative impression about India in the United States, unfortunately—I try to put the ways of India, as a nation or an Asian power, in the right perspective. I appear on CNN World Report every Sunday. For that opportunity, the Fulbright was very well employed.

An Indian scholar: The Fulbright program is excellent, but it is spread too thin. Too many people chasing too few places. [During forty years, 8,000 Indians and Americans have had Fulbright grants.] The opportunity is offered to the person, given his own limitations and constraints, intellectual and academic, to go to a particular university. But some American universities are very good and some are totally indifferent. So much depends on where the person gets accepted. Going to a university like Harvard and Berkeley, as I did, is a memorable experience, wherever I now teach. But there are other countries, particularly in the Middle East, where more people should be invited to go to the United States on a Fulbright. Other parts of the world need the American experience much more than we. But the best course would be to get more money for more Indians, more Pakistanis—and more Arabs.

Professor Ram Karan Sharma: I visited the United States twice as a Fulbrighter—in 1957 as a graduate student in linguistics at the University of California and in 1982 as a visiting professor at Columbia University. I learned very much about America and Indo-European linguistics. I contributed a dissertation on the great *Mahabharata* [the 2,000-year-old Sanskrit epic of India]. It was give-and-take all the time. My Fulbright experience stood me in good stead as a teacher, an official of the ministry of education, where I set up a dozen institutions, and as a chancellor. I also set up the International Association of Sanskrit Studies, headquartered in Paris. I received respect in the United States for my tradition. Sometimes I felt humble before American professors who were so devoted to Indian studies. But for the Fulbright program, I could not have been what I am today. In the future, I say, strengthen Indian studies culturally, intellectually, and in linguistics. Relate Sanskrit and other Indian languages to our internal subjects and systems.

Professor V. Krishna Moorthy, principal, Sri Venkateswara College: I went to the University of California on a Fulbright grant in 1985 to study the functioning of the American university system. Just as India can learn from the United States, I found that the States can learn from us. Those selected for Fulbrights in both the United States and India have benefitted. So the United States is helping itself by this program. It should be strengthened. That would help Indo-American relations a lot.

Professor Susheela Kaushik, director, Women's Studies and Development Center; Department of Political Science, University of Delhi: During two years on a Fulbright at Columbia University in 1964–1965 I did more than collect data for my Ph.D. thesis. I was exposed to important professors and served as teacher as well. I visited many other universities, spending a week in each to collect data and speak to other scholars. The present program has shortened the time spent in the United States. The pre-Ph.D. scholars now go primarily to collect data for their program and get little opportunity to interact with the rest of the academic community.

I also went as a senior Fulbright scholar in 1972–1973 for an eight-month period. That is given to those who teach American studies. My major field is now Indian politics and women's studies but I also offer a course in American studies.

Professor R. P. Kaushik, chairman, Center for American and West European Studies, Jawaharlal Nehru University, New Delhi: My Fulbright began with American studies (1964–1965) and continues with American studies. I would be extremely poor if I had not availed myself the opportunity of visiting the United States. Exposure to its academy was a fantastic experience. With the massive explosion of social sciences and the humanities in the United States it is difficult for any scholar in a Third World country to cope with the material or the resources, or even have a nodding acquaintance with those sciences, without visiting America. To avoid it, would be suicidal. The awareness of American values and cultural baggage would never have been known in a real sense if we had not had these opportunities. My post-doctoral Fulbright was at Berkeley. I specialized in the Civil War and Reconstruction, and studied minorities, particularly blacks, in the United States. It is a disadvantage to a scholar, I found, to have to rush through.

Mrs. Kaushik: There is a case for sending young (pre-Ph.D.) scholars but the post-Ph.D. scholars will be able to draw out a lot more information from the United States. But they must be properly oriented to American studies and well guided in India beforehand. And provided when they get back home they are able to utilize their knowledge not just in writing a book or an article, but in teaching. Postdoctoral scholars are much more useful to the program when they combine it with everyday teaching in the classroom.

Mr. Kaushik: [On the proposal for Americans and Indians, seniors and juniors, working together on a joint research project]: Research is becoming increasingly collective, and the dividends are more feasible, more practical. That can get your work done more quickly. It can help quality when seniors are involved. But it depends on the compatibility of the team. If some of the younger people are very talented it may present ideological hangups among the seniors. When peers disagree, someone must decide.

Mrs. Kaushik: Young people in India wouldn't mind working with a senior American. But do you think the reverse is possible? Would American youngsters work under a senior Indian scholar? It's possible in certain areas, literature and art, for example, but it would be more sensitive in international relations.

Mr. Kaushik: [On government restrictions on research]: There are some sensitive issues: Northeast India near China, Pakistan, Kashmir, some religious and tribal issues. Most of the perception of India in the United States for several decades has been our caste problems, the downtrodden, labor exploitation, tribal primitiveness, less exposure to modernity, exotic things, which may be true or not at all. Researchers coming in to concentrate on those areas create a problem in terms of this society. So the government will discourage it.

Mrs. Kaushik: Since this is a binational board, they must consider such problems.

Mr. Kaushik: In remote parts of the country you can find Indian and foreign scholars working on these problems, but government-sponsored

programs are more sensitive. Americans coming here under other than
binational auspice could probably engage in such studies. I would rather
permit all American scholars to feel free to work in whatever area they
want to work.

Mrs. Kaushik: Our own people sometimes have this problem.

Mr. Kaushik: The issue is the context—what you emphasize—how
you focus.

Participants continuing the discussion stressed the need for greater
collaboration among Indians who have returned from Fulbright experiences, as well as with their collaborators in the United States. They called
for greater continuity by having Fulbrighters arrange seminars as refreshers
to share new developments in their discipline or related field. They
recommended that research, teaching, or lecturing in either country should
be undertaken with a discernible objective that can be measured at the
conclusion of the experience. They also urged that mass media be informed of their work so that the Fulbright program is better understood
in both countries. The editor of *The Times of India* told me that Fulbright, Rhodes, and Nieman were all known in India. And as one interested in the development of ideas, he'd like to hear more about Fulbright.

Apparently, however, hundreds of thousands of Indian students know
where to find the Fulbright office when they plan to study in the United
States on their own. Sarina Paranjape, program director at USEFI-Delhi,
runs that student advisory service and supervises similar operations in
Bombay, Calcutta, and Madras. In 1990 alone, 170,898 students came to
USEFI offices for guidance on attending universities in the United States.
A staff of five, including Paranjape, provide basic orientation, taking
sixty to seventy persons at a time. Most are completing undergraduate-
level work and pointing toward graduate schools in the United States.
The students choose their targets, make their own applications and, if
they come from prestigious Indian schools, often secure scholarship aid
from American institutions. USEFI also provides predeparture orientation for non-Fulbright students. There are 23,000 Indian students in the
United States.

Student advisers from throughout South Asia met in Nepal for the first
time in 1989 to ponder the rapidly mounting demand for their services.
The following year, overseas educational advisers from Asia, Africa,
Europe, and the Americas met in Washington. Clearly, with Indian students—as Japanese, Indonesians, and other Asians—flooding American
colleges and universities, the advisory service is overwhelmed. Only the
most basic, generalized counseling can be provided to all but a handful
of earnest questioners. Such service can hardly be called counseling. In

most cases, the adviser does not, indeed, cannot, try to mesh the individual student's scholastic record and career choice with the most appropriate American college and its record of acceptance. Some assistance, such as that provided, is better than none.

These relatively highly qualified and motivated young people come from obviously favored backgrounds. In their vast numbers, increasing each year, they will become the next generation's leaders in all sectors of a major nation. What a million or more Indian graduate students think about Americans and America must be of some consequence to both countries. Not long ago, the United States lent India a satellite to broadcast educational messages to rural areas. That year-long experiment improved rural health and agriculture. Such an imaginative step is needed to serve thousands of self-selected, upwardly mobile Indian students. They are looking toward the United States for help in fashioning their careers and their nation's future.

Should this advisory service remain a Fulbright function? Certainly not, if it is to continue to be run on a shoestring, and with no clear relationship to the primary objectives of the Fulbright program. The advisory service, important though it is, presently drains funds from the principal program, already under-funded. The service should remain "Fulbright," if it is thoroughly overhauled, properly funded and staffed, and given the same mission as the main Fulbright program; that is, to demonstrate through appropriate mass media as well as academic channels that intellectual and cultural exchanges are the bedrock of mutual understanding between nations and among peoples.

12

Country Model: Italy

Professor Guglielmo Negri, a former Fulbrighter and now legal counselor to the president of the Republic of Italy, declares that the Fulbright program is of "historic importance." What Greece did for ancient Rome, he says, Americans after World War II did for Italy—through the Fulbright program. Here are some examples of the American contribution:

- Italian graduate students in the United States used Fulbrights to acquire academic methods, especially interdisciplinary studies, which had not been tried in Italy.
- Fulbrighters introduced American studies, social science, psychology, women's studies, and linguistics in Italy.
- The Italian government, contemplating changes in its constitutional law, arranged with the Fulbright commission to send Italian specialists to study the American constitutional system.
- In the 1960s, when there were student rebellions against the "baronial" Italian academic system, even the most radical students did not go to the Soviet Union—but began what has become an enormous flow of Italians to American universities.
- When the United States Information Service recently said it must close its Palermo office, which offers Fulbright and non-Fulbright advising, students demonstrated with signs: "Yankee Stay Here!"

Count Carlo Sforza, post-war Italy's foreign minister, told young Professor Negri, "You must go to the United States because, your doctorate notwithstanding, you are a too-provincial boy, still. You must wash

yourself in a great American university. You will change completely."
Forty years later, Negri still recalls that advice, and adds, "Count Sforza
was perfectly right."[1]

Negri was a Fulbright fellow at Harvard in 1951–1952. Though he had
come with "really good cultural preparation," the interdisciplinary organization of the university produced a "revolution in my life." He found
the system more mature than the European mode. Indeed, he believes the
students of the "Roosevelt generation" were generally more mature than
today's students. "When I went to the United States I was 'human history.' I had been in the Italian underground fighting the Nazis, and was
condemned to death. So my first impact with the States was more profound." From his political point of view, Negri believes the Fulbright
program has "strengthened the Atlantic Alliance" through scientific and
cultural exchanges. When the program began, he says, America was fifty
years ahead of Italy in scientific and cultural development. At the beginning, he says, America did not fully know what it was doing. A Fulbright
grant was a "generous overture in the style of Roosevelt democracy—not
consciously doing something of historic importance."

Negri was in the United States at the high point of McCarthyism. "I
saw how a great nation rejected a poison. For me, that was very important. I returned to Italy and wrote a book on the American political system.
It was the product of my Fulbright experience. I was not the same man.
I saw the melting pot, from a spiritual point of view, as astonishing.
From the worldview, it is the most important basis of American politics—it supports, not the military approach but the Fulbright approach."

The new generations, he says, "have not tested the waters" as he.
Nevertheless, when they view many aspects of American civilization they,
too, are "caught," Negri believes. Similarly, American scholars coming
to Italy today are hard-pressed to equal the prominence and scholarly
impact of Charles Rufus Morey, the Princeton professor of art and ar-
chaeology who created the Fulbright commission in Rome, even as he
served as director of the prestigious American Academy there. Morey
forged a chain of high-quality academic relationships that continue to
this day. He moved Dr. Cipriana Scelba out of the U.S.embassy and placed
her in the new binational commission.[2] As its executive director for more
than thirty years, she set a high standard of academic selection and
administration. Scelba, early on, chose as her assistant, Professor Biancamaria Tedeschini Lalli. She, in turn, went to America on a Fulbright
and is mainly responsible for introducing American studies in the University of Rome. This has been a major contribution of the Fulbright
commission.

Observers of the Fulbright program—Italians and Americans—agree there have been fundamental changes since Professor Negri attended Harvard and Professor Morey held forth in Rome. They do not agree on what is now called student or scholarly "quality." Or, for that matter, on "maturity." Clearly, the world has become a more complex place. Today's students and scholars, then, need to assimilate a larger body of fact than the "Roosevelt generation." Systems of analysis of human activity have also become more complex. And, as a consequence, the blood-stirring experiences of Professor Negri are not duplicated in today's more coldly analytical students.

They are not as naive, in some respects, as they may seem. Over the past few years, student organizations in Italy have held strikes to protest their fear that science and technology will dominate the universities at the expense of the humanities. That, indeed, has been a trend resisted by the Fulbright commission. The trend was signaled when the government took the universities, all state run, out of the Ministry of Education and put them in a new Ministry of Industry and Technology. Yet, the Fulbright commission seeks to secure financial support from the private sector for the commission's view of exchanges in higher education. In the Fulbright program, the commission favors greater emphasis on history, political science, and literature. The commission is also concerned with helping Italian universities become more compatible with American as well as European modes of scholarship. The opportunity arises because Italian universities now have greater autonomy in curricular planning and seeking financial support. The U.S. government has been the major funder of Fulbright from the beginning. Since 1968, the Italian government has provided an increasing share. It provides about 30 percent of the cost of the Fulbright program, though the country is the fifth largest economic power in the world. Administrative costs of the Fulbright commission in Italy are said to consume about 25 percent of the expenditure for the program here.

Nearly 10 percent of those funds cover the cost of four student counselors. Some years back, the USIS in Italy as elsewhere dropped student counseling from another budget and had the Fulbright offices continue the service—without added funding for it. "One could argue that this counseling is more important than anything else Fulbright does," observes one American close to the program. The students who seek this help are well educated and have independent means to study in the United States. "It isn't the most democratic part of the program," the observer acknowledges, nor is it directed toward a definable academic or other objective. It is helter-skelter. "But if you're talking about effectiveness," the observer adds, "it may be a very big piece!" It encourages mutual understanding with a large multiplier effect. That view would not be shared fully by American scholars or career counselors who believe that each student's choices deserve highly personalized attention. That is patently impossible with four full-time and several part-time staffers assisting 30,000 students a year in Rome, Genoa, Milan, Florence, Naples, and Palermo.

Inadequate funding for Fulbright generally, not only for counseling, is a serious handicap. The stipend is not competitive with other grantors. "It's hard to make ends meet now, and that takes away from the enjoyment as well as the scholarship," says Jodie Lewinsohn, public affairs officer at the embassy.[3] The Fulbright program in Italy is in her brief. She had a Fulbright award in the Philippines in 1955–1956 and has observed the program in six countries of Southeast Asia, Sweden, and South Africa. Her year on the campus in Manila was "a wonderful time," and largely responsible for her career in the Foreign Service. "But," she says, "the bloom is off the rose. The quality of Fulbrighters moving in both directions—mainly the Americans coming here—is not what it was twenty years ago." Some highly qualified academics cannot be away from home for long. The program has been changed somewhat to accommodate this. There are short trips now. "A serious look is needed," Lewinsohn believes, "at the very special nature of being a Fulbrighter—what once was, and no longer is. Maybe it doesn't matter."

Is the change in "quality" real, or the result of nostalgia for "the good old days"? Or is the change the consequence of a significant deterioration in the general level of American academic standards? Clearly, as Lewinsohn suggests, a serious look is needed. It *does* matter.

It matters to Italian students. This writer recalls the turmoil in Italian higher education in the early 1970s. With Charles Frankel, former assistant secretary of state for educational and cultural affairs, and Paul Seabury, professor of political science at the University of California-Berkeley, I organized the International Council on the Future of the University (ICFU). This small group of leading academics in seven major democratic countries sought to address the disorders in their university systems. ICFU developed studies, conferences, and public policy positions. The European systems of higher education, especially in Italy and West Germany, suffered from what critics called generations of baronial control by a lifetime-tenured professoriat. "Full professors did not even know their students," recalls Professor Carlo Chiarenza who directs the Italian Fulbright commission today.[4] "Professors would come to class once a week, speak for 20 minutes, and then depart. They would go to other universities to lecture and leave an assistant behind to meet the students." The proposals for changing the system, however, often threatened to seriously undermine scholarship. Students in many Italian universities were permitted to devise their own curricula, leading to full degrees. One prominent Italian scholar, who then emigrated to New York, told me that after the university law was radically changed, he would not visit an Italian doctor certified after 1969, depend on a newly minted lawyer, or walk into a building built by an architect licensed after the magic date. The situation has changed, says Chiarenza: "Professors are now more responsible. There are precise rules. So the university today doesn't have the same aura it once had, but its quality has improved."

Chiarenza sees a change as well in the patterns of Fulbright grants. Italians used to want to go to the United States mainly for course work in business administration and sciences. These still lead to high-paying jobs in Italy. But now students also favor literature, history, art, and architecture, as well as political science. Americans used to come to Italy, he recalls, mainly for arts and the humanities, but their range of subjects has broadened. From his view, "there is nothing more powerful than a combination of the Italian undergraduate school and the American graduate school." Now, says Cipriana Scelba, the thirty-year veteran as commission director, "there is greater awareness of the needs in the fields in which Italy and the United States can best contribute to one another." She says she is also told "by American scholars in both the physical and social sciences that the Italian approach to those subjects in which Americans were pioneers, provides Americans now with an additionally useful dimension." There is much talk now, she asserts, by university rectors and industrial leaders of "interacting," "twinning," and "linkages" involving U.S. and Italian institutions. Former Fulbright grantees have inspired this approach, she adds. "Now, we must identify what Fulbright can really do *best*, for resources are meager. We must be very selective."

In the past, the Fulbright program was responsible for the introduction of American studies in Italian higher education. Professor Biancamaria Tedeschini Lalli earned a masters in American literature and a doctorate in English before she went to the United States on a Fulbright grant.[5] During her ten years on the Fulbright commission and as a professor at the University of Rome she created Italy's first department of American studies. It is interdisciplinary, and draws on political scientists, historians, economists, and other Americanists. She specializes in American literature. With assistance from the Fulbright program she also introduced modern linguistics to Italy. The University of Rome now has many Italian professors of linguistics who earned their Ph.D.s in America. Italy was long known for historic linguistics, but Fulbright programs in the 1960s and 1970s helped create additional chairs in modern linguistics.

Since those years, there has been "a relaxing of tension in the Fulbright program," Lalli believes. New ideas and structures were established. Recently, Fulbright chairs have been created at some universities. But Lalli fears these chairs may become fund-raising gimmicks, rather than real additions to scholarship. In the new Italian university climate, institutions are freed to raise funds and control more of their curriculum. Endowed Fulbright chairs are, therefore, welcome. But Lalli notes that the University of Naples, a large institution, wants a Fulbright chair to replace a government-financed chair. "That's ridiculous," she maintains. "We don't want the chair of a retiring Italian professor who taught American history to be replaced by a visiting American professor. A chair should build something, not be just a roving teacher, as the university proposed." In this, as in many aspects of the Fulbright program, a decision on cultural policy is needed.

Lalli regrets that new developments in American studies are not now being followed with adequate attention. "We must not lose one inch of the American subjects we are already covering," she says. There are Fulbright lecturers in American studies in Rome, Genoa and Turin, but their programs need bolstering with matching funds from the universities or the private sector.

Meanwhile, the regular Fulbright selection process continues. For the program year 1992, a budget of $1.8 million is projected, with $511,000 (28 percent) allocated to administration and 7 percent for the student advisory service. The Italian government is expected to provide 31 percent of the total Fulbright expenditure. Between 500 and 600 Italian graduate study candidates apply after taking an English-language test. That leaves between 100 and 120 finalists who are interviewed and tested for 55 grants. Faculty are offered travel grants to lecture or participate in seminars. Altogether, about 75 Italians go the United States each year on Fulbrights, and 65 Fulbrighters come to Italy. Much more Fulbright money is spent on the Americans than on Italians. The Americans are spread all over Italy, but Italians prefer to go to MIT, Stanford, Harvard, and other high-visibility institutions. Few Italians return home after the first year because American universities frequently provide scholarship and other assistance for additional studies. Italian universities do not offer such help to American graduate students or junior scholars. Italians generally do not get Fulbright-financed extensions, only permission to use their air ticket at a later date. Most complete their Ph.D.s in Italian universities.

How many of these 140 Fulbrighters, thirty years from now, will shine as academic "stars," and be heard to say, "The quality of academic exchanges today, this year of 2021, is not what it used to be"?

13

What Should Be Done?

The extensive Fulbright scholarship process is an operational maze. Even after my year-long, close analysis of the program and principal players, I continue to find new facets of the operations. Most active players themselves have only partial glimpses of this far-ranging program. Yet this overriding conclusion must be stated: The Fulbright program, despite its bureaucratic intricacies, is a historic American success. For geographic spread and influence, it surpasses the Marshall Plan, which recreated Western Europe after World War II. While that historic era has passed, the Fulbright program continues. Its influence can still be magnified with each passing generation, into the twenty-first century.

These recommendations, then, are one person's effort to place this unique, effective process—international academic exchange—in the perspective of America's national interest and, no less, in the interest of individual scholarship and its sum, global civilization.

The suggestions stem from cross-checking interviews with active participants, past and present, and careful reading of the record. It should be understood, however, that I am not an inspector general or an auditor, nor do I have subpoena power. I have not seen a full accounting of all expenses of the Fulbright program. I know there has never been an accounting of the real out-of-pocket income generated by the Fulbright program, in the United States and abroad. Nor can there ever be a true estimate of the enormously increased values in personal skills, technological development, and increased trade that can be attributed to Fulbrighters and their personal accomplishments. That said, how can all of us help to improve the Fulbright process?

I. By Promoting a National Cultural Policy

The Fulbright program has been the pacesetter for American educational exchanges. It must resume its leadership role but with a fittingly larger objective, yet a narrower day-to-day operation. The decades ahead require the formulation, finally, of a National Cultural Policy. Most nations have one. The United States has national endowments for the arts and humanities, but these institutions do not lay out broad policy (except insofar as grant making supports one or another creative endeavor). An American ministry of culture is certainly not appropriate. But there is needed, the formulation at the highest level, for example, of the American interest in educational exchange as a requisite for enhancing scholarship, mutual understanding among peoples, and the advancement of American and global civilization. The United States should not regard competitiveness in trade or finance as the sole arenas in which to express American values and aspirations, or assume that military or diplomatic deterrence (even public diplomacy short of cultural diplomacy), can generate mutual understanding among nations without a clearly stated national cultural policy.

1. The president should call to the Oval Office his Foreign Scholarship Board, along with the Librarian of Congress, and the heads of the Smithsonian Institution and the national agencies in the humanities, the arts and sciences, to explore the ramifications of devising a National Cultural Policy. Appropriate American Fulbright alumni should be engaged in formal examinations of such a policy. Later, the full American Fulbright alumni network should be invited to participate (see Chapter 1).

An essential aspect of the presidential promotion of the Fulbright program is recognition that this is not only an important American process, but a long-term commitment. The White House frequently announces relatively short-term projects for economic development, or disaster or refugee aid. Rarely can a president set his sights to benefit generations now and in the future with some degree of specificity. This enables the White House to sound a note of high purpose. The Fulbright awards at their best emphasize scholarship that addresses the history, traditions, and aspirations of other peoples; ignorance of these factors would cloud future American relations with much of the world.

2. The president on a separate occasion should invite to the White House a dozen senior American Fulbright scholars from several disciplines who have agreed to spend a year lecturing abroad. Would he regard

them as a "Dozen Points of Light"? Each would go to several countries for semester-long service. They would receive stipends at least equivalent to their present university salaries. This commitment by these academic "stars" would be welcomed by the president as a signal to the American academy that the Fulbright program is reasserting its leadership role in international academic exchanges. That signal would be well received abroad. Even if the Fulbright program reemphasizes graduate student rather than senior faculty grants to Americans hereafter, the year-long commitment of a few academic "stars" would add luster to the program even beyond the countries directly served. Another year, other countries could be similarly favored.

3. To enhance Fulbright and other U.S. cultural programs around the world, an active effort should be made to attract highly qualified academics to serve as cultural affairs officers abroad. If the government would create three-year stints for this purpose, highly qualified scholars just entering the academy and others in the most senior ranks might be most likely to serve. At its origin, the Fulbright program and the Foreign Service profited from enlisting recognized scholars as CAOs.

4. To demonstrate the extraordinary breadth of the program, an international conference of Fulbright alumni should be called for the fiftieth anniversary (1996). Such an event could take several years to organize. This should engage heads of state of the participating countries as well as the world's leading scholars. An appropriate forward-looking theme should be devised to focus the addresses, discussions, and other events at the conference. The fiftieth year could be initiated by the president sending off from the Oval Office the academics who will spend that year abroad (see Recommendation #2). Before this major undertaking is scheduled, however, the United States should formulate a National Cultural Policy (see Recommendation #1) and the Fulbright program should refine its focus as its 1991 White Paper recommends (see Appendix B) .

II. By Reexamining How Academic Themes and Grantees Are Chosen

Fulbright exchanges must maintain the highest quality of scholarship in selecting grantees and preserving academic integrity in all aspects of the program. Those first principles have clear imperatives:

5. The "quality" of scholars should not be reduced or jeopardized because teaching or research slots, either here or abroad, are requested

in greater numbers than can be filled with high-quality persons. Recruitment to find candidates should be restricted or eliminated when highest-quality scholars cannot be found. The two main nongovernmental screening agencies are committed to high-quality selection but they are under pressure from posts and binational commissions abroad. Both agencies should emphasize the "quality" issue abroad, and keep overseas commissions and posts better informed of each candidate's placement well before the procedure is complete.

6. "Travel grants," which provide funds solely for transportation, should be eliminated and the funds used to provide a better package for fewer people. The travel grant usually enables some specially qualified seniors to be listed as Fulbrighters when they go abroad with other funding. Far better to reduce the number of grants and assure a better package for the most worthy, particularly the younger graduate student.

7. Grants should emphasize scholarship, not occupational study or practice. There are many other sources for professional training. If some professional grants are made, they should include relevant academic elements, not just tools of the trade. Though foreign grant seekers and their governments often want to secure U.S. technological or management expertise, Fulbright should emphasize more scholarly academic slots, or, at least, insist that such courses be included with the occupational. Fulbright should be known for its high-quality, scholarly grants.

8. Even were financial constraints not a factor, the foregoing emphasis and the need for reassessment of basic objectives should lead to greater support for graduate students even at the expense of the senior scholars. Students represent the long-term future of the United States and its commitment to enhancing international understanding. The seniors should not be eliminated from the program. On the contrary, the fewer accepted should be universally recognizable as leading intellectuals in their disciplines. They should receive stipends at least equal to the salaries they earn in their present institutions. In attracting the pointmen and -women of their profession, the Fulbright program will gain added luster. Fulbrights need not excel in numbers transported but in the highest standards of academic accomplishment. The enhancement of "mutual understanding" is still a principal Fulbright goal. Young students rather than senior scholars are more likely to have life-changing experiences. Perhaps graduate-student grants should be titled "dissertation fellowships" to describe grantees who are working on doctoral degrees.

9. Foreign Fulbrighters, soon after returning home, should be invited

to seminars in their own or related disciplines. Reports and papers drawn from their American experience could be presented for other recent and older Fulbright alumni. The overseas commission or post would be the organizer if there is no active alumni association. Alumni should be encouraged to form associations where they do not exist.

III. By Ensuring that Fulbright Is Free of Political Pressures

From the beginning great efforts, perhaps overly extensive, were made to insulate Fulbright scholarships from political influences. Cumbersome, time-consuming procedures resulted. The program can never be apolitical. It is operated by government with mainly taxpayer funds that must be spent in the national interest. But that does not justify tampering with the selection process to favor or disfavor candidates on the basis of their political orientation. Such interference has been rare. But high-level policy based on a current national political objective has occasionally skewed the selection process, and threatens to do so again.

10. The CAMPUS program, created in response to insurgencies in Central America, bringing undergraduates to U.S. universities is highly successful. Yet it is not a typical Fulbright project. It is undergraduate; it is one-track, not an exchange involving North Americans. Other agencies might well have run this effective program. Congress's mandate to select 30 Vietnamese students for commercial law and economics courses in 1992–1993 would presumably draw off $600,000 from other Fulbright programs. Similarly, pressure is on to take Fulbright funds from all other geographic areas to support scholarships in Eastern Europe. Again, the objective is worthy. It is doubtful that the universities of Eastern and Central Europe can be reorganized rapidly to accept a major influx of American scholars. In any event, Fulbright operations elsewhere, particularly in Western Europe, should not be strapped because of this diversion. Western Europe, still the heartland of American civilization, should not receive less attention from the Fulbright program, especially when the European Community is mounting a strongly Euro-centered academic effort. Indeed, IREX, which has spent nearly two decades serving underground scholars of Eastern Europe and the Soviet Union, is eminently qualified to concentrate on the expansion of scholarship in successor states of the Soviet Union where democratic institutions are not yet in place. The Fulbright program is already functioning in several Eastern European countries that are deepening their democratic roots. The Fulbright program should continue to serve those countries with the

highest possible academic exchanges, but without extraordinary funding dislocations that can seriously hamper the rest of the Fulbright program.

11. Debates on and off the campus over "political correctness" focus on the alteration of the academic canon, or classic teaching themes and books, to accommodate more multicultural subjects and personalities. PC debates provide fiery rhetoric. Yet, domestic political objectives aside, fundamental multicultural requirements must be faced. Americans engaging in international trade, cross-border finance, communication, or scholarship will be increasingly hampered by their intercultural and linguistic illiteracy. The Fulbright program, operating in the academy, could divert the bitter PC controversies into constructive efforts to broaden multicultural education through international exchanges.

12. Fulbright, by virtue of being a binational program, must take into account the scholarly objectives of other societies. Even if another country's policies favor science and technology rather than the humanities, the favored Fulbright disciplines, the foreign university should be offered humanities components of U.S. sciences; e.g., how America employs science and technology, the frontiers of science in American society. If science and technology must be provided, then a social scientist should be part of the package. If a medical lecturer is sought, someone who can teach medical ethics should be provided; in hard science, one capable of handling science policy; in architecture, someone familiar with environmental issues. Several U.S. scholars in a developing country can make a significant academic contribution even though the highest level of scholarship may not yet be reflected in the local institutions. Their very presence, however, can have a positive influence on U.S. relations and eventually help raise academic standards. It is in America's interest to share with its partners abroad, as often as possible, the long-term objectives of the Fulbright program. CAOs and PAOs do this as part of their negotiations. Overseas, public meetings or seminars of Fulbright alumni should discuss the program's objectives.

13. The present grantee screening process is cumbersome. Candidates' profiles are sent across the world, sometimes more than once, before they are selected or rejected for narrowly defined assignments. The same process is repeated for each of 130 countries. It would be far simpler for the CIES and the IIE to set forth a simple package of qualified candidates in each of the disciplines and offer all the nominees to all the commissions and posts. Candidates could indicate their country preference if they choose. In that way all commissions and posts would learn more

quickly who is and is not available. Even if some overseas principals engage in competition for candidates, that process would be more open and less disappointing than the present cumbersome method.

14. Studies of American culture should be further expanded in universities abroad. The discipline has been introduced in some countries. In others, courses in American society, politics, and history have been created as well as the more traditional teaching of English and American literature. Fulbright should make the placement of Americanists a higher priority. Admittedly, in many places, there is not yet the perceived need for full-time scholarship in this field. But U.S. scholars who teach other subjects abroad should be encouraged to add curricular material and perhaps a seminar on American cultural aspects of their specialties. It is likely that 90 percent of foreign undergraduates will never study the United States formally except through courses in the English language. That instruction then should have a component that includes even a brief look at American society and governance. The Fulbright program can make a difference in pressing for such inclusion.

IV. By Employing the New Communication Technologies

Fulbrighters should employ the rapidly enlarging global information linkages known as ISDN (integrated systems, or services, of digital networks). ISDN will provide individuals and institutions everywhere with access to scholarly and general data and information. The U.S. Senate late in 1991 authorized $1 billion over five years to build a high-speed supercomputing network to link federal research centers, universities, and corporations. Electronic mail already enables scholars to reach one another across the world instantaneously. Soon, scholarly journals will be accessible over electronic networks. More formal use of electronic systems links academic databases in many countries.

15. Fulbrighters should have access to electronic media. They can be used to maintain contact between Fulbright alumni and their former host institutions abroad. University-to-university ties should be completed at first; many U.S. scholars with private modems will have easier access. Alumni maintaining contact with colleagues would thus keep abreast of current developments in their field. Relatively small grants would purchase access and sustain coverage. Funds could be generated on a binational basis in commission countries. Funds, perhaps from USAID, should be found to establish in each developing country at least one

electronic link to U.S. research databases. The system can also be used
to encourage global conferencing by Fulbrighters. Papers prepared and
circulated in advance can be discussed by electronic meetings.

16. Access to Worldnet, the international telecasting facility of the
U.S. Information Agency, should be offered for classroom instruction or
conferencing abroad. USIA officials had discussed such possibilities with
the University of Maine, which has an extensive university-of-the-air
program in the United States. The concept deserves further consideration. Universities abroad should be asked whether receiving some vari-
ation of the Maine TV system would be acceptable.

17. Institutions as well as individuals engage in bilateral and multi-
lateral educational interactions. The United Nations Educational, Scientific and Cultural Organization (UNESCO) is the most effective multi-
lateral example. The United States withdrew from UNESCO in January
1985. The organization was charged with proposing undemocratic global
communications policies, maladministration, and profligate spending. A
new director-general has dramatically reversed communications programs
in favor of democratizing the flow of news and information. He has
improved administrative and financial operations. It is time for the United
States to consider returning to the only global organization devoted to
the advancement of diverse cultural programs. UNESCO is a useful
channel for Americans to engage in multinational as well as binational
communication on a wide spectrum of issues in science, education, and
culture. The U.S. reexamination should be undertaken by a blue-ribbon
body broader than the State Department bureau or the small advisory
body, which recommended that the United States continue to absent itself
from the universal agency.

V. By Strengthening the Foreign Scholarship Board

The J. William Fulbright Foreign Scholarship Board, under congressional mandate, is composed of twelve members appointed by the president. These members must approve—individually—some 5,000 Fulbright
scholarship grants each year. Yet the FSB itself is not an operational
power base. It depends on two main nongovernmental agencies to screen
all grantees, and relies on 130 overseas commissions or posts to submit
foreign academic project proposals, make grantee nominations, and scruti-
nize American nominations. The FSB sits in the center of this swirl of
activity spread over an eighteen-month cycle.

18. The FSB cannot be a program operator but it can be a highly useful think tank for the planning and development of international academic exchanges. The past two years, the FSB has begun to serve this important purpose. It held a series of roundtable discussions on the future of exchanges. It produced a White Paper, which has already generated diverse responses from academics and bureaucracies associated with the Fulbright program. The FSB should enlarge this activity. It should provide thoughtful papers on the substantive and operational issues with which Fulbright agencies must deal. It should address nongovernmental peer groups that provide screening. Most important, FSB should include in its own board sessions, substantive discussions of academic issues beyond the operational questions. Members of FSB should be asked to prepare papers to introduce such discussions. The best of these may form the basis for other White Papers or occasional publications. To reduce the operational burden, FSB members who are now divided into foreign geographic committees should instead be assigned to theme committees reflecting the main problem areas with which FSB as a think tank should deal. The nongovernmental screening agencies could be given responsibility by contract to make the individual signs-offs on all grants. In present practice, these agencies perform this function de facto, if not de jure. The presidential mandate, I believe, can be extended in this fashion since the FSB would still set general policies and rules of engagement. Whether or not this is attempted, but especially if it is, the FSB should receive from these agencies information about every candidate for a grant who is rejected, as well as candidates recommended. As an alternative to delegating its grant-selection responsibility, the FSB's staff should be enlarged to enable it to deal more selectively with the volume of candidates for awards. Finally, the White House should take appropriate steps to meet the challenge raised by one current FSB member: "Though painful to acknowledge, since 1980 the board's quality of appointments has declined, especially in the proportion of scholars." The president by his appointments can rectify that.

19. Should the FSB and the Fulbright program be moved out of the U.S. Information Agency? This year-long study did not reveal cases of overt politicization in grant selection. We do report some policy-driven activity by both the governmental and academic bureaucracies. The main question, in my view, is whether the Fulbright program would be best served in an agency committed only to academic issues and exchanges. This question was raised even before the FSB was moved into the USIA in 1978. The FSB White Paper, I believe, formally places the question on the current agenda. The FSB does this properly, without making a

judgment by indicating three criteria to be considered: Fulbright must have a link to the foreign affairs community, connections with the private academic world, and a capacity to receive privately donated tax-deductible funds. Several alternative sites for the Fulbright program have been suggested over the years: the Smithsonian Institution, the Library of Congress, and some new agency separate from, but allied to, the State Department. The last was the recommendation of the Stanton Commission, which reported shortly before President Carter moved Fulbright to the USIA. A foreign model is the British Council. It is relatively independent of government but in the American system might not be able to accept private funding. The issue merits continuing consideration.

VI. By Streamlining the Operation at All Levels

While this study does not pretend to have examined all of the Fulbright operations in great depth, we do have some sense of problems and opportunities. These are worth mentioning if only to inspire fuller examination.

20. The Fulbright program itself is a great hidden treasure. And secreted within it is another project that deserves far greater funding, staffing, and promotion as an American asset. That unheralded project is the advisory service for foreign students who will not seek Fulbright grants but make their own arrangement to attend colleges or universities in the United States. In 1990, at least 1,069,197 students were helped at Fulbright offices. In some countries, three or four Fulbright staffers try to counsel some 20,000 to 30,000 students a year. They help students select colleges and courses, and decide on future careers. This is a very important service not only for the vast number of individual young people but for America as well. Over the long term, the student advisory service may influence more friends abroad than the USIA's International Visitors Program, which brings foreign leaders to the United States for short visits. Fulbright aims to enhance mutual understanding. A million or more students have been assisted by this haphazardly designed and impoverished program. At the outset, this was a USIA embassy program, not intended to be a Fulbright activity. There can be no control over the quality of students being counseled. Indeed, there should not be. But then this should not be a Fulbright undertaking. Charging it against the Fulbright budget and staffing reduces support for Fulbright's core work. The advisory service should be returned to USIA's budget and staffing, and upgraded in status reflecting its considerable importance.

21. In most exchanges, more foreign students come to the United States on Fulbright grants than Americans going abroad to the same countries. Some commissions, such as the Japanese, actively seek a larger number of Americans to study in their countries. This may require special arrangements in some places; in others, binational commissions should be urged to equalize the flow, even when foreign governments contribute increasingly more to the funding. Mutual understanding, a basic Fulbright commitment, requires at best an equal two-track movement.

22. Teacher exchanges are particularly important. The USIA-FSB teacher exchange matches foreign teachers with American teachers in the exchange. Each teacher immediately influences a large number of students. This program should be stimulated and extended. The Fulbright program run by the U.S. Department of Education takes U.S. teachers abroad for graduate study and doctoral dissertation research in non-Western language and area studies. USED-assisted teachers do not teach abroad and USED does not invite foreign teachers to the United States.

23. American researchers going overseas on Fulbright grants often want to engage in their research and not teach abroad. Yet foreign universities generally would welcome some teaching along with research. This is a plausible expectation. It enables the researcher to receive information from students and teaching colleagues while contributing to a deeper exchange of ideas. Some teaching abroad, probably at the graduate level, should be required of most researchers going overseas.

24. The Library of Congress should be used as a Fulbright asset. American students going abroad should spend time at the Library researching the country they will visit. That may save important research and adjustment time once they arrive on site. Similarly, foreign students coming to the United States should be expected to use the Library as part of their orientation to America. The Library could provide special seminars for foreign Fulbright scholars. They should also be invited to meet with the congressional leadership during a day-long seminar at the Capitol. The Congress should have a larger role in supporting the Fulbright program. The congressional leadership should appoint some members of the Foreign Scholarship Board, now all presidential appointees.

25. Some members of binational commissions, Americans as well as foreigners, have served for many years. There should be frequent rotation of membership to generate new ideas and improve élan. Some commis-

sion members and executive directors could well serve on the FSB as consultants or evaluators of the program.

26. Briefings on the Fulbright program for CAOs and PAOs going overseas and on home leave should be more extensive. Responsibility for Fulbright programs at posts abroad rests mainly on the CAOs and PAOs. These officers should meet with the nongovernmental selection agencies as well as the FSB. In the past, several days rather than several hours were devoted to such briefings.

27. An advance briefing paper should be given every grantee before he or she leaves home for assignment abroad. The paper should include specific details of the host university's requirements and expectations and information about the country to be visited. Some of the national information is provided now, but adequate details of the specific university's assignment are not always provided in advance.

28. A large governmental bureaucracy separates the FSB from the two nongovernmental screening agencies, and the FSB from the CAOs and PAOs at posts abroad. Area specialists account for some of the parent (USIA) staff. There are, however, sets of area specialists in other parts of the foreign service establishment. Other academic exchanges are also conducted in broader cultural programs. Without suggesting a particular rationalization of these assignments, it seems that a professional management analysis could lead to better deployment of some of these highly skilled officers.

29. The USIA has taken the forward-looking step of opening liaison with the European Community in the interest of advancing cultural activities. The EC's Erasmus program is already inspiring academic exchanges among universities in Western Europe and has expanded to Eastern Europe in the form of the Tempus program. CAOs throughout Europe should urge universities and university systems to include listings of American (as well as European) colleges so that students have a broader choice when applying to colleges. American schools are not yet part of the scheme. The U.S. institutions include tuition charges that are largely absent in the Erasmus system. As long as the Fulbright program operates the student advisory services abroad, this factor is a relevant concern (see Recommendation #20).

30. Public affairs officers, particularly in small countries, understandably seek to use Fulbright grants to advance embassy objectives. The

Fulbrighters, however, distinct from the USIA's International Visitors Program, have scholarly objectives beyond the undoubted value of physical immersion in a second (the American) culture. In countries where the academic establishment has not yet produced adequate numbers of candidates for high-level competition, there should be regional competitions drawing on larger numbers of qualified candidates. Instead of annual grants to any one country, regional competition may discover qualified nominees every other year or so. Geographic distribution should not be the criterion overseas or in the United States. Foreign students should be urged to attend good schools throughout the United States, and American students should be selected for grants to all quality institutions abroad.

31. Funds should be found to enable foreign Fulbright students to spend at least a month traveling around the United States after they complete their academic coursework. Understanding Americans and America is no less educational than formal classes and often makes an impression lasting a lifetime. Funds for this purpose might be sought from corporations and private foundations.

VII. By Making Serious Financial Choices

There should be some streamlining of the Fulbright program. Such rationalization would reduce the time lag in the selection process and cut costs somewhat. Toward that end, some recommendations are made here and elsewhere in this chapter. But cost-cutting will not be sufficient to resolve the basic dilemma of the Fulbright program. As posed on page 112, should the Fulbright program be cut back? Should it receive far greater financial support? Is there a third course?

32. The Fulbright program is hostage to its success. Abroad, the award has high prestige. Demands increase for scholarships coming to and going from America. That demand, however, drains funds faster than they can be provided by current sources. The shortfall particularly affects American grantees. Senior scholars nowadays find it almost impossible to live abroad on the meager Fulbright stipend. It has been kept low in order to spread the generally flat budgets (inflation considered) over more grantees and countries. Even graduate students find other scholarships more financially remunerative. The funding dilemma must be faced as a matter of high policy. The objective: to assure the traditional Fulbright stature among Americans as well as foreigners. Some guidelines:

a. The Fulbright program should secure private as well as governmental funding. Universities already provide substantial tuition-waiver and other in-kind assistance to Fulbright grantees. A fund-raising "Friends of Fulbright" should be formed in the United States comparable to groups in Japan, which provide substantial resources for the Fulbright program. Prominent Americans, including Fulbright alumni, should enlist corporate and other support. That effort would generate new interest in the program and demonstrate Fulbright's impressive constituency.

b. Increase the Fulbright budget substantially. The added funds should be used to attract the most qualified candidates and provide them longer and richer experiences in the countries they visit. Only a very small portion of new funds should be used for administration.

c. If the budget cannot be substantially increased, add to the number of graduate student grants by reducing the number of American senior scholars and researchers going abroad. To secure the highest quality of seniors they should be given substantially increased stipends at least equal to those provided by competitive grantors.

d. In every country, do not allow the demand for more scholarship slots or more candidates to determine the actual number of awards to be made. Although larger numbers add to the growing society of Fulbrighters worldwide, the program should be regarded in far longer terms: Over time, a few grantees more or less will not alter the general impact of the program. But maintaining the highest possible standard of academic quality, by wisest use of available funds in the screening process, will influence positively the entire program and all its recipients. This policy may be difficult to pursue in some countries that provide matching funds or, as in several cases, more funds than the United States. In such places, the increased U.S. funding (b. above) will be needed to equalize the two-way exchange.

33. Unfreeze Fulbright funds in a commission where the original purpose for this money cannot be fulfilled and the dollars cannot be transferred to other projects or sent to another commission.

VIII. By Improving Liaison Between the USED and USIA Fulbrights

The U.S. Department of Education operates Fulbright programs apart from the USIA's Fulbright programs. The USED sends abroad only

Americans: teachers, professors, school administrators, curricular specialists. This is not an exchange. Its purpose is to train Americans in foreign language and area skills, particularly of developing countries not generally visited by Americans. USED's Fulbright budget is about $5.8 million a year; USIA's is around $91 million. The J. William Fulbright Foreign Scholarship Board signs off on all USED as well as USIA Fulbright grants.

34. Should the FSB continue to be responsible for all USED grants? The FSB must find it difficult to pass on programs the board has not helped plan, organize, or conduct. If these programs are to remain in USED some mechanism other than the FSB, perhaps situated in USED, should be mandated to approve those grants. Perhaps an amendment to USED's Title VI NDEA legislation is needed. The Fulbright-Hays Act vests the responsibility for foreign-area and language training programs in the FSB, though under an executive order USED was given operational responsibility.

35. Better coordination between USED and USIA is needed in the United States and countries abroad where both agencies operate Fulbright programs. They should act neither aloof nor competitively. USED should routinely inform Fulbright commissions overseas well before a USED grantee or group is scheduled to arrive in the country. Commission facilities are automatically provided after arrival, but liaison from the beginning is likely to improve the quality of the visit.

36. USED should not offer a higher stipend for the same kind of Fulbright grant that USIA provides.

IX. By High-level Examination of the Fulbright Program

I fully endorse the conclusion of the FSB's White Paper that "a presidential commission be convened on the future of international educational exchange with a particular eye to furthering useful planning of exchange efforts." The FSB properly makes the point: "The federal government must retake the leadership it has abdicated in this area so vital to the national interest and to the perception of American commitment abroad." I would expand this by calling on the White House to formulate a National Cultural Policy (see Recommendation #1). Other monitoring is needed.

37. At least every five years, the Fulbright program should be thor-

oughly reassessed by an independent organization for the following: standing of the Fulbrights in the eyes of observers in the United States and abroad, academic quality of grantees, disciplines to be emphasized, special projects to be considered in light of changing conditions in the world and the academy, balance between Americans and other nationalities in the country-by-country exchange, level of stipends in relation to other grantors, efficiency in approving scholarship positions and screening grantees,and general operational efficiency.

38. There should be a management study of the cost and degree of efficiency, in the United States and abroad, in designing academic offerings and screening scholars to fill the positions. This should not focus on academic policies but solely on the operational factors. Clearly, too much paperwork handicaps the policy making and screening process at every step. After forty-five years, any process requires a complete reexamination—even one run with as dedicated individuals as those in the USIA, USED, FSB, State Department missions abroad, Fulbright commission directors overseas, and the CIES and the IIE in the United States. The study should be conducted by a nongovernmental management specialist familiar with governmental agencies.

Epilogue

The Culture of Freedom depends greatly on expanding human insights through intellectual exchanges. Academic exchange is no zero-sum matter. Sharing information and wisdom does not deprive the donor while it helps the receiver.

This is especially true in the exchanges the Fulbright program pioneered. It works on a track between two nations. That makes the program complex to administer, but its policies hard to distort for partisan or even national purposes.

The administrative difficulties, even the occasional efforts to politicize (whether originating in governments or in the academy) are far outweighed by the enormous values generated by the Fulbright process itself.

The United States and especially its people are the chief beneficiaries of the Fulbright legacy. Each of the cooperating nations has also gained markedly. Some 180,000 scholars have had their lives transformed by the Fulbright experience.

Fulbrighters, then, are a small world that quietly closes gaps of ignorance and misunderstanding, and thereby links countless pairs of people across the globe.

May their number and influence go from strength to strength.

Appendix A
Interviewees for the Study

Boston/Cambridge, Massachusetts

Brigette Berger, Professor of Sociology, Boston University
Derek Bok, President, Harvard University
Robert S. Brustein, Director, Loeb Drama Center, Harvard University
Jan Graham Geidt, American Repertory Theatre, Harvard University
Nathan Glazer, Professor of Education and Sociology, Harvard University
Marshall I. Goldman, Professor of Economics, Harvard University
Oscar Handlin, Professor of History, Harvard University
Mary Rose Maybank, Fogg Gallery, Cambridge
Walter A. Rosenblith, Institute Professor, Massachusetts Institute of Technology

Bronxville, New York

Alice Stone Ilchman, President, Sarah Lawrence College

Clemson, South Carolina

Charles W. Dunn, Chairman, J.W. Fulbright Foreign Scholarship Board

Middletown, Connecticut

Fredrik E. deBoer, Chairman, Theater Department, Wesleyan University

New Haven, Connecticut

Robin Winks, Professor of History, Yale University
C. Vann Woodward, Professor of History, Yale University

New York City

Peggy Blumenthal, Vice President, Educational Services, IIE
Boonrak Boonyaketmala, Dean, Thammasat University, Thailand
Thomas Farrell, Vice President, Exchange Programs & Regional Services, IIE
Denka Gabal, Fulbright graduate student from Czechoslovakia
Vartan Gregorian, President, Brown University
Salud Hernandez-Mura, Fulbright graduate student from Spain
Ada Louise Huxtable, architectural critic
Hans Janitschek, United Nations Population Fund
Maria Japa, Fulbright graduate student from the Philippines
Stanley Katz, President, American Academy of Learned Societies
Alfred Kazin, author; professor, City University of New York
Imad Khachchan, Fulbright graduate student from Lebanon
Joseph Lelyveld, Managing Editor, *New York Times*
I.C. Madubuike, Director, *Daily Champion*, former Minister of Education, Nigeria
Philip N. Marcus, consultant; FSB board member
William Plowden, Director, U.K. Harkness Fellowships
Norman Podhoretz, Editor, *Commentary* magazine
Cassandra A. Pyle, Executive Director, CIES
Roger Rosenblatt, Essayist, *Life* magazine; MacNeil/Lehrer News Program
Stacey K. Simon, Executive Director, Metro International
Alberto Vitale, President, Random House
Doris Wibunsin, Executive Director, Thailand-U.S. Educational Foundation
Yassen Zassoursky, Dean, Faculty of Journalism, Moscow University

Princeton, New Jersey

Allen Kasoff, Director, International Research and Exchanges Board (IREX)

Washington, D.C.

John C.T. Alexander, Director, CIE, U.S. Department of Education
Richard T. Arndt, President, Fulbright Association
James H. Billington, Librarian of Congress
Daniel J. Boorstin, Librarian Emeritus of Congress
Guy S. Brown, Director, Academic Programs, Educational & Cultural Affairs/USIA
Csaba Chikes, Deputy Director, Office of European Affairs/USIA
Barbara Crossette, *The New York Times*
J. William Fulbright, Former United States Senator
Georgie Anne Geyer, syndicated columnist
William P. Glade, Associate Director, USIA
Mark Glago, Regional Affairs Officer, NEA/USIA
Tom Haran, American Republics Affairs/USIA
David I. Hitchcock, Director, Office of East Asian & Pacific Affairs/USIA
Lee James Irwin, CAO, Gulf States & Iraq/USIA
William Jones, CAO, Pakistan, Bangladesh, Nepal/USIA
Maryanne McKaye, Acting Branch Chief, NEA/USIA
Jennifer Newton, Deputy Director, J.W. Fulbright Foreign Scholarship Board
Lea Perez, CAO, Israel/West Bank, Jordan, Lebanon, Syria/USIA
John Richardson, former Assistant Secretary of State/CU
Ronald Ungaro, Chief, Academic Exchange Programs Division/USIA
Ralph Vogel, Executive Director, J.W. Fulbright Foreign Scholarship Board
Stanley A. Zuckerman, Director, American Republics Affairs/USIA

New Delhi, India

Leonard J. Baldyga, Minister Counselor for Public Affairs, U.S. Embassy, Delhi; Director, USIA/India
O.P. Bhardwaj, Executive Officer, U.S. Educational Foundation in India (Fulbright Commission)
R.K. Chhabra, former Secretary, University Grants Commission for academic awards and standards for all academics in India); member of Fulbright board for more than a decade
Mary D. Connors, Acting Cultural Affairs Officer, USIS/India; Treasurer of the Fulbright Commission

R.P. Kaushik, Chairman, Centre for American & West European Studies, School of International Studies, Jawaharlal Nehru University; former Fulbrighter

(Mrs.) Susheela Kaushik, Political Science Dept.; Director, Women's Studies & Development Center, University of Delhi; former Fulbrighter

A.M. Khusro, Chairman, Aga Khan Foundation; Resident Editor, the *Financial Express* and the *Indian Express*; former Indian Ambassador to Germany; Vice Chancellor, Aligarh Muslim University; member, planning commission (directing development of India); former Fulbrighter

S.G. Mankad, Joint Secretary, Dept. of Education, Ministry of Human Resource Development, Government of India; member Fulbright Commission (his office gives clearances/GOI approvals for all Fulbright scholars)

Sarina Paranjape, program coordinator, USEFI, directs advisories for thousands of students going to the U.S. independently

Group Interviews with Former Fulbrighters

Current Fulbrighters attending Journalism School of Syracuse University

G.K. Kapoor, Principal, Birla Vidya Niketan, New Delhi

R.K. Kaushik, Principal, A.R.S.D. College, New Delhi

Rajiv Kumar, producer, news and current affairs, national network, Door Darshan Kendra (TV), government net; also, weekly correspondent CNN

D. Raj Mahajan, cardiac surgeon to President of India; Governor, American College of Surgeons; pioneer in open-heart surgery in U.S. and India

V. Krishna Moorthy, Principal, Sri Venkateswara College, New Delhi

M.S. Rajan, professor emeritus, School of International Studies, Jawaharlal Nehru University, New Delhi

*K.V. Rajaram, TV cameraman, Door Darshan Kendra, Punjab

*Raj Kiran Sangwan, TV producer, Indira Gandhi National Open University, New Delhi

Ram Karan Sharma, former Vice Chancellor

*Ajmer Singh Shokar, TV producer, Door Darshan Kendra, Punjab

Jagjit Singh, senior professor and chief editor, Institute of Marketing and Management, New Delhi

Conversations

Cushrow Irani, Managing Director, *The Statesman*, daily newspaper
Dileep Padgaonkar, Editor, *The Times of India*, daily newspaper

Bali, Indonesia

I. Made Bandem, Director, STSI (Indonesia School of Arts); worldwide reputation as performer (dance) and ethnologist/musicologist

Jakarta, Indonesia

Pia Alisjahbana, Chair, AMINEF (American Indonesian Exchange Foundation); Publisher of *Femina,* a leading women's magazine
Harsja W. Bachtiar, head of the Ministry of Education's Research and Development
Robert W. Hornaday, Professor of Management, University of North Carolina, Charlotte; senior Fulbright lecturer at Gadjah Mada University
Aristides Katoppo, Chief Editor, *Mutiara* magazine
Ann vB. Lewis, Executive Director, AMINEF
Don Q. Washington, CAO, U.S. Embassy/Jakarta
Putu Widjaja, author, filmmaker, editor of *Tempo*, popular newsmagazine
Michael M. Yaki, PAO, U.S. Embassy/Jakarta

Rome, Italy

Gil Callaway, CAO, U.S. Embassy/Rome
Carlo Chiarenza, Executive Director, Fulbright Commission for Cultural Exchange between Italy & USA; professor of comparative literature
Luigi Filadoro, Deputy Director, Fulbright Commission for Cultural Exchange
Biancamaria Tedeschini Lalli, Chair, Department of American Studies, University of Rome
Jodie Lewinsohn, PAO, U.S. Embassy/Rome

Guglielmo Negri, Legal Counselor to the President of the Italian Republic; Professor of Constitutional Law at LUISS, prestigious private university; former Fulbrighter

Cipriana Scelba, Executive Director of the binational commission for more than thirty years

Kyoto, Japan

Yasunori Nishijima, President, University of Kyoto

Tokyo, Japan

Akira Fujishima, Justice, Supreme Court of Japan

Ryuici Hirano, former president, University of Tokyo

Keiko Jones, educational and information officer at JOSEK

Kazuko Kamimura, program officer, Japan-U.S. Educational Commission

Shigekuni Kawamura, President, Dai-Nippon Ink Chemical, Inc.; chairman, Japanese GARIOA/Fulbright Alumni Association; board member, IIE

Ray McGunigle, First Secretary, cultural division, U.S. Embassy/Tokyo

Robert L.M. Nevitt, Director, U.S. Information Service Japan; Minister-Counselor of Embassy for Public Affairs

Yuji Tsushima, member of the House of Representatives (Diet); former cabinet member and minister

Kenichi Takemura, critic/commentator; popular journalist in Japan

Port of Spain, Trinidad and Tobago

Felipe Noguera, Secretary General, Caribbean Association of National Telecommunication Organizations

Appendix B
1991 White Paper
J. William Fulbright Foreign
Scholarship Board

Chairman: Dr. Charles W. Dunn
Chairman, Department of Political Science, Clemson University
Vice Chairman: Mr. T. Kenneth Cribb
President, Intercollegiate Studies Institute, Inc.

Mr. Michael D. Antonovich, Member, Los Angeles County Board of Supervisors

Dr. Shu Park Chan, Acting Dean, School of Engineering, Santa Clara University

Mr. Tyrone C. Fahner, Attorney, Mayer, Brown & Platt

Dr. Vartan Gregorian, President, Brown University

Dr. Philip N. Marcus, Consultant

Mr. Ewell Murphy Jr., Attorney, Baker & Botts

Dr. Nelson V. Nee, Vice President for International Services & Studies, United States International University

Mr. John W. Sears, Trustee

Ms. Margarita Tonkinson, Associate Director, Office of International Programs, University of Miami

Mr. James R. Whelan, The Whelan Company

White Paper
on The Future of the Fulbright Program
Prepared by The J. William Fulbright
Foreign Scholarship Board
Charles W. Dunn, Chairman

Preface

Strangled by too few resources and subverted by too many demands, the Fulbright Program is in jeopardy, its historic mission and hard-earned reputation endangered.

   This White Paper on the future of the Program culminates a year of work by the J. William Fulbright Foreign Scholarship Board. Included among the authorities called upon by the Board during this time are James Billington, Librarian of Congress; Stanley Katz, president of the American Council of Learned Societies, Charles Blitzer, director of the Woodrow Wilson International Center for Scholars; and officials from the Institute of International Education, the Council for International Exchange of Scholars, the U.S. Agency for International Development, the National Association of State Universities and Land-Grant Colleges, the Fulbright Association, and the U.S. Information Agency, which administers the Fulbright Program.

A Global Trust

   The Fulbright Program is the world's best known and most prominent symbol of international education. In its 44-year history, it has offered 180,000 people worldwide the means to become wiser international citizens, people who have gone on to become leaders in their chosen fields and in their communities and nations. In the United States, these include Librarian of Congress James Billington, Senator Daniel Patrick Moynihan, University of Chicago President Hanna Holborn Gray, journal editor Norman Podhoretz, and writers Eudora Welty, Joseph Heller, and Alfred Kazin. From Aaron Copland and Virgil Thomson to Philip Glass, an extraordinary number of prominent American composers of the past 40 years held Fulbrights early in their careers. A dozen Nobel Prizewinners in physics, medicine and economics—Hans Bethe and Milton Friedman among them—were also Fulbrighters.

   Fulbright alumni overseas include Alexander Yakovlev, longtime advisor to Soviet leader Mikhail Gorbachev, and the Prime Minister of

Sweden, Ingvar Carlsson. Dozens of former and current cabinet ministers are Fulbrighters, including Pedro Aspe, the new Finance Minister of Mexico, who is surrounded by fellow Fulbrighters advising the Mexican government on trade-related matters.

In Japan in the last five years, the list of prominent former Fulbrighters has included seven Diet members, the Chief Justice of the Supreme Court and three other justices, the presidents of 27 universities, over 100 senior executives of major business corporations, and more than 30 ambassadors to other nations. Our current American Ambassador to Japan, Michael Armacost, was himself a Fulbrighter, and he recently called the program "the most successful, farsighted element of America's—or perhaps any nation's—international cultural policy."

While promoting human interaction on an individual scale is its central spirit, the Program can legitimately point to some more tangible benefits to the interests of the United States and other countries.

* It has done much to build American knowledge of foreign peoples and languages and, conversely, to improve the quality of foreign scholarship about the culture, history and government of the United States. This in turn affects the intellectual context for public policy debates in the United States and elsewhere, and strengthens this country's capacity to participate effectively in the emerging international community.

* The Program has successfully fostered private institutional relationships between American and foreign universities, leading to joint research, further exchange and a ripple effect among students who may never set foot from their countries.

* The Program has helped to expand the influence of the American model of higher education and of American research methodologies, which are admired worldwide. Even as American technological progress is viewed as waning, the demand for study in the United States continues to grow dramatically. As one European Fulbright administrator noted recently, higher education is now America's best export.

* The Program has created 46 active binational agreements establishing independent, nonpartisan bodies called Fulbright commissions. By these acts, other nations join us in affirming the importance of peaceful relations, the enduring effect of education, and the mutual responsibilities to support international un-

derstanding. Substantial sums of foreign monies support these efforts, with the foreign government in some cases exceeding the American in its support of Fulbright exchanges between the two nations.

The Changed World Situation

There was a time when Fulbrights were about the only game in town. Now the Program is dwarfed, by waves of self-financed students from overseas, by the proliferation of private exchange programs it helped to foster, and by other governmental activity, foreign and American. Consider this:

- In 1948, there were 500 British graduate students in the U.S., 200 of whom were Fulbrighters; today, there are roughly 6,000, only 30 whom are under Fulbright auspices.

- Fulbrighters now make up only 6% of the international exchange participants funded annually by the U.S. Government alone.

The playing field is different, too. In 1949, the Fulbright Program was active in ten countries, mostly in Western Europe. Today it serves 130 countries in every corner of the globe. The years in between highlight America's need for in-depth knowledge of peoples and cultures previously considered marginal. They also demonstrate the extent to which American principles and way hold worldwide interest, if not attraction.

To continue this valuable but long-term investment into the 21st century, the Fulbright Program needs two things: adequate funding and refined focus.

First, funding.

The U.S. Government appropriates 530 times as much money annually for development and humanitarian assistance as for the Fulbright Program. Yet, as Librarian of Congress James Billington recently put it to the Board, what can be a more faithful projection of American values than giving the brightest individuals the opportunity to find their own way through education?

In constant dollars, the Program's annual budget has only little more than doubled during the ten-fold expansion of participating countries since its inception. (See graph.) The cost of thus extending the Program has been diminution of the award itself, to the ultimate detriment of the entire enterprise. We have been able to ride for a time on the Program's established reputation, particularly given the increased financial support af-

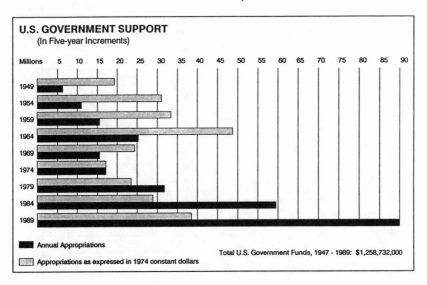

U.S. GOVERNMENT SUPPORT
(In Five-year Increments)

Millions 5 10 15 20 25 30 35 40 45 50 55 60 65 70 75 80 85 90

1949
1954
1959
1964
1969
1974
1979
1984
1989

■ Annual Appropriations
▒ Appropriations as expressed in 1974 constant dollars

Total U.S. Government Funds, 1947 - 1989: $1,258,732,000

forded the Program by other participating nations (See graph). But the programmatic effects of stretching so thin are doing damage that may be irreparable if not addressed soon.

- Low stipends have reduced the attractiveness of a Fulbright award for American scholars to the point where many outstanding people no longer consider participating.

- In the name of having a Fulbright presence in as many countries as possible, we end up actively recruiting candidates for many awards, or taking almost anyone who applies, whatever their qualifications.

- On the foreign side, bright scholars are asked to forgo admission to a top American graduate school that wants them in favor of a less prestigious one that has offered financial aid. Others are offered a "travel grant," basically a round-trip airline ticket, as their Fulbright. Increasingly, the Fulbright is only a part—sometimes an inconsequential part—of a financial package, rather than an award of excellence.

Hence, the second need of the Fulbright Program: refined focus, or—put another way—product differentiation in a crowded market that is partly a creation of its own success. After two decades in which new initiatives and targeted programs have coincided with erosion of the financial base, what is sorely needed is "a redefinition of purpose for the

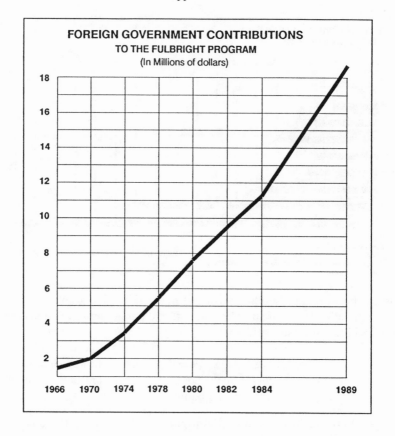

FOREIGN GOVERNMENT CONTRIBUTIONS
TO THE FULBRIGHT PROGRAM
(In Millions of dollars)

Fulbright Program," in the words of Stanley Katz, president of the American Council of Learned Societies.

The Board believes that it is time to go back to the Program's roots, which predate the Cold War. Its reputation, the activities and prominence of many of its early participants, and we suggest, even the improved international atmosphere in the world today argue for the long-term value of the investment in international networking that exchanges build so well. But there are certain practices that must be re-evaluated as we do so.

First, the Program is a long-term proposition. This is its legislative intent and its vision, imperatives to demonstrate its effectiveness or hone its results notwithstanding. Stringent mechanisms of accountability will diminish the Program or turn it to goals too narrowly defined or too short-term.

Second, the Program must stand for quality. Our efforts should go into selecting the best minds and enabling them to do the work that interests them. This is consistent with the Program's history and reputation, and also makes good sense in distinguishing Fulbrights from the competition, which increasingly favors targeted or institutional awards. More than any other single action that could be taken under current budget constraints, allowing the balance to go to fewer but more substantial grants will underscore the Program's prestige.

Third, geographical dispersion must not be viewed as an end in itself. The unintended result of much of the process of defining country-by-country programs and filling openings has been to compromise quality, sometimes to extreme extents in the American side of the Program. We must not try to cover every country every year, nor pretend that each country of the world is equally interesting to Americans. (If there are no viable institutions of higher education operating in a given country, Fulbright dollars are surely better spent elsewhere.) It is clearly in the national interest to disperse Fulbright awards to all regions of the world, but this can be accomplished through regional competitions without the distortions that are currently undermining the Program.

Fourth, the Program must embody scholarship, not training or work in applied or developmental fields, however valuable those efforts may be. The Program is too small to serve adequately any serious utilitarian interests, particularly when compared with other governmental efforts like those of AID. Even if funding were to be dramatically increased, grants to individuals are an inefficient mechanism for problem-solving, particularly in the short-term, and should not be used as such.

Fifth, pressures to shorten the length of Fulbright awards must be resisted. Our goal is not to fill "slots" however we can but to further mutual understanding, which can only happen over time. The need for in-depth knowledge and instinctive appreciation of other cultures is even more crucial in this age of faxes, jets and teleconferences.

Sixth, the administrative apparatus and the types of awards offered must be simplified. As one program administrator has commented, we have come to be managing a process, not a program. Reducing or eliminating the imperatives discussed above will go a long way toward making the Program comprehensible again. So will simplifying the type of grants awarded.

The Board believes that the student grants are the lifeblood and raison d'être of the Program, and that grants to American students have been woefully neglected in recent times (see graph). We should once again turn our sights to the longer term, toward replenishing the future. The effect of these grants is less immediately apparent, but presenting young people with an international experience at a crucial point in their lives will have the lasting human impact Senator Fulbright sought. It is also what the Fulbright Program stands for in the general public eye. The Board believes that student grants in both directions should form at least half of the Program.

The faculty grants need to be revamped as well. The false dichotomy—or the supposed quid pro quo—between lecturing and research grants should be eliminated in favor of a simplified faculty award that combines time for quality research with a small concomitant obligation to "give back," with a seminar, lectures, or faculty development work, as can most usefully be arranged. But the driving force must be choosing

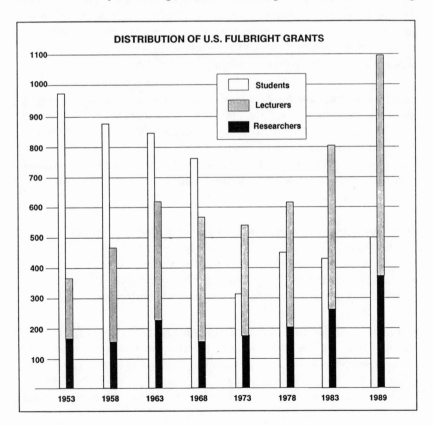

the best applicants and making it possible for them to go where they want to go and do the work that will eventually enrich American knowledge and scholarship. Within a given institution or field, those few recognized by all as outstanding should be the ones who are tapped for Fulbrights.

No discussion of program administration would be complete without comment on "siting" Fulbright within the U.S. Government. The Program was administered largely by the Department of State until 1978, when the Department's Bureau of Educational and Cultural Affairs was folded into the U.S. Information Agency (USIA). Certain smaller programs have been housed at the Department of Education and its predecessor institutions. The issue of where the Fulbright Program is best administered—or most carefully protected—is one that flares up periodically, with the Smithsonian Institution, the Library of Congress, and an independent foundation or endowment being recently put forth as alternatives to the USIA.

There is no perfect answer to this recurring question, which indeed recurs because of the nature of the Fulbright Program as a foreign policy initiative but only in the broadest, long-term sense. The Board believes, however, that any viable "home" for the Program should have certain features, including:

- a link to the foreign affairs community

- connections to the private academic world

- capacity to receive privately donated, tax-deductible funds

Conclusion

In recent years, we have been trying to do more and more with less and less, and this is an increasingly destructive dynamic. The Board believes strongly that the exchanges we describe above are in the long-term interest of this nation and of the interdependent world in which we find ourselves, and that a program along these lines should be funded accordingly. The federal government must retake the leadership it has abdicated in this area so vital to the national interest and to the perception of American commitment abroad. We urge:

- That Congress double the current appropriation level without specifications or earmarks.

- That a Presidential commission be convened on the future of international education exchange, with a particular eye to furthering useful planning of exchange efforts.

- That Fulbright program administrators apply increased funds toward more student grants for Americans, and toward making individual senior scholar grants more commensurate with a first-
  rate program. This is the responsible course for the flagship of
  international educational exchange, a program that has truly
  become a global trust.

Nearly 20 years ago, in its "Statement on Exchange in the Seventies,"
the Board called for innovations and directions that would make the
Fulbright Program—"an activity that began almost as a postwar 'impro-
visation'"—more relevant in a complex and changed world. Today we
are convinced that—with or without funding increases—simplification,
a return to the basics, is the approach that should guide our actions in an
even more complex and changing environment. There are very few bad
ideas in international exchange; the important thing now is for the Fulbright Program to do what it is known for well. To stray even further
from our path will mean losing the name recognition—and its aura of
value—that 44 years of success have built.

Appendix C
Fulbright Grants Awarded, 1949–1990

USIA (Foreign Nationals)

	Africa	American Republics	East Asia/Pacific	Europe	Near East/South Asia	Total
1990	180	658	323	1,598	256	3,015
1949–1990	5,240	16,692	17,049	66,956	11,581	117,518

USIA (U.S. Citizens)

	Africa	American Republics	East Asia/Pacific	Europe	Near East/South Asia	Total
1990	99	270	227	992	160	1,748
1949–1990	1,816	6,305	6,841	43,674	5,076	63,712

Department of Education

	Africa	American Republics	East Asia/Pacific	Europe	Near East/South Asia	Total
1990	111	100	202	218	280	911
1949–1990	2,393	2,075	5,106	7,156	8,891	25,621

USIA (Foreign Nationals)

	University Study	Advanced Research	Teaching or Educational Seminars	University Lecturers	Practical Experience & Training	Hubert H. Humphrey Scholars	Total
1990	1,457	835	347	161	80	135	3,015
1949–1990	66,107	22,243	19,391	6,000	2,253	1,523	117,518

USIA (U.S. Citizens)

	University Study	Advanced Research	Teaching or Educational Seminars	University Lecturers	Total
1990	504	352	213	679	1,748
1949–1990	25,780	8,835	11,416	17,681	63,712

Department of Education

	Doctoral Dissertation	Faculty Research	Group Projects	Seminars Abroad	Curriculum Consulants	Total
1990	86	26	644	155	0	911
1949–1990	3,042	1,226	19,241	1,785	327	25,621

Notes

1. Toward a National Cultural Policy, Pages 1–14

1. Bob Woodward, *The Commanders*; New York: Simon & Schuster, 1991, page 370.

2. The idea of the "small world" phenomenon was conceived in the 1950s by Ithiel deSola Pool of Massachusetts Institute of Technology. Efforts to devise a mathematical formulation were taken by Manfred Kochen. See *The Small World*, edited by Manfred Kochen, Norwood, NJ: Ablex, 1989.

3. Letter of Arnold Toynbee to Lyle Nelson, former chairman of the Board of Foreign Scholarships, published in the twenty-fifth annual report of the Fulbright program.

4. Author's interview with Derek Bok, October 12, 1990.

5. *Harper's* magazine, December 1990, page 31.

6. Gerald Prillaman, "Some Notes on the CAOs: A Dying Breed?," delivered December 12, 1988 at a USIA meeting in Salzburg; mimeo.

7. Author's interview with Robin Winks, April 23, 1990.

8. Author's interview with John Richardson, May 7, 1991.

9. *China Daily*, September 12, 1991.

10. Isaiah Berlin, *The Crooked Timber of Humanity: Chapters in the History of Ideas*, Henry Hardy, ed., New York: Knopf, 1991, page 2.

2. A History of the Fulbright Program, Pages 15–38

1. Author's interviews, with Richard T. Arndt, October 18, 1990 and Cipriana Scelba, July 1, 1991.

2. Author's interview with J. William Fulbright, October 18, 1990.

3. See J. Manuel Espinosa, *Inter-American Beginnings of U.S. Cultural Diplomacy, 1936-1948*; Washington: Bureau of Educational and Cultural Af-

fairs, U.S. Department of State, Cultural Relations Programs of the U.S. Department of State, 1976.

4. See Wilma Fairbanks, *America's Cultural Experiment in China, 1942-1949*; Washington: Bureau of Educational and Cultural Affairs, U.S. Department of State, Cultural Relations Programs of the U.S. Department of State, 1976.

5. Clark Clifford, *Counsel to the President*, New York: Random House, 1991, page 125.

6. See Henry J. Kellermann, *The Educational Exchange Program Between the United States and Germany, 1945-1954: Cultural Relations as an Instrument of U.S. Foreign Policy*, Washington: Bureau of Educational and Cultural Affairs, U.S. Department of State, Cultural Relations Program of the U.S. Department of State, 1978.

7. Ibid., "The Cumulative Report of Cultural Affairs, May 1, 1948-April 30, 1949," WNRC, RG 260, Box 335 3/5.

8. Estimates of the value of some four million items ranged from $60 to $105 million.

9. Senator Fulbright had several precedents. In 1908, the U.S. allowed China to use $16 million for Chinese students studying in the United States. China had been made to pay this amount as restitution after the Boxer Rebellion. In 1920, Herbert Hoover applied to Belgian-American educational exchange, funds not spent when the Belgian Relief Commission was liquidated.

10. Author's interview with Fulbright, October 18, 1990.

11. Public Law 402, 80th Congress, 2nd session.

12. See John T. Gullahorn and Jeanne E. Gullahorn, *Professional and Social Consequences of Fulbright and Smith-Mundt Awards*, East Lansing: Michigan State University, June 1958 mimeo; prepared for the U.S. Department of State.

13. Ibid., Gullahorn and Gullahorn, pages 11-13.

14. Ibid., page 14.

15. See Divo Institut, *A German Appraisal of the Fulbright Program*, Frankfurt am Main, Germany, March 1961.

16. Ibid., Divo, page III.

17. Ibid., Divo, page IV.

18. Ibid., Divo, page V.

19. The U.S. Information Agency provides funds for programs in Cambridge, New York, and other cities for foreign Fulbright scholars. They visit cultural and historic sites and have social events as well. The New York program is known as Metro International.

20. Public Law 87-256, H.R. 8666, 75 Stat. 527, approved September 21, 1961.

21. See *A Beacon of Hope: The Exchange-of-Persons Program*, Washington: The U.S. Advisory Commission on International Educational and Cultural Affairs, John W. Gardner, chairman, April 1963; see also the sequel, August 1964.

22. Ibid., Gardner Report, 1963, pages 56-57.

23. Author's interview with Fulbright, October 18, 1990.

24. Op. cit., Clifford, page 529.

25. Charles Frankel, *The Neglected Aspect of Foreign Affairs: American Educational and Cultural Policy Abroad*, Washington: The Brookings Institution, 1965.

26. Charles Frankel, *High on Foggy Bottom: An Outsider's Inside View of the Government*, New York: Harper & Row, 1968-1969, page 71.

27. Ibid., Frankel, *Foggy Bottom*, page 30.

28. John Richardson, who came after Frankel at CU, does not recall this problem.

29. Op. cit., *Foggy Bottom*, pages 31-32.

30. Op. cit., Frankel, *Neglected Aspects*, pages 9-23.

31. Author's interview with John Richardson, September 18, 1990.

32. *International Information, Education and Cultural Relations: Recommendations for the Future* (The Stanton Report), Center for Strategic and International Studies, 1975, page 77.

33. Leo Cherne, acting chairman, U.S. Advisory Commission on International Education and Cultural Affairs, letter to President Nixon, July 27, 1973, transmitting the commission's resolution notifying the President that under the Fulbright-Hays Act the commission is obligated to examine international educational and cultural exchange activities; at pages vi-vii and 43-44 of *The Stanton Report*.

34. The Center for Strategic and International Studies was requested by the State Department and the U.S. Advisory Commission on Information to undertake the study.

35. Op. cit., *The Stanton Report*, pages 3-4.

36. Ibid., *Stanton*, page 4.

37. Ibid., *Stanton*, page 5.

38. Gifford Malone, "Public Diplomacy: Organizing for the Future," in *The Stanton Report Revisited*, Kenneth W. Thompson, ed., University of Virginia, the White Burckett Miller Center of Public Affairs, 1987, page 19.

39. See *Commission on the Organization of the Government for the Conduct of Foreign Policy*, June 1975, Robert D. Murphy, chairman, Washington: Government Printing Office, 1975.

40. Ibid., The Murphy Report, page 138.

41. Op. cit., *Stanton Revisited*, page 49.

42. Memorandum, Jimmy Carter to John Reinhardt, director, International Communications Agency, March 13, 1978.

43. Richard T. Arndt, "Public Diplomacy, Cultural Diplomacy: The Stanton Commission Revisited," in *The Stanton Report Revisited*, Kenneth W. Thompson, ed., University of Virginia, the White Burckett Miller Center of Public Affairs, 1987, page 100.

44. Enrique Gonzalez-Manet, *The Hidden War of Information* (translated by Laurien Alexandre), Ablex, 1989, page 75.

45. Letter from Senator Fulbright to Lester S. Jayson, director, Congressional Research Service, January 15, 1974.

46. See *The United States Communicates with the World: A Study of U.S. International Information and Cultural Programs and Activities*, by the Foreign Affairs Division of the Congressional Research Service, Library of Congress, for the Committee on Foreign Relations, August 1975.

47. Ibid., *The U.S. Communicates*, page XLI.

48. Ibid., page XLIV.

49. Ibid., page XLV.

50. Op. cit., Richardson, May 7, 1991.

51. Letter to the author, November 20, 1991, from James H. Billington, Librarian of Congress.

52. United States Comptroller General, Report to the Congress of the United States: *Flexibility—Key to Administering Fulbright-Hays Exchange Program*, Washington: U.S. Accounting Office, December 10, 1979, ID-80-3.

53. Ibid., *GAO Report*, page 61.

54. Ibid., *GAO Report*, page 62.

55. Michael G. Stevens and Ronald A. Ungaro, "Fulbright at 40," *Foreign Service Journal*, November 1986; both are associated with the USIA's exchange programs.

3. How Do You Get a Fulbright Grant?, Pages 39–51

1. Author's interview with Maria Japa, November 21, 1990.

2. Author's interview with Charles Dunn, May 24, 1991.

3. Author's interview with Thomas Farrell, February 28, 1991.

4. *Manual of Operations and Administration (MOA), USIA, Part XII, Academic Exchange Under the Fulbright Program*, December 28, 1990, pages 214d-214.2.

5. Ibid., *MOA*, December 28, 1990, pages 223-223.3c.

6. Author's interview with Alfred Kazin, September 27, 1990.

7. Author's interview with Cassandra Pyle, October 19, 1990.

8. Op. cit., *MOA*, December 28, 1990, pages 241, 248, 248.3, 252.4.

9. Author's interview with Peggy Blumenthal, February 28, 1991.

10. *Manual of Operations and Administration (MOA), USIA, Part XII*, February 15, 1991, pages 200-209c.

11. Author's interview with Joseph F. Belmonte, March 19, 1991.

12. Author's telephone interview with Richard Corby, June 11, 1991.

13. Author's telephone interview with Ralph T. Nelson, June 11, 1991.

14. Interview with USED executives, March 19, 1991.

15. This paragraph from an untitled, undated CIE-USED memorandum.

16. *Open Doors: Report on International Education Exchange*, 1989-1990, New York: Institute of International Education.

5. Who Are the Fulbrighters?, Pages 59–76

1. Kay Larson, "Art: Foreign Intrigue," *New York* magazine, May 20, 1991, page 62.

2. Author's interview with Zdenka Gabalova, April 29, 1991.

3. Author's interview with Imad Khachchan, March 25, 1991.

4. The Fulbrighters were organized by Metro-New York, the year-round agency funded by the USIA to assist visiting scholars. The West Point conference was the 41st Annual Student Conference on United States Affairs. Political science students from 110 colleges representing thirty countries participated in the 1989 sessions.

5. Memorandum from Eric T. Wang, commander SCUSA 41, Department of the Army, United States Military Academy.

6. Author's interview with Joseph Lelyveld, May 10, 1991.

7. Joseph Lelyveld in *Young Americans Abroad*, Roger H. Klein, ed., New York: Harper & Row, 1963, page 1.

8. Ibid., *Young Americans*, page 22.

9. Op. cit., Lelyveld, May 10, 1991.

10. Author's interview with Hans Janitschek, April 10, 1991.

11. Author's interview with Robin Winks, April 23, 1991.

12. Author's interview with Ada-Louise Huxtable, November 28, 1990.

13. Author's interview with Robert Brustein, September 26, 1990.

14. Author's interview with Roger Rosenblatt, September 3, 1990.

15. Author's interview with Derek Bok, September 12, 1990.

16. Author's interview with Alberto Vitale, January 8, 1991. John Brademas, president of New York University (host to fifty-eight foreign Fulbrighters as he spoke), presented a 1991 Metro-New York award to Alberto Vitale. Said Brademas, "He brings to his profession great understanding and appreciation for other nations and peoples. His experiences as a Fulbright scholar had more than a little bearing on his tremendous business successes in the global arena."

17. Hsi-Huey Liang, *Berlin Before the Wall: A Foreign Student's Diary with Sketches*, New York: Routledge, 1990, page 12; the book is dedicated to the late Jay H. Cerf.

18. Ibid., *Berlin Before the Wall*, page 136.

19. Author's interview with Georgie Anne Geyer, September 18, 1990.

20. Author's interview with Norman Podhoretz, October 27, 1990.

21. Author's interview with James Billington, October 18, 1990.

22. Michael J. Berlin, *Washington Journalism Review*, September 1989, page 32.

23. Ibid., Berlin, page 37.

24. Author's interview with Daniel Boorstin, September 18, 1990.

25. Author's interview with Alfred Kazin, September 27, 1990.

26. Author's interview with Nathan Glazer, September 26, 1990.

27. Author's interview with Marshall E. Goodman, September 26, 1990.

28. Harrison H. Schmitt in *The Fulbright Experience, 1946-1986: Encounters and Transformation*, Arthur Power Duden & Russell R. Dynes, eds; New Brunswick: Transaction Books, 1987.

29. *Forty Years: The Fulbright Program, 1946-1986*, Board of Foreign Scholarships, page 15.

30. Minutes, September 6-7, 1990, Board of Foreign Scholarships.

31. Embassy cable to USIA, R-031844Z, October 1990.

32. Letter to the author from Gonzalo Cartagenova, executive director, Comision Fulbright, Ecuador, October 17, 1990.

33. Edward T. Purcell, *Report on a Survey of U.S. Student Fulbright Grantees to Latin America, 1964-68*, J. William Fulbright Foreign Scholarship Board, December 1, 1990, mimeo.

34. Ibid., Purcell, page 3.

35. "Sir Zelman: 'Fulbright outstanding act of statesmanship,'" *The Fulbrighter*, vol. 2, no. 2, June 1989, Australian-American Educational Foundation.

36. See Geraldine McDonald, Pam Kennedy, Barb Bishop, *Coming and Going: Forty Years of the Fulbright Programme in New Zealand*, New Zealand-United States Educational Foundation and New Zealand Council for Educational Research, 1989.

37. See Wilma Fairbanks, *America's Cultural Experiment in China, 1942-1949*; Washington: Bureau of Educational and Cultural Relations Programs of the U.S. Department of State, 1976, page 185.

6. Is the Program Effective?, Pages 77–89

1. Charles Frankel, *High on Foggy Bottom: An Outsider's Inside View of the Government*, New York: Harper & Row, 1968-69, page 223.

2. Author's interview with Allen Kassof, November 18, 1990.

3. Richard Schifter, Assistant Secretary of State for Human Rights and Humanitarian Affairs at seminar of the Center for Strategic and International Studies, October 8, 1990, in Moscow, USSR, page 1, mimeo.

4. John T. Gullahorn and Jeanne E. Gullahorn, *Professional Consequences of Fulbright and Smith-Mundt Awards*, East Lansing: Michigan University, June 1958, appendix 1, mimeo.

5. From USIA, Bangkok, Thailand, 1987.

6. Crawford D. Goodwin and Michael Nacht, *Fondness and Frustration*, New York: Institute for International Education, 1984.

7. Ibid., page 8.

8. Ibid., page 15.

9. Ibid., page 27.

10. In Arthur Power Dudden and Russell R. Dynes, eds., *The Fulbright Experience: Encounters and Transformations*, New Brunswick, N.J.: Transaction, 1987, page 261.

11. Ibid., page 43.

12. Author's interview with Daniel Boorstin, September 18, 1990.

13. Author's interview with Derek Bok, October 12, 1990.

14. *Fortieth Anniversary Proceedings*, Board of Foreign Scholarships.

15. *1991 Annual Report*, J. William Fulbright Board of Foreign Scholarship.

7. Problems: Tensions in Policy, Performance, and Support, Pages 91–105

1. Author's interview, July 17, 1991, Guy S. Brown, director, academic programs, Bureau of Educational and Cultural Affairs, USIA.
2. Author's interview with Walter Rosenblith, October 12, 1990.
3. Beijing embassy cable #07098, 1310302, March 1991.
4. Author's interview with William P. Glade, associate director, USIA, April 25, 1991.
5. Ibid., Glade.
6. Ibid., Glade.
7. Ibid., Glade.
8. Furthering American studies abroad is mandated in Section 102 b4 of the Fulbright-Hays Act.

8. Who Pays and for What?, Pages 107–112

1. *Manual of Operations and Administration (MOA), USIA*, December 28, 1990, page 212.
2. Ibid., *MOA*, page 221d.
3. Letter to the author, November 12, 1991, from Gloria H. Ilic, director of Foreign Fulbright Programs Division, IIE.
4. Author's interview with Ronald A. Ungaro, March 19, 1991.

9. Country Model: Japan, Pages 113–119

1. Author's interview with Kenichi Takemura, June 19, 1991.
2. Author's interview with Akira Fujishima, June 18, 1991.
3. Author's interview with Yuji Tsushima, June 17, 1991.
4. Author's interview with Yasunori Nishijima, June 19, 1991.
5. Author's interview with Shigekuni Kawamura, June 18, 1991.
6. Author's interview with Rob Nevitt, June 17, 1991.

10. Country Model: Indonesia, Pages 121–127

1. Author's interview with Harsja W. Bachtiar, June 22, 1991.
2. Author's interview with Ann vB. Lewis, June 21, 1991.
3. Author's interview with Michael M. Yaki, June 21, 1991.

4. Author's interview with Fredrik deBoer, November 16, 1990.
5. Author's interview with I. Made Bandem, June 11 and 23, 1991.
6. Author's interview with Putu Widjaja, June 22, 1991.
7. Author's interview with Aristides Katoppo, June 24, 1991.

11. Country Model: India, Pages 129–139

1. Moments before Rajiv Gandhi was killed, he was riding in a car with Barbara Crossett, correspondent for the *New York Times*, a former Fulbright scholar. Her firsthand report of the assassination and her narrow escape was one of her two historic stories appearing on the *Times*'s first page within hours of the assassination. Crossett won the prestigious Polk Award for her coverage.
2. Author's interview with A. M. Khusro, June 27, 1991.
3. Author's interview with R. K. Chhabra, June 26, 1991.
4. Author's interview with S. G. Mankad, June 27, 1991.
5. Author's interview with Leonard J. Baldyga, June 27, 1991.

12. Country Model: Italy, Pages 141–146

1. Author's interview with Guglielmo Negri, July 2, 1991.
2. Author's interview with Cipriana Scelba, July 1, 1991.
3. Author's interview with Jodi Lewinsohn, July 1, 1991.
4. Author's interview with Carlo Chiarenza, July 1, 1991.
5. Author's interview with Biancamaria Tedeschini Lalli, July 2, 1991.

Index

About the Author

Leonard R. Sussman has written three books on international communications and organized an international council on the future of the university. He served on U.S. delegations to UNESCO, the information forum of the Commission on Security and Cooperation in Europe, and the Geneva conference to plan humanitarian aid to Africa. He was also a member of the congressional panel on competition and cooperation in outer space. For 21 years, he was executive director of Freedom House, the monitor of political and civil rights worldwide. He is now senior scholar at the organization and adjunct professor in journalism and mass communication at New York University. Earlier, he was a journalist in New York and the Caribbean, and press secretary to the governor of Puerto Rico.